The Purpose of Banking

Transforming Banking for Stability
and Economic Growth

ANJAN V. THAKOR

OXFORD
UNIVERSITY PRESS

Oxford University Press is a department of the University of Oxford. It furthers
the University's objective of excellence in research, scholarship, and education
by publishing worldwide. Oxford is a registered trade mark of Oxford University
Press in the UK and certain other countries.

Published in the United States of America by Oxford University Press
198 Madison Avenue, New York, NY 10016, United States of America.

Library of Congress Cataloging-in-Publication Data
Names: Thakor, Anjan V., author.
Title: The purpose of banking : transforming banking for stability and
economic growth / Anjan V. Thakor.
Description: New York : Oxford University Press, [2019]
Identifiers: LCCN 2018031498 | ISBN 9780190919535 (hardcover) |
ISBN 9780190919542 (updf) | ISBN 9780190919559 (epub)
Subjects: LCSH: Banks and banking. | Banking law. | Economic development.
Classification: LCC HG1601 .T355 2018 | DDC 332.1—dc23
LC record available at https://lccn.loc.gov/2018031498

9 8 7 6 5 4 3 2 1

Printed by Sheridan Books, Inc., United States of America

To the latest inspirations for my higher purpose: Aiden and Lily.

Contents

ACT IV. Financial Crises: Causes, Effects, and Cures

ACT V. Reforming Banking and Looking Ahead: Improving Banking and the Potential Interactions with Fintech

The Purpose of Banking

Introduction

The Columbo Approach

A BIRD'S-EYE VIEW OF THE BOOK

IN THE TYPICAL mystery novel, say an Agatha Christie classic like *Murder on the Orient Express*, there is an intriguing mystery about whodunit, and you have to wait until the end of the novel to find out. Well, this is not a mystery novel. Rather, it is a synthesis of a large body of research in banking to answer one of the most important questions: How do we design a banking system to achieve the "right" balance between financial stability and economic growth? That is, how do we get banks to help the economy grow, but without recurring crises? You will not have to wait until the end of the book to find out the answer. Instead, you will have it in this chapter.

If there is an analogy to a murder mystery, a more fitting one is to the TV show *Columbo*. Invariably, the show tips the audience off to who the killer is right at the outset. The rest of the show is then devoted to a discovery of how Columbo found out who the killer was and how he went about proving it. So it is with this book. I will give you the answer to the question above, as well as the most important takeaways from the book in this chapter. The rest of the book is devoted to how these conclusions can be reached by accessing the vast body of research that has been done in the past three or four decades.

The Four Biggest Takeaways

Takeaway #1: A key to understanding how to develop a banking system for economic stability and growth is first understanding the *core economic functions* banks serve. There are three core functions:

1. Banks create funding liquidity and private money by gathering deposits and lending money to borrowers who they screen, monitor, and develop lending relationships with.

2. Banks provide safekeeping services for valuables, maintain the confidentiality of clients' information, and develop trust.
3. Banks process different sorts of information that helps to reduce contracting costs and costs of verification of cash flows, asset ownership, and so on.

Takeaway #2: These core economic functions help to crystalize the higher purpose of banks and their corporate culture. The banks' clearly articulated higher purpose should be built around the provision of these services, but not in a conventional way. The purpose should be defined not in terms of an economic transaction but in terms of a contribution. An authentic higher purpose expresses the true intent of the bank in serving these core functions, but it requires delivering these services in a way that exceeds the conventional expectations of the customer. It is thus a prosocial goal that transcends the usual business goals of the bank but intersects with these goals, and it encourages the development of a corporate culture that generates trust in the bank. When the higher purpose is the arbitrator of all decisions, the culture of the bank is continually reshaped to serve and exceed the changing needs of the customer.

Takeaway #3: In performing their core economic functions in accordance with the higher purpose, banks engage in activities like depository services, relationship lending, selling loan commitments and standby letters of credit, and securitization. These activities put banks on center stage within the overall financial system, and thus banking stability and health also affect the health of financial markets and the whole financial system. This has numerous implications:

1. Banks are crucial for economic growth.
2. Financial markets cannot be developed effectively without first developing banks.
3. The centrality of banks makes it very tempting for politicians to influence banking, and politics can contribute to financial crises.
4. The centrality of banks means that a sufficiently high number of bank failures can generate financial crises that have significant effects on the real sector (Main Street)—the 2007–2009 crisis cost the US economy $22 trillion.
5. The specter of such costs creates a powerful incentive for the government to intervene to prevent financial crises or minimize the damage they cause. Interventions include ex ante safety nets like deposit insurance for financial institutions and bailouts of failing institutions. These safety nets encourage these institutions to take excessive risks and be excessively leveraged (too little equity capital). Many of these behaviors are due to

deep-seated attributes of the corporate culture in some banks, a culture that is not shaped by an authentic higher purpose for the bank's existence.

Takeaway #4: Although extensive regulations seek to limit such risk-taking behavior by banks, regulators tolerate undercapitalized and risky banks because they believe that there is a tradeoff between economic stability and growth. Asking banks to keep more capital will make them safer, but it is believed that it will be at the expense of economic growth because it will reduce lending and liquidity creation. However, this is a false tradeoff. Extensive research points to the fact that we can get long-run stability as well as economic growth if we:

- increase equity capital significantly in banks without burdening them with onerous liquidity requirements
- strengthen bank culture and encourage it to be linked to an explicitly articulated higher purpose that is prosocial, and
- develop a more integrated regulatory structure, keeping fintech developments on the radar and permitting banks to integrate these developments into their activities.

With these changes, banks will become more trusted by their counterparties and taxpayers; they will create more liquidity, lend more, contribute to higher long-term economic growth, and be less crisis-prone, leading to a much lower exposure for taxpayers.

Recent Proposals to Fundamentally Reform Banking

In the wake of the 2007–2009 financial crisis, some countries (e.g., Iceland and Switzerland) have recently contemplated a fundamental remaking of banking. The proposals they have considered rest on the premise that the crisis that led to the Great Recession was a liquidity crisis. So the proposals seek to end the specter of bank runs and panics by changing banks themselves.

The proposed new system is one in which all bank branches would disappear. All deposit gathering would be done by the central bank, which would then distribute deposits to banks at a price determined by supply and demand forces, subject to banks posting sufficient equity capital. The central bank would be the counterparty for all depositors. Deposit insurance as presently designed, bank bailouts, and bank-level liquidity requirements would all be eliminated. Gone would be "liquidity crises" in which healthy (solvent) banks fail because liquidity unexpectedly dries up.

I explain that this proposal is a logical consequence of the research that argues that a central problem in financial crises—including the 2007–2009 crisis—is *liquidity risk.* In this view, liquidity risk arises from the likelihood of massive deposit withdrawals from banks that are due to the sudden liquidity needs of depositors and unrelated to the financial health of the bank's assets; nonetheless, these withdrawals can cause the bank to collapse. Centralizing deposits at the central bank helps to address this risk of bank runs. I then evaluate the pros and cons of this proposal in light of the overall empirical evidence available and other considerations discussed throughout the book.

The Future

The book closes with some thoughts about the potential impact of fintech on banking. In particular, how will banks respond to blockchain technology, cryptocurrencies, P2P lending, and other developments? In a nutshell, I do not view these developments as threatening banking, but I do see them changing the core economic functions of banks. One important way in which this change will occur is that banks will become more integrated with the financial market, and the lines delineating banks from the market will become increasingly blurred. Another is that the provision of financial services will become increasingly "decentralized" and customized to the needs of customers. Their ability to engender trust with their customers and counterparties may remain the last distinctive asset of banks. And the ability of banks to engender trust will depend on their ability to articulate and implement an authentic higher purpose.

The Purpose of Banks

What Banks Do and Why

1

Money, Guns, and Lawyers

THE BUSINESS OF BANKING

Introduction

Few outlaws are more notorious than Jesse James in the history of the Wild West. In the annals of Minnesota banking is the story of how the James-Younger gang, led by Jesse James, was nearly wiped out attempting a bold daytime robbery of the Northfield First National Bank in 1876. The robbery started in the classic manner depicted in countless movies—a gang rides into town firing pistols, scaring people away and creating a diversion, while some other gang members walk into the bank brandishing guns. On this fateful day—September 7, 1876—however, one of the bank employees managed to escape and sound the alarm, which led to the people in the town surrounding the bank with guns blazing. In the aftermath, most of the gang was wiped out, but the James brothers managed to escape.

The Minnesota Historical Society has a Northfield bank note from the time of this raid. Signed by the bank cashier, G. M. Phillips, and bank president, F. Goodsell, this note survived the raid.[1] Such bank notes were a part of the money supply then.

Why were the good folks of Northfield so determined to confront a dangerous gang and risk their lives? Because banks matter for the lives of everyday people. They provide a host of economic services, create money, and lubricate economic growth. For bankers, this means that it matters not only what they do but how what they do is perceived. As John Maynard Keynes put it:

> It is necessarily part of the business of a banker to maintain appearances and to profess a conventional responsibility, which is more than

human. Lifelong practices of this kind make them the most romantic and least realistic of men.

Perceptions shape the confidence people have in banks. And confidence shapes their willingness to do business with banks. Not only must banks be trusted by their customers and various other counterparties in terms of the actions, but those they deal with should also have confidence in their financial viability. Indeed, this is one of the fundamental conundrums of banking—bankers can serve you only if you *believe* they will. A lot that happens in banking depends on perceptions and confidence. But what do banks really do? How do they serve you?

While "Lawyers, Guns, and Money" is a song by Warren Zevon from his 1978 album *Excitable Boy*, these are three things that go hand in glove with banking. Not just today; they always have. Money is a much older creation than guns, and banks were involved in the original creation of money. But money has always attracted weapons of war, so the association of guns with money is no surprise. And the centrality of banks in money creation and the payment system typically invites banking regulations. Of course, regulations are laws, and where there are laws, there are lawyers. And in some cases, politics too.

These literal interpretations aside, the phrase "lawyers, guns, and money" is often used as an analog for *resources* in general. And this is where the crucial economic role of banks comes in. They not only play a central role in how resources are allocated in the economy but also help *create* resources. This has been true for millennia. And while modern banks look very different from their ancient ancestors, it is striking how much of the original DNA still exists in modern banks. As we will see, this historical perspective is useful for informing contemporary issues.

The Bright and Dark Sides of Banking

The people of Northfield bravely defended their bank because it provided valuable economic services to them. But this bright side of banking is only one side of the equation. Like the moon, banking has a dark side, too, and it is most visible during financial crises.

After the Civil War, US banking grew rapidly. But then came the crisis of 1873. It started with a stock market crash in Europe. European investors began selling their investments in US railroads, and many American railroads went bankrupt. As is typically the case, bankruptcies in the "real economy" spilled over to banks, and they began to experience an increase in their risk of insolvency. A big New York bank, Jay Cooke & Company, went bankrupt due to its large investments in the now-troubled railroads. Shocked by the failure of such a large bank, investors and depositors in banks panicked and began withdrawing their money from other banks.[2] Over one hundred banks failed as a result. The New York Stock Exchange was closed for ten days. Credit began to shrink dramatically. Factories were shuttered. Thousands lost their jobs. The resulting economic pall lasted until 1879 in the United States, and even longer in Europe.

Banking Is Old, But We Can't Do Without It

Neither the value provided by banks nor the economic carnage that accompanies banking crises is a new phenomenon. Some economic historians tell us that banking predates even the invention of coinage. Grain loans to farmers and traders by grain warehouses that evolved into banks probably began around 2000 BCE in ancient Egypt, Assyria, and Babylon. Others claim that the Venetian goldsmiths in the fourteenth century CE were the immediate predecessors of modern banks, and the antecedents of these early banks can be found in the goldsmiths in Athens around 700 BCE, which is roughly the time coinage first came into existence.[3] The first credit crisis apparently occurred in the fourth century BCE when Dionysius of Syracuse ordered that all metal coins be collected under penalty of death, restamped one-drachma pieces as two drachmas, and used his newly inflated coins to pay off his IOUs.[4] So banks and financial crises have a long and hoary tradition.

But what about the state of banking today? While no one denies that banks are still important in modern times, the spectacular development of financial markets—especially in the United States—has led many to believe that the importance of banks is fading. Indeed, many research papers were written in the 1980s about the demise of banks, as mutual funds emerged and drained deposits out of banks.[5] Today people talk of Bitcoin and digital currencies replacing the bank-dependent, fiat-currency-based payment systems we have and P2P platforms taking loan market share away from banks.

Nonetheless, we underestimate the importance of banks at our own peril. This lesson was brought home to me forcefully in 2001–2002 when I was at the University of Michigan. My colleague Anna Meyendorff and I worked on a project (requested by the Central Bank of Romania) under the auspices of the Davidson Institute to study the Romanian financial system and make recommendations for reform.[6]

The prevailing wisdom at the time was that economies like Romania's that had recently made the transition from a Soviet-style, centrally planned economic system to a free-market system ought to focus on developing their stock and bond markets by establishing exchanges on which the formerly state-owned companies could be traded. In other words, following the example of the United States, which has deep and liquid securities markets, the path to economic development lies in focus on developing such markets.

Romania had taken this advice and focused on the development of their stock exchange in Bucharest, called RASDAQ, patterned after NASDAQ in the United States. However, when we studied the Romanian financial system, we found that it faced a number of challenges. It had weak corporate governance in (formerly state-owned) firms. It had weak banks that relied on fee income but loaned little. This was in part because the banks felt they lacked the skills to make risky loans that might have to be restructured later. The other reason was that there was no securitization then, so some forms of lending—like home mortgages—were just considered too illiquid and risky. Moreover, even though the former state-owned enterprises were privatized and listed on RASDAQ, most of them were not involved in raising capital. So corporate investment was low. Companies were not getting enough credit, and they were not making up for that by capital market financing. Economic growth was hindered because the financial system was not lubricating this growth.

Why was this transition to a free-market economy not flourishing?

The answer, we discovered, was simple—the banking system had not been developed. It is wrong to focus on securities markets before developing a robust banking system. Markets do not work well without a strong banking system. This is reminiscent of Adam Smith, who wrote in *The Wealth of Nations* (1776):

> That the trade and industry of Scotland, however, have increased very considerably during this period, and that the banks have contributed a good deal to this increase, cannot be doubted.

There is now extensive academic research that explains why financial markets cannot function well without robust banks; I will discuss some of it later. But what matters for now is that we concluded that banks had to become the central focus of development, and we came up with a specific set of recommendations to achieve this. This was Romania in 2002, and it is a story we saw repeated in other former Soviet-bloc countries. Let us now turn to the banks of today.

From the Old to the New: What Do the Banks of Today Do and Affect?

Highgrove Partners is a family-owned landscaping business in Atlanta. It provides commercial landscape, development, and water management to property managers and owners. Its CEO, Jim McCutcheon, decided to do his banking with Atlantic Capital. McCutcheon describes his relationship with the bank as follows:

> By now I've worked with Atlantic Capital on many things—real estate loans, lines of credit, and equipment lines of credit. . . . I even went through the challenging situation of buying out two partners, and ACB worked through that with me.[7]

Like the experience of Hargrove Partners, today's banks touch our lives in many ways. They safeguard our money, allow us to write checks, give us loans to buy houses and finance our businesses, enable us to use credit cards, participate in securitizing loans of all kinds, buy the bonds that finance our state and federal governments, and act as market makers in various securities. Today's banks are as essential to our daily lives as the roads we drive on and the electronic devices we are addicted to.

This centrality of banking in our lives is time honored. In a report submitted to the lord commissioners of trade for the foreign plantations on January 9, 1740, Governor Richard Ward of Rhode Island wrote: "If this colony be in any respect happy and flourishing, it is paper money and a right application of it that hath rendered as so."[8]

As the principal conduit for the creation and flow of paper money, banks were an important part of economic growth in the eighteenth century. That role is an important part of banking even today. But it is augmented by a plethora of other economic functions that include off-balance-sheet activities like loan commitments and letters of credit, securitization, and others. The core economic functions banks perform are threefold: (1) they create funding liquidity (and money) by gathering deposits and developing lending relationships; (2) they provide safekeeping services, protect the confidentiality of their clients' information, and engage in activities that require the trust of their counterparties; and (3) they reduce transactions costs of contracting by more efficiently processing various sorts of information and reducing verification costs of all kinds (e.g., verification of asset ownership, borrower cash flows, etc.). As a result of these core functions, it is difficult to talk about banking in isolation from the rest of the financial system, and we will talk later about the *architecture* of the financial system and how banks fit into that.

It is because of their central role in economic activity that the real sector experiences serious indigestion when the banking system has a hiccup. This was brought home to us forcefully during the 2007–2009 financial crisis. What began as defaults on US subprime mortgages grew into a fire that ravaged the global financial system. Employment dropped, consumption dropped, and companies cut back on investments. Research estimates put the damage done to the US economy alone at between $6 trillion and $14 trillion.[9] These were the direct costs. When the estimated indirect costs—like productivity losses and the costs of mortgage foreclosures—are taken into account, the General Accounting Office puts the losses at around $22 trillion.[10] When banks bleed, we all do.

Of course, crises are not new. They are as old as banking itself. The first banking crisis in the United States occurred in 1792. The first emerging market crisis occurred in Latin America in 1825. Not only are banks are disrupted by crises and thus more likely to fail during those times; crises are the fire in which the shape of banking is itself forged.

Preventing Banking Crises

An enormous amount of research, both theoretical and empirical, has been done on what causes financial crises.[11] Less has been done on how to design banking systems that are less crisis-prone. In fact, some believe that avoiding financial crises may be impossible.

The problem then is not that we lack theories of what causes banking crises. Rather, we probably have too many. Many of these are elegant and complex, but the challenge is to find a parsimonious set of theories that explain a large set of facts about crises and are also possible to test empirically. That is, we would not only like them to explain what we have documented about crises, but we would like these theories to predict things we do not know so we can test them. Accurate predictions would give us greater confidence in these theories, so we could take their policy implications more seriously.

Whether it is the lack of a dominant theory of financial crises that is widely endorsed and fits the facts or it is our unwillingness to learn from the vast amount of research about crises, our response to any financial crisis is predictable. Politicians point fingers at greedy bankers, typically representing newer parts of the financial system,[12] then they pass new regulations—often too many—to "solve" the problems that they think led to the crisis, and then they complain about how banks behave by being innovative in getting around the new regulations. "Never waste a good crisis" is a statement often used to indicate that a crisis provides increased opportunities for politicians to enact new rules and regulations. As we will see later, the ever-present potential for the intrusion of politics into banking can severely limit the attractiveness of many reform proposals.

Do these regulations work? Some do. Some don't. Can we tell which will work well and which will do more harm than good? How do we avoid this reactive regulatory dynamic? How much does research help us here?

These are important questions. As we work on answering them, we will begin to see a picture that emerges about what a healthy, relatively crisis-free banking system would look like.

As a society, we value stability. It facilitates planning and encourages individuals and corporations to invest. But achieving stability at the expense of economic growth is not always desirable. If it were, it would be easy to simply restrict all our banks with insured deposits to be "narrow banks" that can invest only in very safe assets like US Treasury securities. This is akin to an individual planning for retirement. If all you care about is stability, then you invest all your wealth in federally insured deposit accounts and US Treasury bonds. But if you are also interested in the growth of your wealth, then you have a blended portfolio that also includes riskier securities like common stock and claims on real estate. So any theory of financial stability must confront the stability-growth tradeoff. Moreover, the theory should focus on the *common elements* that are found in most crises and avoid the trap of being tailored to deal with those that were particular to the last crisis.

In discussing these issues, I will attach special importance to three things: bank capital, bank culture, and bank higher purpose. Capital is a heavily researched topic, so my task is relatively easy—I can borrow from that vast body of knowledge. Bank culture is a newer topic, and much work remains to be done. But increasingly, bank regulators are realizing the limits of their regulatory effectiveness and the need for a greater focus on culture to ensure that banks maintain their role as trusted intermediaries. That is, there is growing recognition that the trust of counterparties is an essential asset of banks, and bank culture has to ensure that this trust is maintained. Nonetheless, issues of bank culture have been alluded to over many past decades. Consider the example of Jacob Franklin Butcher, known to most as Jack Butcher, who built a financial empire in Tennessee and was the Democratic Party nominee for governor of Tennessee in 1978. He was convicted of banking fraud after pleading guilty in 1985; he got a twenty-year prison term. The *New York Times* (September 6, 1984) reported:

> Eighteen months after the collapse of the Butcher brothers' Tennessee banking empire, the Federal Deposit Insurance Corporation fears that its losses on the episode may total several hundred million dollars more than it initially expected. . . .
>
> The agency also said it found that the Butchers had been shifting bad loans from bank to bank to keep regulators from noticing them. On Valentine's Day 1983, Tennessee had the F.D.I.C. arrange the sale of Jack Butcher's flagship, the United American Bank of Knoxville, and the unraveling began.
>
> The following month, C. H. Butcher's Southern Industrial Banking Corporation, a consumer finance company that attracted uninsured deposits by paying high interest rates, filed for protection from creditors under Chapter 11. . . . In May 1983, the F.D.I.C. sold five more Tennessee banks that were owned or formerly controlled by the Butchers.
>
> . . . Since then, nine more Tennessee banks have failed at least in part because of problems related to the Butchers.

These kinds of bank failures are not just due to bad luck. Rather, they reflect systematic failures of culture that jeopardize the trust taxpayers place in the banking system.

Finally, there is the issue of higher purpose, a reason for the bank to exist—typically a prosocial goal—that transcends typical business goals but intersects with these goals. This is an issue of great import, but one that has received little attention from banks, and even less in research.[13] When an organization has higher purpose, decisions are made that are in line with both prosocial goals and the business goals. A higher purpose expresses the deepest authentic intent of the organization. Steve Jobs described it thus:

> Great companies must have a noble cause. Then it is the leader's job to transform that noble cause into such an inspiring vision that it will attract the most talented people in the world to want to join it.

Higher purpose is not charity or corporate social responsibility. These terms mean different things to different people, but to me they are distinct from an authentic (not PR), organizational higher purpose.

What should a bank's higher purpose be? Since we are interested in how the bank makes decisions at the intersection of its business goals and its higher purpose, this question is difficult to answer until we understand what banks do and why they do it. That is, we first need a deeper understanding of the business of banking. After these ideas have been established, I will return to a discussion of how higher purpose interacts with bank culture and the role it can play in financial stability.

Notes

1. See Nicholson 2000–2001.
2. Banks runs are typically triggered by worries about economic fundamentals. That is, they are not completely random phenomena, but are caused by observed economic stresses caused by things like asset price declines, loan defaults, layoffs, and so on. In 1873, this shock to fundamentals came from bankruptcies in the real sector. More generally, bank runs are typically triggered by a decline in the values of assets banks hold on their balance sheets due to stresses in the real sector. In the 2007–2009 crisis, this decline was in the values of home mortgages and mortgage-backed securities due to falling house prices.
3. See Donaldson, Piacentino, and Thakor 2018.
4. See Reinhart and Rogoff 2009.
5. See, for example, Gorton and Rosen 1995.
6. See Meyendorff and Thakor 2002.
7. See the website of Atlantic Capital: http://www.atlanticcapitalmanagement.com/.
8. See chapter 2 in Mayer 1975.
9. See Atkinson, Luttrell, and Rosenblum 2013 and Thakor 2015.
10. See General Accounting Office 2013. The Bank for International Settlements estimates that a typical crisis costs 158% of the nation's GDP.
11. See Thakor 2015.
12. See "Financial Crises" 2014.
13. See Quinn and Thakor 2018.

References

Atkinson, Tyler, David Luttrell, and Harvey Rosenblum. 2013. "How Bad Was It? The Costs and Consequences of the 2007-09 Financial Crisis." Staff Papers 20, Federal Reserve Bank of Dallas, July.

Donaldson, Jason, Giorgia Piacentino, and Anjan V. Thakor. 2018. "Warehouse Banking." *Journal of Financial Economics* 129:250–267.

General Accounting Office. 2013. *Financial Regulatory Reform: Financial Crisis Losses and Potential Impacts of the Dodd-Frank Act.* Report to Congressional Requesters, January.

"Financial Crises." 2014. *Economist* online, April.

Gorton, Gary, and Richard Rosen. 1995. "Corporate Control Portfolio Choice, and the Decline of Banking," *Journal of Finance* 50 (5):1377–1420.

Mayer, Martin. 1975. *The Bankers.* New York: Weybright & Talley.

Meyendorff, Anna, and Anjan V. Thakor. 2002. *Designing Financial Systems in Transition Economies: Strategies for Reform in Central and Eastern Europe.* Cambridge, MA: MIT Press.

Nicholson, Claudia, J. 2000–2001. "Bankers with Shotguns and Other Minnesota Banking Stories." *Minnesota Historical Society* (Winter): 183–197.

Quinn, Robert, and Anjan V. Thakor. 2018. "Creating a Purpose-Driven Organization." *Harvard Business Review,* July–August, 2–9.

Reinhart, Carmen, and Kenneth Rogoff. 2009. *This Time Is Different: Eight Centuries of Financial Folly,* Princeton, NJ: Princeton University Press.

Smith, Adam. 1776. *An Enquiry into the Nature and Causes of the Wealth of Nations.* London: W. Strahan & T. Cadell.

Thakor, Anjan, V. 2015. "The Financial Crisis of 2007–09: Why Did It Happen and What Did We Learn?" *Review of Corporate Finance Studies* 4 (2):155–205.

2

The Origins of Banking and the Services Banks Provide

CUSTOMERS, INVESTORS, AND OTHER
STAKEHOLDERS

From Warehouses to Banks

In *The Daily Life of Christians in Ancient Rome*, James Ermatinger writes of
Rome in the third and fourth centuries:

> The Aventine, named for the Aventine Hill, was the chief river port
> of Rome, since the river traffic coming up the Tiber from Istia would
> unload its wares there. . . . The shore line, dotted with numerous
> docks and granaries, offices and warehouses, became the great granary
> for Rome and the commercial and government distribution source.
> Here grain, wine, olives, and olive oil contained in amphorae were
> unloaded. . . . The amphorae were unloaded where the customs of-
> ficer, a government accountant, removed two stamped handles of each
> amphorae, one handle staying at the office where they were counted
> and divided into separate piles for each shipper, the other handle acting
> as a receipt for the buyer. . . . For large shipments the bullion remained
> in Rome and was merely credit from *one account to another, much the
> way modern commodity brokers work.*[1]

But this function of warehouses predates by centuries the Roman
warehouses. In Genesis, there is a description of Joseph being appointed by

the Pharaoh in Egypt in 1707 BCE to provide grain warehouses all over the land and levy a tax on all farm products during the seven years of plenty.[2] This was meant to insure against the prophesied seven years of famine. These warehouses were located in the cities and designated "the king's warehouses."

It was from these ancient warehouses that banks originally evolved. The story of this evolution goes something like this: Say a farmer has some grain that needs to be stored safely. Because storage has huge economies of scale, it is better for the farmer to store his grain in the king's warehouse—where the likelihood of theft is low—than in his own farmhouse. The farmer will pay the warehouse a fee and get a receipt as proof of deposit. In some instances, the farmer had no choice but to deposit in the King's warehouse because that is how he was taxed (equivalent to a storage fee). If the farmer then needed to purchase services—say labor to till the fields—he could go to the warehouse, withdraw some grain, and pay the workers. Indeed, in ancient Egypt, grain formed the most extensively used medium of exchange, even after coinage was introduced.

Over time, people realized that going back and forth to the warehouse to withdraw grain was inefficient. Instead of giving grain to pay for purchased services, the farmer could simply give some of his grain receipts. These receipts were "payable to the bearer upon demand," that is, they did not bear the farmer's name. Consequently, they could be "cashed" by anyone the farmer gave them to. These warehouse receipts effectively became *private money*.[3] See figure 2.1.

Even though private money was created this way, these warehouses were not banks. That transformation had to await a breakthrough. The

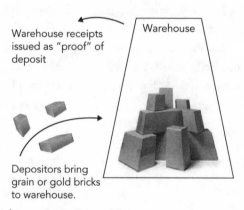

Warehouse receipts issued as "proof" of deposit

Warehouse

Depositors bring grain or gold bricks to warehouse.

FIGURE 2.1 Warehouses Create Private Money.

warehouse manager realized that there was not much happening to the inventory of grains, other than new deposits; withdrawals were limited. This is where the warehouse manager had a brilliant insight. Why not write additional receipts—those with no grain deposits to back them— and lend them to those in need of "private money"? We can call these "fake receipts," because they are not issued in response to actual grain deposits, but they are indistinguishable from deposit-backed receipts and are every bit as authentic as those receipts in terms of payments and settlements.[4] There will now be more warehouse receipts in circulation than grain, so the warehouse will be in trouble if everyone decides to withdraw grain at the same time. But absent that remote possibility, the warehouse will have enough grain to meet withdrawals, as long as too many fake receipts are not created.[5] See figure 2.2.

This issuance of fake receipts has numerous important implications. First, it means that the warehouse bank allows individuals and companies to consume and invest more at any given point in time than the entire endowment of the economy. That is, if we imagine everything everybody owns in the economy is either deposited, consumed, or invested, the fact that the fake receipts are leading to *additional* investments means that money has essentially been created out of thin air. We call this funding *liquidity creation*—banking *expands* the resources available for investment (or consumption) beyond what the economy has on its own without banks.

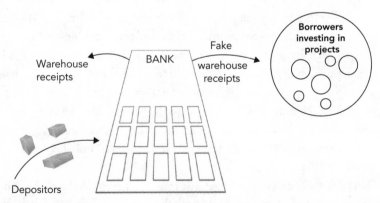

FIGURE 2.2 Fake Warehouse Receipts and Banking: Warehouse Becomes a Bank.
Key: Receipts are "payable to bearer upon demand" (i.e., name of depositor is *not* there ⇒ fake and authentic receipts are identical).

Second, most people think of a bank as an entity that takes in deposits and then invests these deposits in loans. That is, deposits create loans. This is a very literal way of thinking about the process. I deposit $100 in bills in the bank, and the bank then lends this $100 to you. This is a process that does happen in practice, of course. But it is dwarfed in many countries by the process described here, which shows that *loans also create deposits*. That is, when the bank lends fake receipts to farmers and merchants, in its books it has to record an offsetting deposit liability in recognition of the fact that if the fake receipt is presented for deposit withdrawal, it must be honored. In other words, when you go to the bank to request a $100 loan, the bank does not literally reach into its vault and pull out $100 in bills to hand to you. Rather, the bank creates a deposit account for you (either in that bank or any other bank of your choice) and credits that deposit account with $100. Thus, its $100 loan to you creates a $100 deposit. This somewhat unfamiliar notion of loans creating deposits was recognized by John Maynard Keynes many decades ago:

> It is not unnatural to think of deposits of a bank as being created by the public through the deposits of cash representing either savings or amounts which are not for the time being required to meet expenditures. But the bulk of the deposits arise out of the actions of the banks themselves, for by granting loans, allowing money to be drawn on an overdraft or purchasing securities, a bank creates a credit in its books which is the equivalent of a deposit.[6]

Third, this shows that the private claims created by banking can function without fiat currency issued by the government. As you can see, this process of lending by creating deposits leads naturally to "fractional reserve banking." Indeed, the invention of fractional reserve banking—wherein the bank always has liquidity on hand to meet deposit withdrawals that is less than its deposit obligations—was not dependent on the invention of coinage. Interestingly, some of the earliest recorded laws pertaining to banks were part of the code of Hammurabi in ancient Mesopotamia. The deposits in these ancient warehouse banks were cattle, grain, and precious metals. However, a banking system in which credit transfers occurred was probably introduced during the Ptolemaic era (323–30 BCE) in Egypt.

Fourth, it was not a coincidence that these ancient banks were the "king's warehouses" or located near temples and other places of power and influence. Such locations gave these banks an added aura of being safe havens for storing valuables, by either the force of the royal army or the presence of God. This generated trust in banks. The consequence was an advantage for people to use these as the places to store valuable commodities. As we will see, this advantage was critical to the emergence of the warehouse as banks. It is an advantage that is of pivotal importance to banks even today.

How Many Fake Receipts?

If a bank can create money out of thin air by printing fake receipts and lending them out, in this case to farmers, why not do it ad infinitum? Some might think that it is the fear of losing credibility and risking a run on the bank that keeps the bank from creating excessive amounts of private money. This may be so, but there is another powerful deterrent—*incentive compatibility*. This means the number of fake receipts issued by the bank and loaned to farmers must be compatible with the incentives of these farmers to repay the loans. Imagine a world in which the borrowers cannot reliably pledge their output (say, harvested grain or olives) to repay the loan. This may be because they can simply hide it from the bank. What then would induce them to repay their loans?

This question is similar to a question a student once asked me when I was teaching a banking course: "If people deposit all their money with the bank, why does the bank do all the hard work of operating the bank? Why not just take the money and run?" This is similar to asking why a borrower would ever bother to repay the bank.

The borrower's repayment incentive arises from his need to continue to have access to the bank. If the borrower were to harvest his grain, after having taken a bank loan to pay his workers, then he must decide where to store the grain. If the output is deposited in the warehouse bank, it can be seized by the bank as repayment for the loan. On the other hand, keeping the output away from the warehouse can allow the borrower to avoid repaying the loan. But this comes at a cost. The borrower can no longer make use of the safekeeping services offered by the warehouse. If the advantage of the warehouse over private storage is big enough, the borrower will prefer to deposit his output with the bank and repay the loan. This puts an upper bound on how big a loan the bank can make to the borrower using fake receipts.[7] One can solve mathematically for exactly the number of fake receipts that can be loaned out before the borrower will default with certainty.[8] Thus, the system has its own checks and balances, and just the right amount of liquidity is created through private money.

Whither Fiat Money?

Just as private money existed side by side with fiat money (coins) in ancient Egypt, so it does today as well. There are actually many forms of money today. The paper currency and coins we use are "fiat money," since they are legally acceptable by government fiat and have value because they are accepted in payments. The check you write that instructs your bank to pay from your deposit account is another form of money. Our financial system creates money in a variety of ways. See table 2.1.

Money has value because people *believe* it has value. At the top of the hierarchy is fiat money, the most liquid form of money with the most credibility in the sense that the assets backing the claims have the lowest likelihood of default.

Table 2.1 Hierarchy of Money Claims in the Economy

	Money or money-like claim issued	Assets backing the claim
Central bank	Currency in circulation and bank reserves (liabilities of central bank)	Treasury bills (federal government debt), agency debt, and residential mortgage-backed securities (RMBS)
Depository banks issuing insured deposits	Insured deposits (liabilities of commercial banks)	Loans and deposit insurance
Dealer banks	Repurchase agreement or repos (liabilities issued by dealers' credit trading desks)	Collateralized by corporate bonds, asset-backed securities, and private-label RMBS
Money funds	Constant net asset value (NAV) shares.	Commercial paper, Treasury bills, and other short-term assets
Depository banks issuing uninsured deposits	Uninsured deposits	Loans and securities

Source: Thakor 2015b.

How Does Money Creation Interact with Lending?

Banks act as warehouses for valuables, including things that serve as a medium of exchange (grain, olives, fiat money). This is true even today. Banks are not only depositories but also trusted custodians who provide safekeeping services. They are also experts in screening borrowers and lending.[9]

This lending expertise evolved quite naturally from the warehousing function. The bank *creates* liquidity only when it lends fake receipts to borrowers. Just the act of opening a deposit account for a borrower does *not* create liquidity. That is merely the warehousing function. It is important, but it is not banking.

Banking arises when liquidity is created, not just when liquidity is stored safely. This necessarily involves lending. So lending is an essential part of the liquidity creation that is the raison d'être for the bank. We sometimes use the term "qualitative asset transformation" to describe what the bank is doing—on the asset side it has illiquid loans, and on the liability side it has liquid deposits. But, of course, lending is typically risky. Even creditworthy borrowers default sometimes. And some are not even creditworthy.

Given the centrality of risky lending to banking, it is no surprise that over time, banks developed specialized expertise in managing this risk by screening borrowers to identify the creditworthy borrowers, monitoring those who are given credit, and designing loan contracts with covenants and collateral provisions to limit credit risk. In the process of managing these risks, they also developed expertise in processing a wide range of credit-related information and in verification of cash flows, asset ownership, and contract compliance, so as to reduce the transactions costs of contracting.[10]

Because banks developed information processing expertise, they also routinely acquired sensitive (confidential) information about their customers. Therefore, it became essential for them to become *trusted* by their clients and other counterparties to protect the confidentiality of this information.[11] Trust evolved inevitably as a central attribute for banks to focus on.

This perspective also highlights the fact that research that focuses on only the liability or asset side of the bank's balance sheet misses the important link between the bank's warehousing function (deposits) and its liquidity creation (lending fake receipts). Any policy discussion that does not simultaneously consider both sides of the bank's balance sheet runs the risk of being misguided.[12] The magnitude of liquidity created by banks is huge. For example, research shows that in 2003 US banks created over $2.84 trillion in liquidity. It was 39 percent of bank total assets. Every dollar of bank equity capital was associated with $4.56 of liquidity creation.[13] In 2017, the total assets of the US banking system were about $16.711 trillion, so applying the 39 percent to this number gives liquidity creation of about $6.517 trillion.

This view of lending-based liquidity creation by the bank is not the way most of the existing research views liquidity creation in banking. The dominant view is that banks create liquidity by providing risk-averse depositors with insurance against uncertain future liquidity needs.[14] A simple way to see the argument is this: You have $100 today, and if you invest it, you will get $120 in a year. You are not sure whether you will need money in six months or in a year. If you need it in six months, you have to liquidate your investment and recover $100. So you get to either consume $100 in six months or $120 in a year. What a bank can do is ask you to deposit the $100 now and promise to give you, say, $106 if you withdraw in six months and $110 if you withdraw in a year. Your consumption stream (106, 110) is "smoother" than (100, 120) without a bank, so you are better off with a bank, because your risk is lowered. A deposit contract is considered liquid because it gives you instantaneous access to liquidity. Improved risk sharing is viewed as being synonymous with liquidity creation.

This view of bank liquidity creation is very different from what I have described as lending-based liquidity creation. In this risk-sharing view, banking does not expand the investable resources of the economy beyond the endowment of the economy. A second difference is that with warehouse banking, loans create deposits, whereas in the risk-sharing (consumption insurance) views, deposits create loans.

To sum up, banks serve three core economic functions, as shown in figure 2.3.

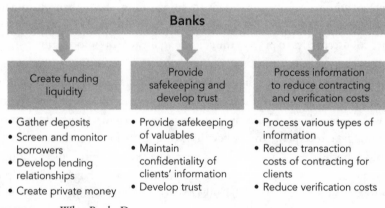

FIGURE 2.3 What Banks Do.

At this point, the casual observer might say: "Wait, I know banks do a lot more. They make loan commitments, provide market making services, act as counterparties in swap contracts, and so on." True. But, as we will see later in this book, the three main economic functions I have listed will suffice to develop a coherent argument for how to achieve growth-friendly banking stability.

Banking Is Not a One-Night Stand: Relationship Lending

Every company knows the value of customer loyalty. Having repeat business from your customers is a great thing. For most companies the reason for this is that it is costly to acquire new customers. This is why airlines, cruise ships, and hotels have customer loyalty programs that reward customers with greater benefits the more business they do with the company.

For banks there is an added benefit of customer loyalty in its lending business. The longer the relationship of the borrower with the bank, the more the bank learns about the borrower, and this knowledge can be used in subsequent contracts with the borrower. Economists call this "intertemporal information reusability."[15] Simply put, it means that, unlike a scoop of ice cream, which disappears when you eat it, the same information can be consumed or reused time and again without diminishing its value. Having done credit analysis on the borrower once and having observed the borrower's behavior on the first loan, the bank has a lot less work to do when it lends to the borrower again. This provides the bank with a big advantage over new lenders who might wish to lure the borrower away. After all, the incumbent bank now knows "for free" what competing banks have to invest to learn. This repeated interaction between the bank and the borrower is called "relationship lending."

Relationship lending has interesting consequences.[16] One is that as the bank learns more about the borrower, the terms of lending may become better over time for borrowers. Another is that borrowers who start out getting only secured loans may over time be able to switch to unsecured loans. This is beneficial for the borrower because it frees up collateral that can be used to support other types of financing.[17] Finally, because the relationship is valuable for both the bank and the borrower, both have incentives to behave better in order not to jeopardize the relationship. The borrower is less likely to take actions that may hurt the bank, and the bank is less likely to engage in exploitative pricing to fleece the borrower.

From What Banks Do to How It All Breaks Down: Stakeholders and Financial Crises

In the fall of 2007, Sam Smith was a young aspiring assistant professor of finance at a lending business school in the United States. He had been an assistant professor for two years and was struggling with the disappointment of his papers being rejected by the top journals. Then came the financial crisis.

All of a sudden, Sam found himself engaged in conversations with his colleagues and students about the crisis. Every conversation raised questions no one knew the answers to. How did this happen? What are its effects? What are the magnitudes of the effects? What kind of crisis is this—a liquidity or an insolvency crisis? What should the government do in the short run and in the long run?

As the questions grew, Sam felt a strange sense of excitement. If everybody is so interested in the answers, why not start doing research on these questions? Over the next five years, Sam completely switched his research agenda to addressing a host of interesting questions about the crisis. There seemed to be no end to the ideas one could explore. A whole new continent of opportunities had opened up. He found great success in publishing his papers, and his career took off.

This story is fictitious. But I know many whose research careers were boosted by the research they did on the crisis. It is a fact that the financial crisis generated a plethora of fascinating research questions that many young scholars attacked with creativity and vigor. A large number of excellent books and research papers have been written on the subject.[18] The body of knowledge is indeed very rich.

In light of this vast body of knowledge, why do we need to revisit the issue of what banks do and how they do it? The answer is suggested by the following quote from Ben Bernanke:

> In the analysis of the crisis, my testimony before the Financial Crisis Inquiry Commission drew the distinction between triggers and vulnerabilities. The triggers of the crisis were the particular events or factors that touched off the events of 2007–09—the proximate causes, if you will. Developments in the market for subprime mortgages…were a prominent example of a trigger of the crisis. In contrast, the vulnerabilities were the structural, and more fundamental, weaknesses in the financial system and in regulation and supervision that served to propagate and amplify the initial shocks.[19]

To understand the fundamental structural weaknesses in the financial system—at whose epicenter banks sit—we need to focus on the core economic activities of banks, how the very performance of these activities set in motion the forces that generate financial crises, how regulation then attempts a correction, and how this in turn reshapes the economic activities banks engage in and the services they provide, as shown in figure 2.4.

The point of figure 2.4 is simple. It is the very nature of the services that banks provide (and the reasons why they exist) that leads to these institutions being crisis-prone. And a crisis invariably invites new regulation, which in turn changes banking. This is the sense in which a crisis is the fire that not only threatens the existence of banking but also forges its very shape. Without starting with why banks exist and the services they provide, it is extremely challenging to think of ways to enhance banking stability. So it is useful to start with the first box in figure 2.4.

For now, I want to stress one point. The warehousing function of banks defines three groups of stakeholders: customers who finance the bank, customers who receive financing from the bank (borrowers), and investors.[20] The bank's depositors represent customers who finance the bank; banks are unusual in that a lot of their financing comes from their customers. Financing also comes from investors—shareholders and bondholders. A key distinction between these two groups of financiers that was emphasized by Robert C. Merton[21] is that investors are willing to bear the credit risk associated with the bank and they reflect it in the pricing of the bank's securities, but customers (depositors) are unwilling to bear this risk. This means that they will rush to withdraw their deposits as soon as there is even a whiff of elevated credit risk in the bank.

Banks rely on deposit funding to a large extent—deposits account for 70 percent or more of a bank's total funding typically. So a precipitous decline in this funding can bring down the bank. This is costly to society for various reasons, one of them being relationship lending. When a bank shuts down due to failure, the information it has about its relationship borrowers is lost. Even if these borrowers can go to other banks, they are likely to get less credit, because these new banks lack the information the failed bank had about them. The specter of such losses encourages regulatory protection of banks—things like deposit insurance and other safety nets.[22] But once these safety nets are in place, they generate structural incentives for banks to take greater risks.[23] These risks can then lead to overinvestments in risky assets, excessive leverage, and asset price bubbles—a potent admixture for igniting a crisis. What research has shown is that an important way to diminish these

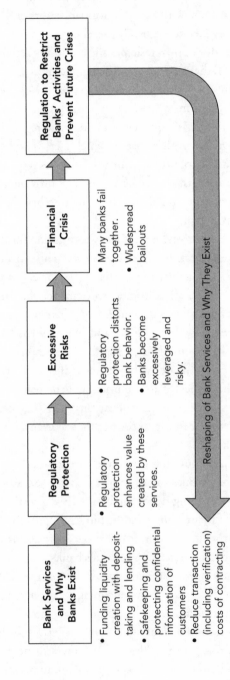

Bank Services and Why Banks Exist

- Funding liquidity creation with deposit-taking and lending
- Safekeeping and protecting confidential information of customers
- Reduce transaction (including verification) costs of contracting

Regulatory Protection

- Regulatory protection enhances value created by these services.

Excessive Risks

- Regulatory protection distorts bank behavior.
- Banks become excessively leveraged and risky.

Financial Crisis

- Many banks fail together.
- Widespread bailouts

Regulation to Restrict Banks' Activities and Prevent Future Crises

Reshaping of Bank Services and Why They Exist

FIGURE 2.4 The Existence-Failure-Regulation Cycle in Banking.

risk-taking incentives is by asking banks to keep more equity capital. Better-capitalized banks are safer and have stronger incentives to develop a safety-oriented culture.[24] Such banks are thus better at earning the trust of their counterparties. Opponents of higher capital in banking would say that this will sacrifice economic growth.

Banks and Society

What we have discussed thus far gives us a glimpse of how banks fit into society at large. The various actors in the drama are banks and their shareholders, households who are both depositors and borrowers of banks, businesses who depend on bank credit for their operations, central banks that provide safety nets for banks and regulate them, taxpayers who pay for these safety nets, and the financial markets that banks compete with and complement as well. That is, we are all involved in the business of banking in one way or the other.

The manner in which banks interact with these other actors in the drama shapes banking itself. For example, when competition for borrowers that banks face from investment banks and the capital market heats up, banks deepen their relationships with borrowers.[25] Trust becomes more important, and banks invest more in relationships that add greater value to borrowers.

Because banks have both a bright and a dark side for society, banks must take into account their relationships with these other actors in striking a balance between the role of banking in promoting economic growth and its role in providing economic stability. By articulating an authentic higher purpose that serves society and developing a culture that strikes the right balance between growth and stability, banks can engender *trust,* which is central to society being willing to continue to provide the safety nets that are so crucial for banks. Banking without trust is like prayer without faith. As we shall see, both organizational higher purpose and capital play important roles in the ability of banks to support economic growth in society without sacrificing growth and to earn society's trust.

So far, we have seen only the *on-balance-sheet* activities of banks. This is like observing the tip of the iceberg that is visible above the water—over 90 percent is below the water. A large portion of what banks do is actually *off the balance sheet*, like the iceberg below the water. Even the loans banks make do not necessarily stay on their balance sheets, because of things like securitization, a process by which a bank that originates a loan then proceeds to sell it into a pool from which market-traded securities are issued, so a piece of that loan will be held eventually by some investor. For example, do you know which institution holds your home mortgage? It is most likely not the bank you borrowed from. What exactly do banks do off the balance sheet? Let us turn to this in the next chapter.

Notes

1. See Ermatinger 2007, 34 (emphasis added).
2. See Davies 2016.
3. Interestingly, this kind of money coexisted with metallic money (coins) during the Egyptian empire of the Ptolemies (323–30 BCE). See Davies 2016.
4. But these fake receipts are not fiat money, which is money created by the government and has the authority of the government backing it. Economists refer to these fake receipts as "private money" created by banks.
5. I am using the terminology used in Donaldson, Piacentino, and Thakor 2018. What is described here is a simplified version of their general equilibrium model.
6. Macmillan Committee 1931, 34.
7. See Donaldson, Piacentino, and Thakor 2018
8. In information economics, incorporating this consideration means taking into account an "incentive compatibility constraint."
9. See Coval and Thakor 2005, Millon and Thakor 1985, and Ramakrishnan and Thakor 1984.
10. The costs of verifying things like borrower cash flows, to ensure that debt contracts are being appropriately serviced, leads not only to an economic justification for using debt contracts but also to a justification for banks to serve as intermediaries to reduce verification costs.
11. See Bhattacharya and Chiesa (1995), who develop a theory in which some borrowers prefer bank financing to market financing because the former better protects information confidentiality.
12. Fortunately, we have plenty of theories that deal both with what banks do on the asset side and what they do on the liability side. See Diamond 1984, Diamond and Dybvig 1983, Ramakrishnan and Thakor 1984, Millon and Thakor 1985, and Coval and Thakor 2005. See Bhattacharya and Thakor 1993 for a review.
13. See Berger and Bouwman 2009.
14. See Bryant 1980 and Diamond and Dybvig 1983.
15. See Greenbaum, Thakor, and Boot 2015.
16. These consequences were derived by Boot and Thakor 1994 in a theoretical model of relationship lending with collateral.
17. Collateral is typically costly for borrowers to post. See Besanko and Thakor 1987a, 1987b.
18. Lo 2012 reviews twenty-one books on the subject. See Thakor 2015a for a recent literature review.
19. Bernanke 2012.

20. I am using the terminology used in Merton and Thakor forthcoming in their theory of financial intermediation based on the "functional perspective."
21. See Merton 1993, 1997.
22. See Merton and Thakor forthcoming.
23. See Merton 1977.
24. Weaknesses in corporate culture often lead to reckless behavior in banking, so a more safety-oriented culture is typically welcome news.
25. See Boot and Thakor 2000 for a foundational theory of relationship banking using this idea.

References

Berger, Allen N., and Christa H. S. Bouwman. 2009. "Bank Liquidity Creation." *Review of Financial Studies* 22 (9): 3779–3837.

Bernanke, Ben S. 2012. "Some Reflections on the Crisis and the Policy Response." Speech at the Russell Sage Foundation and the Century Foundation Conference "Rethinking Finance," New York, April 13, 2012.

Besanko, David, and Anjan V. Thakor. 1987a. "Collateral and Rationing Sorting Equilibria in Monopolistic and Competitive Credit Markets." *International Economic Review* 28 (3): 167–182.

Besanko, David, and Anjan V. Thakor. 1987b. "Competitive Equilibrium in the Credit Market Under Asymmetric Information." *Journal of Economic Theory* 42 (1): 449–471.

Bhattacharya, Sudipto, and Gabriela Chiesa. 1995. "Proprietary Information, Financial Intermediation, and Research Incentives." *Journal of Financial Intermediation* 4 (4): 328–357.

Bhattacharya, Sudipto, and Anjan V. Thakor. 1993. "Contemporary Banking Theory." *Journal of Financial Intermediation* 3 (1): 2–50.

Boot, Arnoud, and Anjan V. Thakor. 1994. "Moral Hazard and Secured Lending in an Infinitely Repeated Credit Market Game." *International Economic Review* 35 (3): 679–705.

Boot, Arnoud, and Anjan V. Thakor. 2002. "Can Relationship Banking Survive Competition?" *Journal of Finance* 55 (2): 679–714.

Bryant, John. 1980. "A Model of Reserves, Bank Runs and Deposit Insurance." *Journal of Banking and Finance* 4:335–344.

Coval, Joshua, and Anjan V. Thakor. 2005. "Financial Intermediation as a Beliefs Bridge Between Optimists and Pessimists." *Journal of Financial Economics* 75 (3): 535–570.

Davies, Glyn. 2016. *A History of Money: From Ancient Times to the Present Day.* 4th ed. Cardiff: University of Wales Press.

Diamond, Douglas. 1984. "Financial Intermediation and Delegated Monitoring," *Review of Economic Studies* 51 (3): 393–414.

Diamond, Douglas, and Philip Dybvig. 1983. "Bank Runs, Deposit Insurance and Liquidity." *Journal of Political Economy* 91 (3): 401–419.

Donaldson, Jason, Giorgia Piacentino, and Anjan V. Thakor. 2018. "Warehouse Banking," *Journal of Financial Economics* 129:250–267.

Ermatinger, James. 2007. *The Daily Life of Christians in Ancient Rome*. Westport, CT: Greenwood.

Greenbaum, Stuart, Anjan V. Thakor, and Arnoud Boot. 2015. *Contemporary Financial Intermediation*. Amsterdam: Elsevier, 2015.

Hull, Stephen, A. 2013. "Warehouses: Their Development and Latest Mode of Construction." *Rotarian* 3 (8): 31–32.

Lo, Andrew, 2012. "Reading about the Financial Crisis: A Twenty-One Book Review." *Journal of Economic Literature* 50: 151–178.

Macmillan Committee. 1931. *British Parliamentary Reports on International Finance: The Report of the Macmillan Committee*. London: H. M. Stationery Office.

Merton, Robert, C. 1977. "An Analytic Derivation of the Cost of Deposit Insurance and Loan Guarantees: An Application of Modern Option Pricing Theory." *Journal of Banking and Finance* 1 (1): 3–11.

Merton, Robert C. 1993. "Operation and Regulation in Financial Intermediation: A Functional Perspective." In *Operation and Regulation of Financial Markets*, edited by Peter Englund, 17–67. Stockholm: Economic Council

Merton, Robert C. 1997. "A Model of Contract Guarantees for Credit-Sensitive, Opaque Financial Intermediaries." *European Financial Review* 1 (1): 1–13.

Merton, Robert, and Richard Thakor. Forthcoming. "Customers and Investors: A Framework for Understanding the Evolution of Financial Institutions." *Journal of Financial Intermediation*.

Millon, Marcia, and Anjan V. Thakor. 1985. "Moral Hazard and Information Sharing: A Model of Financial Information Gathering Agencies." *Journal of Finance* 40 (5): 1403–1422.

Ramakrishnan, Ram T. S., and Anjan V. Thakor. 1984. "Information Reliability and a Theory of Financial Intermediation." *Review of Economic Studies* 51 (3): 415–432.

Thakor, Anjan V. 2015a. "The Financial Crisis of 2007–09: Why Did It Happen and What Did We Learn?" *Review of Corporate Finance Studies* 4 (2): 115–205.

Thakor, Anjan V. 2015b. *International Financial Markets: A Diverse System Is the Key to Commerce*. Washington, DC: US Chamber of Commerce.

3

Out of Sight, Out of Mind?

OFF-BALANCE-SHEET BANKING

Introduction: Tales from the Twilight Zone

The first tale is about the December 2015 Paris Climate Accord. Major enthusiasm followed because there was widespread agreement on global emission reductions and pledges to increase investments in renewable energy. This was welcome news to supporters of clean energy in light of diminishing enthusiasm on the part of traditional venture capitalists to invest in renewable-energy companies.[1] However, not long after the Paris Accord, there was bad news. SunEdison filed for bankruptcy in April 2016. The company was planning to become a big player in renewable energy. But its bankruptcy cast a pall over the prospects of private-sector initiatives to promote clean, renewable energy. What should be done to regain momentum?

For the second tale, imagine that you own a house in an area in which there is plenty of sunshine most of the year, and you spend a fortune on air conditioning, which you also need most of the year. Along comes a company that wants to sell you solar panels for the house so you can convert the whole house to solar energy. You like the idea because you care about the environment. The problem is the cost. The estimate is $100,000. You just can't afford that right now. What do you do?

For the third tale, imagine a somewhat different challenge. There is a community with a large inventory of unsold houses—some of these are houses that were foreclosed on during the Great Recession, and others are houses the homeowners want to sell but are unable to get a good price for. There are just not enough homebuyers. In the community there is ironically also a shortage of rental housing. What should be done?

The answers to all three questions are the same—securitization. In the first case, the big challenge is to stimulate demand for the output of the clean energy company, especially in an era of low oil prices. This is reflected in the second case—an individual who simply lacks the wealth or liquidity for a major outlay on solar panels. It is estimated that the national average residential solar price was around $3.70 per watt during 2014–2015, which includes installation and ongoing maintenance costs.[2] The median US household income was $53,657 in 2014, which puts solar panels out of reach for most Americans. The third case reflects an imbalance in the availability of rental property vis-à-vis homes for sale, relative to demand. How is securitization the answer in all cases?

Let us begin by summarizing how securitization works. A large number of similar assets—essentially claims to future cash flows—are pooled together. Then multiple tranches or classes of asset-backed securities (ABS)—that is, securities whose holders will be paid with the cash flows from the pooled assets—are created. These are multiple prioritized claims against the stream of cash flows from the asset portfolio pool. These tranches have differing seniorities, so all of the portfolio cash flows are first used to pay off the seniormost tranche. Once this tranche is fully paid off, the next most senior tranche begins to be paid off, and so on. So the seniormost tranche has the lowest risk as well as the shortest duration. Each tranche is typically given a rating by the credit rating agencies. So securitization creates different debt claims against a relatively homogeneous pool of assets (which are themselves debt claims). The ABS are purchased by capital market investors, which provides the funding for the assets being securitized.

So consider the first two cases. Suppose the solar panel company tells you that you do not need to pay anything for the solar panels to be installed. They will do it at no cost to you. However, all of the power generated will be given by you to the grid. They will then sell it back to you, but it will cost you less than what you are paying for power right now.

How can the solar panel company do this? By securitizing solar panel sales. The idea is for the company to raise the financing for the purchase and installation by selling claims to investors and then repay these investors from the revenue from the sale of power back to the consumers. This is not just an idea anymore. It is already being done. In this new residential solar business model for households, consumers have become "prosumers" of electricity—producing, consuming, and reselling electricity to the grid. A commonly used contract is a solar "power purchase agreement" (PPA). With this contract, there is typically a twenty-year lease agreement in which the solar company provides the panels to consumers, and consumers then make predetermined payments that are below their current payments.[3] See figure 3.1.

Now consider the last story. Instead of ill-advised government initiatives like rent controls, with all of the distortions and unintended consequences, why not use securitization? The way it would work is as follows. Investors buy the unsold houses. They then refurbish them, and then these houses are rented. The financing for this is raised by setting up a special purpose vehicle

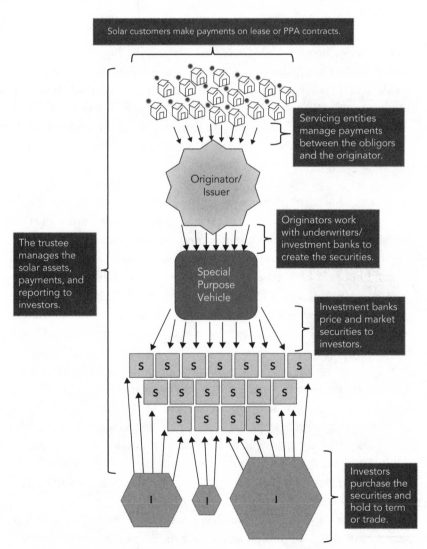

FIGURE 3.1 Securitization for Solar Panels.

for securitizing these properties. The investors who purchase the asset-backed securities are paid out of the rental income.

Again, this is no longer just a theoretical possibility. It is already being done. After the 2007–2009 crisis, institutional investors like hedge funds and private equity firms purchased hundreds of thousands of houses, worth billions of dollars, and leased them to renters. The money to buy the houses was raised by securitizing the rental income. Investors who purchased the asset-backed securities to provide the financing essentially acquired claims on the future rental income.[4]

As William Cohan writes:

> Whether or not Blackstone, Hyperion, and other big investors suc-ceed, what they are doing is in fact a classic example of the role that risk capital is supposed to play in broken markets: to make bets that others are fearful of making, and to profit from them if things work out.... And if it really does provide a growing rental population with better options and better service, that will also serve a nation still recovering from the excesses of the past decade.[5]

These are not far-fetched stories, although they may seem that way to some. Despite being maligned for its role in the 2007–2009 financial crisis, securitization may well be the greatest contribution to finance since the de-velopment of the Black-Scholes-Merton option pricing model.[6] The reasons are many, but here are a few examples. First, it is a way to liquefy illiquid as-sets. Consequently, liquidity premia that investors demand on these assets go down, and investments in these assets increase. Second, securitization can help stimulate demand for certain things that were previously unafford-able for consumers, such as solar panels. Third, securitization can help stim-ulate urban renewal and a host of other prosocial activities by channeling investments into these activities that are otherwise not possible. And finally, it allows banks to more efficiently manage a variety of risks.

What is most relevant is the last point. At its core, securitization improves balance-sheet risk management in banks, and the fundamental economic purpose of banks is to create liquidity and stimulate economic growth. So anything that reduces financial stability and detracts from this role of banks is inimical to economic growth in the long run.[7]

From this perspective, securitization is a boon to banking because it si-multaneously does two things that enhance the core economic functions of banks: it enables banks to create liquidity in areas of the economy that banks might shy away from, and it also reduces banking risk in serving these parts of the economy.

A Fly in the Ointment

While securitization is a brilliant innovation, it also has some well-known problems. The biggest one is caused by what is referred to as the originate-to-distribute (OTD) model of banking, which is how securitization is described. In traditional banking, banks originate loans to hold them on their balance sheets, engaging in a variety of relationship lending activities. With securitization, banks originate loans to distribute them to others. Banks are screening and monitoring experts, but these activities are costly. Depositors rely on banks to screen properly and make loans only to creditworthy borrowers, and then monitor them using their relationship lending expertise to make sure loans are repaid. But banks may not live up to these expectations, because doing so is costly. How can depositors and investors be sure that banks will indeed live up to their expectations?

With traditional banking, incentives to screen and monitor are sustained because banks have skin in the game—the fortunes of the bank's shareholders depend on the quality of its loans. But, with the OTD model, the bank has no skin in the game, because the loans are sold and are no longer on its balance sheet. This means there is a risk that the bank may originate bad loans.[8] In a sense, this is like *syndicated lending,* in which the lead bank originates a loan but then participating banks provide much of the funding for the loan, which reduces the lead bank's skin in the game.

Countless papers have been written on the adverse incentives generated by the OTD model of banking. Weakened screening incentives have been empirically documented with clever designs. For example, one study found that mortgage loans with FICO scores of 621 actually turn out to have significantly higher default rates than those with FICO scores of 619.[9] How can this be? We would expect these two types of loans to have virtually identical default probabilities, or if they differ, then the 621 loans to be less risky. The answer is that a score of 620 is the threshold for mortgage securitization—banks can securitize mortgages with FICO scores of 621 or more, whereas the 619 loans stay on its books. The evidence suggests that banks are more careful in screening loans they will hold on their books than the ones they will securitize.

Of course, investors who buy asset-backed securities in the market are rational and understand these distorted incentives due to the OTD model. They will therefore price asset-backed securities accordingly. Banks, faced with these unattractive prices, have incentives of their own to improve these prices. There is really only one way to achieve this—put some skin back in the game. One way is to provide some recourse to investors in case the asset-backed securities underperform due to loan defaults. That is, the banks that originate these loans agree to compensate investors for some of their losses. The other is overcollateralization, meaning the pool of assets transferred to the trust is bigger than the face value of the claims of the investors purchasing the asset-backed securities. Once skin in the game is restored, screening incentives for banks are strengthened. And of course the power of skin in the game is greater the higher the bank's capital.[10] The reason is simple. The higher the capital, the more of the bank's owners' wealth is at risk; hence, the stronger the bank's incentives are to reduce risk with greater due diligence.

This means that higher bank capital can help to minimize the downside of the OTD model of banking as long as originating banks have enough skin in the game. Some skin in the game comes from explicit recourse—meaning that investors who buy the asset-backed securities have recourse to the loan originator for compensation in case of losses due to loan defaults—and overcollateralization. And additional skin in the game comes from reputational incentives associated with loan originators playing a "repeated game" in the securitization market. The idea here is that most loan originators do not securitize just once. Rather, they do it on an ongoing basis. This means that if they securitize poor-quality loans, they will develop a bad reputation, making the market unreceptive to the next securitization. This will induce loan originators not to securitize bad loans.

An interesting aspect of this relates to an issue we saw in the previous chapter, which is the blurring of boundaries between banks and markets. Nowhere is this blurring more evident than with securitization. The quality of securitized assets affects the risk investors are exposed to in the market for asset-backed securities, which in turn affects the risk premia on these securities and the liquidity of the market in which they are traded. Thus, the capital market is significantly affected by the perceived quality of asset-backed securities. And since capital levels in the originating banks causally affect the quality of these securities, we can infer that bank capital has a potentially significant effect on the financial market.[11] With higher levels of bank capital, we may be able to have the best of both worlds—getting inherently illiquid assets off the balance sheets of banks and still preserving sufficient incentives for these banks to diligently screen the assets they choose to originate. This can then facilitate the coevolution of banks and capital markets.[12]

Other Interesting Things off the Balance Sheet

In an address to the American Bankers Association in October 1985, Paul Volcker, then Chairman of the Board of Governors of the Federal Reserve System, said: "Has the attention paid to simple capital ratios driven risks off balance sheet, and is off balance sheet also out of mind?"[13] Volcker was almost prophetic in worrying about the issue. Once negligible in amount, off-balance-sheet (OBS) banking now amounts to trillions of dollars. For many large money-center banks, the notional value of OBS claims may be as large as thirty times what is on the balance sheet.[14] In other words, when we look a bank's balance sheet, what we see is only the tip of the iceberg.

OBS claims are essentially *contingent liabilities* for banks.[15] The largest among these are loan commitments and standby letters of credit. A loan commitment is simply a promise by the bank to make credit available to the borrower in the future at terms that are (at least partially) predetermined. The table below (table 3.1) is an example of a loan commitment.

As this example shows, the loan commitment contract specifies a maximum amount of the credit line that the borrower can tap for a loan; this

Table 3.1 **An Example of a Loan Commitment Contract**

Blockbuster Entertainment	
Amount	$200,000,000
Maturity	48 Months
Beginning	8-31-1990
Lender	Security Pacific
Use	General Corporate Purposes
Fee Structure	
Commitment fee	0
Annual servicing fee	12.5 basis points
Usage fee	12.5 basis points
Cancellation fee	0
Take-down interest rate alternatives	
Prime	
LIBOR + 50 basis points	
CD + 62.5 basis points	

Source: Greenbaum, Thakor, and Boot (2015)

maximum does not have to be tapped in one fell swoop—it can be done gradually over time. It also stipulates how the interest rate and fees on the loan will be determined.

Although in this case the commitment fee is zero, there may sometimes be a commitment fee that the borrower has to pay just in order to buy the option to borrow under the commitment. This makes economic sense; a loan commitment is basically a put option. If the borrower can borrow in the spot credit market (when the loan is needed) at a rate lower than the commitment rate, it will do so. Think of this market borrowing rate as the true cost of debt for the borrower. This is the rate at which the borrower's future repayments should be discounted back to the present to arrive at the *value* of the borrower's debt security that is being sold by the borrower to raise financing, that is, the loan.

This means that when the spot credit market borrowing rate is lower than the loan commitment rate, the borrower can sell its security in the market at a higher price than it can to the bank under the loan commitment (i.e., it can borrow at a cheaper rate in the market—the value of a debt security rises as the borrowing rate falls), so it will choose to do so and let the option to borrow under the commitment expire unexercised. On the other hand, if the loan commitment borrowing rate is lower than the spot market rate, the borrower will get a higher price for selling the debt security to the bank by exercising its commitment option and taking a loan under the commitment. When it does so, it is selling the bank an *overpriced* debt security, since this security would sell at a lower price in the market (i.e., the market borrowing rate would be higher). This is similar to a common stock put option in which you sell stock to the option writer at a higher price than the stock price at the time of exercise. The commitment fee can be viewed as the price of the put option.

There may also be a host of other fees. For example, the usage fee can be either a fee on the actual amount borrowed under the commitment or the amount of the commitment *not* used. The commitment contract will also specify the uses to which borrowed funds will be put.

Loan commitments are extremely widely used. Research shows that 77 percent of new commercial and industrial loans in an average US bank's portfolio are made under loan commitments, with only 23 percent being spot loans, and many banks make no spot commercial and industrial loans at all.[16]

Like loan commitments, standby letters of credit also have option characteristics. When a bank issues a standby letter of credit, it guarantees the performance of an "account party," usually in a commercial or financial transaction. Typically it would arise as follows. Let us say John has placed an order for one hundred thousand fresh flowers to be delivered from a farm owned by Mary. Mary ships the flowers to John and expects John to pay $200,000 upon delivery of the flowers. But how can Mary be sure John will pay after he takes possession of the flowers? One way for John to reassure Mary is to have his bank issue a standby letter of credit, which guarantees that the bank will make up any deficiency in John's repayment to Mary. The bank will charge John an upfront fee for providing this guarantee.

Connecting the Dots from Warehouse Banking to OBS Banking

One might think therefore that the explosion of OBS banking has little to do with the origins of banking and the basic liquidity creation function of banks. But quite the opposite is true. Think of a bank as a warehouse for safe storage of deposits (commodities in the past and fiat currency now). To this day, banks play a critical role in providing a safekeeping function. Indeed, there is now quite a bit of research on the "creation of safe assets" in the economy.[17] We already saw how this allows the bank to create private money via fake receipts that are loaned out. This is spot lending. But why limit the bank to that? Inject a little uncertainty like the possibility that a borrower cannot be sure it will be able to get a loan from the bank at a future date when it needs the loan. Economists refer to this as "quantity rationing," meaning that there is no price at which the borrower can get credit.[18] Now the borrower will have an incentive to approach the bank and purchase a loan commitment as a sort of insurance policy against future rationing.[19] The bank, as a warehouse of liquidity, will sell the commitment because it boosts its profits now. If we imagine that the bank incurs a warehouse storage cost (for modern banks this can be the combining of many operating costs), then we can imagine that the bank faces a cost of keeping liquidity in its coffers, and it does so because it faces the prospect of depositors arriving at the bank to make actual withdrawals in circumstances in which (fake) receipts may not suffice. Similarly, loan commitment customers may in some cases wish to access the actual liquidity stored by the bank rather than simply accepting (fake) receipts. So liquidity storage may kill two birds with one stone—satisfying the withdrawal needs of depositors who want actual liquidity (commodities or fiat money) and the borrowing needs of loan commitment customers who have a similar liquidity need. From a cost perspective, therefore, it makes the most sense for a depository institution—with liquidity safekeeping as one of its primary economic functions—to sell loan commitments.[20]

The argument for standby letters of credit is similar. Inject a bit more uncertainty to see why. Suppose the customer of a bank wishes to purchase some goods and realizes that the bank knows its creditworthiness from previous dealings, but the seller it wishes to purchase the goods from does not. Asking the bank to substitute its good name for the borrower's (unknown) name is economically beneficial. Moreover, the customer may suffer an unexpected liquidity crunch in the future that may impair its ability to pay the supplier. Having a standby letter of credit is like having an emergency line of credit.

So the bottom line is this. OBS banking is a natural outgrowth of the original liquidity creation service provided by banks that we discussed in connection with the evolution of banks; indeed, about half of all bank liquidity creation is off the balance sheet.[21] A lot of loan commitments and standby letters of credit back up commercial paper and municipal bond issues, so in this way banks also help the capital market function better. Moreover, the claim that is sometimes made that bank liquidity creation will decline in importance as markets develop is not borne out by the facts. US bank liquidity creation grew every year from 1993 to 2003.[22] While it declined during the 2007–2009 crisis, the trend of increasing liquidity creation over time has resumed.

There is evidence, however, that banks do not always honor their commitments.[23] For example, some banks reneged on their loan commitments during the financial crisis. One might ask: How can you renege on contracts? The answer lies in the fact that loan commitments are what lawyers call "illusory promises," which means they are not legally binding. Why borrowers would be willing to enter into such contracts and why such contracts actually make economic sense is a fascinating topic unto itself,[24] but a bit tangential to the discussion here.

The point is that when a bank reneges on a commitment contract, it is disruptive for the borrower. It is costly for a borrower to lose credit supply from a relationship lender. And it depreciates the bank's reputation for being trustworthy. Even though giving the bank the discretion to act in this manner was efficient (or made economic sense) for the bank, it costs the bank in terms of reputation, and it may be costly for the borrower. How can these costs be minimized?

The answer lies again in having financially sounder banks. Banks are less likely to renege on their commitments if they are financially sounder.[25] Banks with higher capital are usually financially sounder for three reasons. One is that they simply have more capital, and this makes a direct contribution to soundness.[26] The second reason is that banks with more capital make asset-portfolio and monitoring choices that reduce their risk.[27] And third, banks with more capital are more willing to incur a financial cost by honoring their commitments in order to preserve their reputational capital and trust.[28] Thus, having more capital in banking will reduce the uncertainty in OBS banking.

Summing Up and Questions

OBS banking is here to stay and grow. It adds to the aura and mystique of banking, because it makes banks more opaque to investors. I was once at a conference organized by the Federal Reserve Bank of New York, and the topic of information disclosure by banks was being discussed by a panel of equity analysts who specialized in valuing banks. One of them said that the problem was not that banks did not disclose enough information; rather, it was that banks were so opaque and complex that it was difficult to know what any disclosure meant for the value of the bank. OBS banking obviously makes this problem worse, and in the end it may increase the cost of equity capital for banks. This, in turn, makes building up equity capital in banks more challenging.[29]

Now that we have seen the basics of what banks do on and off the balance sheet, we can turn to how they make their most important decisions. No bank decision is more important for the financial stability and growth of the economy than the bank's capital structure decision. This raises some interesting questions:

1. Given the growth of OBS banking and the positive contribution of bank capital to the value of OBS banking, how do banks determine their capital structure?
2. Will banks with more capital lend more or less?
3. How will bank capital affect bank values and the growth-stability,

We will take up these questions in the next chapter.

Notes

1. See O'Sullivan and Warren 2016.
2. See O'Sullivan and Warren 2016. The comparison of the cost of solar power with electricity is not straightforward, because you would typically *install* solar panels in your home at some initial cost, whereas you would *consume* electricity generated at

a power station. This is why the solar power cost is stated on a *per-watt* basis (an average home would need a 3–4 kW system), whereas the cost of electricity is stated on a *per-kilowatt-hour* basis; the national average price of electricity is 12 cents per kilowatt-hour. For apples-to-apples comparison, we could look at the cost of solar power based on leasing the panels with a fifteen-year or twenty-year term. In 2018, in Colorado, this cost is about 16.9 cents per kilowatt-hour with a fifteen-year lease. See https://www.solar-estimate.org/solar-panels/colorado. Compare this to the national average price of 12 cents per kilowatt-hour people in the United States pay for electricity.

3. See O'Sullivan and Warren 2016.

4. See DePillis 2013.

5. See DePillis 2013. William Cohan is a regular contributor to *The New York Times* and author of the book *Money and Power*.

6. In my opinion, the option pricing model (OPM) of Black, Scholes, and Merton is the most significant contribution not only to economics but to the social sciences as well, when one considers both its academic and practical impact.

7. This means we can have spurts of economic growth with excessively leveraged banks that make excessively risky investments, but this is growth that will generally not sustain; most likely it will end in a crisis, with subsequent economic contraction. Such boom-bust cycles not only are disruptive and discourage long-term investments, but they also elevate risk premia, even when crisis probabilities are low.

8. Most banks are repeat players in the securitization market, so reputational concerns can mitigate some of these adverse incentives, but there are factors that can weaken reputation-based incentives. See Cortes and Thakor 2017. Greenbaum and Thakor 1987 provided a theory of securitization in which, absent reputational concerns, banks choose to securitize their *best* assets.

9. See Keys et al. 2010. The term FICO stands for "Fair Isaac and Company," which is a data analytics company based in San Jose, California, focused on credit scoring services. FICO scores are used as proxies to measure individual creditworthiness. Higher scores are better.

10. Empirical evidence supports this. For example, Purnanandam 2011 finds that banks with higher capital exhibit less of the screening-dilution incentives with the OTD model than banks with lower capital.

11. Future research will need to uncover all of the dimensions of this effect as well as the magnitudes of the various effects. There is opportunity here for both good empirical research and good theoretical research.

12. See Song and Thakor 2010 for a theoretical analysis.

13. See Volcker 1985, 5–6.

14. For data related to this, see Berger and Bouwman 2016.

15. Thakor, Hong, and Greenbaum 1981 showed how OBS claims can be viewed as put options sold by banks, and thus the Black-Scholes-Merton OPM can be used to price them. Boot, Thakor, and Udell 1987 provide one of the earliest economic

justifications for why loan commitments exist, whereas Thakor and Udell 1987 provide an economic rationale for the pricing structure of loan commitments. Shockley and Thakor 1997 provide evidence on the structure of loan commitment contracts and how bank loan commitments affect the capital structures of their borrowers.

16. See Greenbaum, Thakor, and Boot 2015.

17. See Gorton and Pennacchi (1990), who suggest that uninformed people are at a disadvantage in trading with informed investors, so they prefer safe assets like bank deposits that are "informationally insensitive." Merton and Thakor (forthcoming) propose that depositors want deposits to be delinked from the bank's credit risk because they do not want the bank's provision of liquidity services to depend on the bank's financial health. Krishnamurthy and Vissing-Jorgensen (2012) provide evidence that investors are willing to pay a premium to hold safe assets like US Treasury instruments. Boot and Thakor (1993) develop a theory that explains why firms create and supply safe assets.

18. See the theoretical papers by Besanko and Thakor (1987) and Stiglitz and Weiss (1981, 1983) on why credit rationing of this sort makes economic sense in some circumstances.

19. See Thakor 2005 for a theory along these lines. Another motivation to purchase a loan commitment is to insure against an increase in the loan interest rate.

20. See Kashyap, Rajan, and Stein 2002 for a theory along these lines and empirical evidence.

21. See Berger and Bouwman 2016.

22. See Berger and Bouwman 2009.

23. See, for example, Huang 2009.

24. See Boot, Greenbaum, and Thakor 1993 for a theory that explains this in great detail. "Illusory promises" is a legal term that describes the nature of the loan commitment contract.

25. See Boot, Greenbaum, and Thakor 1993.

26. See, for example, Berger and Bouwman 2013.

27. See Mehran and Thakor 2011.

28. See Boot, Greenbaum, and Thakor 1993, which develop this theory.

29. This may not be such a big challenge after all, since most banks build up equity capital via retained earnings.

References

Berger, Allen, and Christa Bouwman. 2009. "Bank Liquidity Creation." *Review of Financial Studies* 22:3779–3837.

Berger, Allen, and Christa Bouwman. 2013. "How Does Capital Affect Bank Performance during Financial Crises?" *Journal of Financial Economics* 109 (1): 146–176.

Berger, Allen, and Christa Bouwman. 2016. *Bank Liquidity Creation and Financial Crises*. Amsterdam: Elsevier.

Besanko, David and Anjan V. Thakor. 1987. "Collateral and Rationing: Sorting Equilibria in Monopolistic and Competitive Credit Markets." *International Economic Review* 28 (3): 671–689.

Boot, Arnoud W. A., Stuart I. Greenbaum, and Anjan V. Thakor. 1993. "Reputation and Discretion in Financial Contracting." *American Economic Review* 83 (5): 1165–1183.

Boot, Arnoud, Anjan Thakor, and Gregory Udell. 1987. "Competition, Risk Neutrality and Loan Commitments." *Journal of Banking and Finance* 11 (3): 449–471.

Cortes, Felipe, and Anjan V. Thakor. 2017. "Loan Securitization, Career Concerns and Screening: Does Securitization Increase Systemic Risk?" Working Paper, Washington University in St. Louis.

DePillis, Lydia. 2013. "Wall Street Figured Out How to Securitize Your Rent." *Washington Post*, November 8.

Gorton, Gary, and George Pennacchi. 1990. "Financial Intermediaries and Liquidity Creation." *Journal of Finance* 45 (1): 49–71.

Greenbaum, Stuart, and Anjan Thakor, 1987. "Bank Funding Modes: Securitization Versus Deposits." *Journal of Banking and Finance* 11 (3): 379–401.

Greenbaum, Stuart, Anjan Thakor, and Arnoud Boot. 2015. *Contemporary Financial Intermediation*. 3rd ed. Amsterdam: Elsevier.

Huang, Rocco. 2009. "How Committed Are Bank Lines of Credit? Evidence from the Subprime Mortgage Crisis." Federal Reserve Bank of Philadelphia and Wharton Financial Institutions Center. https://papers.ssrn.com/sol3/papers.cfm?abstract_id=1659986.

Kashyap, Anil K., Raghuram Rajan, and Jeremy C. Stein. 2002. "Banks as Liquidity Providers: An Explanation for the Coexistence of Lending and Deposit-Taking." *Journal of Finance* 57 (1): 33–73.

Keys, Benjamin, J. Tanmoy Mukherjee, Amit Seru, and Vikrant Vig. 2010. "Did Securitization Lead to Lax Screening? Evidence from Subprime Loans." *Quarterly Journal of Economics* 125:307–332.

Krishnamurthy, Arvind, and Annette Vissing-Jorgensen. 2012. "The Aggregate Demand for Treasury Debt." *Journal of Political Economy* 120 (2): 233–267.

Lowder, Travis, and Michael Mendelsohn. 2013. "The Potential of Securitization in Solar PV Finance." Technical Report NREL/TP-6A20-60230, available at www.nrel.gov/publications.

Mehran, Hamid, and Anjan V. Thakor. 2011. "Bank Capital and Value in the Cross-Section." *Review of Financial Studies* 24 (4): 1019–1067.

Merton, Robert, and Richard Thakor. Forthcoming. "Customers and Investors: A Framework for Understanding the Evolution of Financial Institutions." Working paper, MIT Sloan, June 2017, *Journal of Financial Intermediation*.

O'Sullivan, Francis, and Charles H. Warren. 2016. "Solar Securitization: An Innovation in Renewable Energy Finance." MIT Energy Initiative WP-2016-05.

Purnanandam, Amiyatosh. 2011. "Originate-to-Distribute Model and the Subprime Mortgage Crisis." *Review of Financial Studies* 24:1881–1915.

Shockley, Richard, and Anjan Thakor. 1997. "Bank Loan Commitment Contracts: Data, Theory and Tests." *Journal of Money, Credit and Banking* 29 (4): 517–534.

Song, Fenghua, and Anjan V. Thakor. 2010. "Financial System Architecture and the Co-evolution of Banks and Markets." *Economic Journal* 120 (547): 1021–1255.

Stiglitz, Joseph E., and Andrew Weiss. 1981. "Credit Rationing in Markets with Imperfect Information." *American Economic Review* 71 (3): 393–410.

Stiglitz, Joseph E., and Andrew Weiss. 1983. "Incentive Effects of Terminations: Applications to the Credit and Labor Markets." *American Economic Review* 73 (5): 912–927.

Thakor, Anjan V. 2005. "Do Loan Commitments Cause Overlending?" *Journal of Money, Credit and Banking* 37 (6): 1067–1100.

Thakor, Anjan, Hai Hong, and Stuart I. Greenbaum. 1981. "Bank Loan Commitments and Interest Rate Volatility." *Journal of Banking and Finance* 5:497–510.

Thakor, Anjan, and Gregory Udell. 1987. "An Economic Rationale for the Pricing Structure of Bank Loan Commitments." *Journal of Banking and Finance* 11 (2): 271–289.

Volcker, Paul. 1985. "Remarks at the 1985 Annual Convention of the American Bankers Association, New Orleans, Louisiana." October 21. In *Statements and Speeches of Paul A. Volcker, 1979–1987*, compiled by the Board of Governors of the Federal Reserve System. Available on FRASER, Discover Economic History, Federal Reserve. https://fraser.stlouisfed.org/title/451/item/8332.

Bank Decision-Making and the Regulation of Banks

Capital, Regulation, Purpose, and Culture

4

When Your Chickens Come Home to Roost

BANK CAPITAL REGULATION AND THE SEARCH
FOR FINANCIAL STABILITY

Introduction: The Bank Capital Structure Dance

I suggested in the previous chapters that better capitalized banks serve their core economic functions more efficiently. But the issue of bank capital structure is highly contentious. Consider the following three statements:

Economics Nobel Prize winner Merton Miller stated that "an essential message" of the Modigliani-Miller theorem, "as applied to banking, in sum, is that you cannot hope to lever up a sow's ear into a silk purse. You may think you can during good times; but you'll give it all back and more when the bad times roll around."[1] In response to the decision of US bank regulators to adopt a 5 percent leverage ratio,[2] higher than the 3 percent required by the Basel III Capital Accord, the American Bankers Association, a trade association, stated that US banks would be less competitive than their European counterparts. They would make fewer loans, and the ones they made would be more expensive. This was also the theme of a statement by the Financial Services Roundtable:

> While we support financial institutions holding more capital, this new proposal, combined with existing capital and leverage requirements, will make it harder for banks to lend and keep the economic recovery going.[3]

And then there is this:

> Banks had losses far in excess of 6% in 2008, and that was even after massive taxpayer and government bailouts. These few banks pose a grave and unique threat to our financial system and economy.[4] Regulators must require them to have enough capital to be able to absorb all their losses so that the American people don't have to bail them out again. That means capital of at least 20%. Until then, taxpayers will continue to be on the hook for Wall Street's losses!![5]

Now let us evaluate each in turn. The statement by Nobel laureate Merton Miller basically says that banks cannot benefit from leverage, because while leverage can amplify shareholders' earnings in good times, it also crushes earnings in bad times. So Miller questions the claim that asking banks to hold more capital will hurt their shareholders. The second statement says that having more capital in banking is likely to lead to less lending and hence less economic growth. This is the typical banker's view, and it has been one of the reasons why regulatory capital requirements are not higher than they are. The third statement also asserts that bank capital matters. But it says we need more of it to protect taxpayers. Collectively, these three statements span the entire spectrum of arguments for and against higher capital requirements in banking.

These arguments repeatedly crop up in what is now a fierce debate on this issue in both academia and policy circles. It is fair to say that the debate is essentially around the second and third positions above. Most people do agree that higher bank capital will foster safety and soundness in banking, with all of the attendant benefits. But there are many who think this enhanced safety and soundness will come at the expense of lower lending and liquidity creation by banks—hence at the expense of economic growth.

Herein lies the fundamental dilemma or tradeoff facing society, and it is at the heart of the academic debate and research on this issue. There is a large body of research on both the second and third viewpoints, and consensus has proved elusive, although there is now mounting evidence on the nature of the tradeoffs and calibrating the right amount of capital in banking, evidence that I will go over later in the book. The Holy Grail for researchers is: What is the right capital structure for a bank?

Taking a Step Back: Bank Decision-Making

To understand the role of capital in the overall functioning of the bank, we need to peer inside the bank and look at its major decisions. This is displayed in figure 4.1.

At the risk of oversimplification, figure 4.1 shows the major decisions a bank makes. The first of these is capital structure—the mix of equity, subordinated debt (i.e., non-deposit debt that is junior to deposits), and deposits to have in the overall financing it raises. This is basically the money flowing into the bank. The second major decision is how to invest this money. This involves deciding how much to lend to borrowers, how much to keep as cash in vault (for operating expenses and meeting deposit withdrawals), and how much to invest in securities like Treasury bonds and the like.

These decisions determine the bank's risk. The capital structure decision determines the bank's appetite for risk. Generally, the lower the equity capital, the stronger is the bank's preference for risk. This is because the bank's equity capital has *incentive effects* on the bank. More capital means more skin in the game for the bank's owners (shareholders) and hence a lesser propensity to bet the farm on risky gambles. This risk is then reflected in the bank's investment decisions—the care it takes in screening borrowers before making loans, the diligence with which it monitors them after lending, and the riskiness of

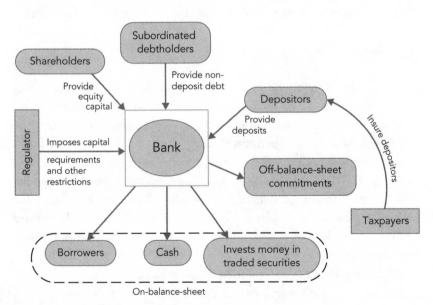

FIGURE 4.1 Banks' Decision-Making.

the borrowers it lends to and the securities it invests in. The amount the bank decides to keep as cash affects its ability to cope with withdrawal risk—to meet withdrawals by depositors.

Many of the loans the bank makes will be *relationship loans*. These borrowers will be especially sensitive to the bank's equity capital. Higher bank capital means a higher likelihood that the bank will be financially healthy enough to survive the bumps in the road and be around in the future. Since relationship lending involves long-term relationships, relationship borrowers value higher-capital banks more highly. This means higher loan demand for such banks.

We also know from our discussion of loan commitments in the previous chapter that banks with higher capital are more likely to honor their loan commitments, so they will be more *trusted* by their loan commitment customers and will have stronger reputations in this market.

While the bank's capital can affect the decisions that influence its reputation, the bank's reputation can also affect the risk to which the bank is exposed. The bank's counterparties—its subordinated debtholders and (uninsured) depositors—are more likely to continue to provide financing if the bank has a stronger reputation for being a good caretaker of other people's money.

To sum up, those who regulate banks, provide their safety nets, and do business with banks care a lot about the riskiness of these banks. This risk is affected by a host of factors, but at the heart of these factors is bank capital. The bank's decision about its capital affects almost all of its other decisions.

Why Do We Care?

One might ask: Why are we so concerned about the mix of debt and equity with which banks finance themselves? After all, it is a decision for the bank to make, and we do not have public debates about that with other firms. The reason, of course, is government safety nets. Unlike other firms, banks have deposit insurance and bailout protection even beyond that. Why these safety nets? Well, if the role of banks is to be safe warehouses of liquidity (commodities, fiat money, etc.), then ensuring that safety becomes paramount. We provide safety nets to banks because even rumors of diminished safety can cause depositors to run on banks, and this can have seriously negative economic consequences.[6] Safety nets like deposit insurance and bailouts of failed institutions can prevent these negative consequences.

The problem with safety nets is that they encourage banks to be excessively leveraged. This is a point that was elegantly recognized by Nobel

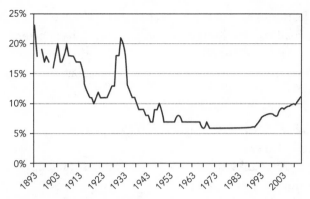

FIGURE 4.2 Mean Book Equity Ratios for US Banks, 1893–2010.

laureate Robert Merton in an important paper decades ago.[7] This can be seen from the mean book equity ratios graph (figure 4.2), which shows how bank capital ratios began to decline significantly after the adoption of deposit insurance in the United States in 1933.

When banks keep low capital levels, it increases the contingent liability faced by taxpayers, because it increases the value of the deposit insurance put option. Merton's analysis likened deposit insurance to a put option in which the bank's shareholders can essentially "put" (sell) the bank to the deposit insurer when the total value of the bank's assets falls below the value of its liabilities and the bank's economic net worth is negative. Merton showed that this option increases in value as the bank's capital ratio falls, thus providing an incentive for the bank to keep too low a level of capital and to take excessive risk. This jeopardizes the financial stability of the whole economy. This is why risk-based deposit insurance pricing and regulatory capital requirements are needed.[8] On the other hand, if raising bank capital requirements causes banks to lend less and create less liquidity—as some have argued—then economic growth is sacrificed.

What Does the Evidence Say about the Tradeoff between Stability and Economic Growth?

Stability is valuable. But if stability through more robust, higher-capital banks can only be achieved by sacrificing economic growth, then we need to recognize a tradeoff.

Economists love tradeoffs. They set up answers to research questions nicely and lead to testable predictions. Sometimes the consideration of tradeoffs leads to a convergence toward a specific conclusion. But at other times it actually causes divergence. On the issue of bank capital, the latter seems to be the case, although I will argue that this should not be so. In what follows, I will summarize what we know about the following three questions:[9]

1. Will higher capital levels in banking lead to lower lending and less liquidity creation by banks?
2. Will requiring banks to keep more capital increase funding costs for banks and diminish their values even if doing so benefits society?
3. How will higher bank capital affect systemic risk?

I believe these three questions are at the heart of the debate about whether we should have more or less capital in banking. The answers may surprise you.

As for the effect of bank capital on lending, we need to recognize first a subtle point, which is that an increase in bank capital *levels* has an effect that differs from that of an increase in bank capital *requirements*. The former is a result of the voluntary choices of banks—such as raising capital for retaining more earnings—or perhaps some exogenous shocks due to either good or bad luck. The latter is due to a change in capital requirements by regulators that calls for a proactive adjustment by the bank. Very broadly speaking, the effect of an increase in capital levels on bank lending is positive, whereas the short-run effect of an increase in bank capital requirements on lending is negative. Shortly it will become clear why this is so.

To set the stage for a discussion of how bank capital affects lending, it would be useful to first start by asking: What is the theoretical argument for why higher bank equity capital might diminish bank lending? There are two arguments—one wrong and one right. The wrong argument confuses bank capital with cash asset reserves. That is, it thinks of bank capital as cash set aside on the bank's balance sheet. Hence, the more capital the bank has, the more cash is sitting idly on the bank's balance sheet and not available for lending. In other words, capital is mistaken for cash, a lazy asset that directly and mechanically reduces bank lending because it is not loaned out. This is all wrong, of course. A bank's equity capital is loaned out by the bank—it does not sit idly on its balance sheet.[10]

The correct argument goes something like this. Equity capital has a higher cost than debt for the bank. The simplest reason for this is taxes—debt interest payments are tax deductible, whereas dividends are not. So the more equity there is in the bank's capital structure, the higher its weighted average cost of capital will be. This will mean that fewer investments will clear the bank's hurdle rate, and lending will decline.

The issue must therefore be decided empirically. However, it is quite challenging to uncover a *causal* link between bank capital and lending, something that goes beyond just showing a correlation in the data. This is because simply observing that higher bank capital is accompanied by higher bank lending does not suffice to tell us whether this was due to higher loan demand from borrowers who deemed higher-capital banks to be safer or due to banks increasing their credit supply. We cannot even rule out the possibility that bank capital went up at the same time that the economic outlook brightened and loan demand increased in the wake of a stronger economy. In this case, the observed positive correlation between bank capital and lending tells us next to nothing about the effect of bank capital per se on lending.

Empirical researchers have picked up the gauntlet and designed clever tests to isolate the effect of bank capital on the *supply* of credit by banks. In one such effort, the researchers examined German savings banks, which operate in specific regions and are required by law to serve only local customers.[11] In each area there is a regional bank called a *Landesbank*, which is owned by the savings bank in that area. These regional banks had varying degrees of exposure to US subprime mortgages during the 2007–2009 financial crisis. Thus, each suffered different losses. Since a loss depleted the equity capital of the Landesbank, the savings banks that owned them had to inject equity capital into them to make up for the losses. The key is that different savings banks had to make different injections, so they were hit by these losses in different amounts. What the researchers document is that the savings banks that were hit harder cut back on lending more. This shows that a decrease in bank capital leads to lower lending.

Such lending reductions have numerous real consequences. One of them is higher unemployment. This comes from two sources. One is that when firms face reduced credit supply, they may cut back on production and employ fewer people. The other is that consumers are also not able to borrow as much from banks. So they cut back on purchases of durables and nondurables. This reduced demand for goods and services causes firms to cut back further on production and employment.[12] Research has uncovered a causal link between a reduction in the credit supply and an increase in unemployment during a crisis.[13]

What about liquidity creation? This is a broader measure of the economic services banks provide than lending. For example, it includes off-balance-sheet claims and also takes into account how the bank funds itself.[14] What the research has found is that for the vast bulk of liquidity creation by US banks—about 80 percent—higher capital is associated with more liquidity creation.

Higher capital levels also make banks stronger competitively.[15] Banks with higher capital grow faster and have an edge over lower-capital competitors in both loan and deposit markets. Higher-capital banks of all sizes also display higher probabilities of surviving financial crises.[16]

So on the issue of whether higher capital in banking leads to more lending, liquidity creation, and economic growth, the answer is a resounding yes. So far, the popular bankers' argument that there is a tradeoff between economic growth and financial stability (through higher capital levels in banking) is not holding up well. The empirical evidence simply does not support the tradeoff story. Higher capital levels in banks seem to be delivering both higher stability *and* more economic growth, and also more competitive banks to boot.

Then Let's Require Banks to Post Dramatically Higher Amounts of Capital, Shall We?

The S&L crisis in the 1980s forcefully reinforced the lesson for regulators that banks needed to be required to post more equity capital to avoid a recurrence of the reckless risk-taking behavior exhibited by the S&Ls in the years leading up to the collapse of the industry. The Basel I Capital Accord of 1987 and the FDIC Improvement Act (FDICIA) of 1991 followed. The most important component of these regulations was the adoption, for the first time, of formal risk-based capital requirements that linked the amount of capital banks needed to keep to the riskiness of their assets and also imposed capital requirements on off-balance-sheet items.

As the US economy was coming out of the recession in the late 1980s, regulators were desperate to jump-start bank lending. The Federal Reserve adopted an easy-money monetary policy that pumped liquidity into the banking system, in the hope that this liquidity infusion would be channeled into higher lending by banks.

But what happened is that banks simply took the money and bought US Treasury bonds with it. They did not increase their lending significantly. This was frustrating to the Federal Reserve. Research has shown that this behavior by banks was in part due to the phased transition to risk-based capital requirements under Basel I and FDICIA.[17] The reason is that new capital requirements for the first time linked the amount of capital that the bank needed to keep to support an asset on its books to the credit risk associated with that asset. Put a loan on your books, and you need to support 8 percent of that loan with equity. Keep US government bonds on your books, and you need no capital to support it. Thus, the "capital charge" associated with bank loans increased compared to the capital charge associated with Treasury securities.

Banks issue equity securities to build up their capital only in very special circumstances, such as an imminent threat of violating capital requirements. The preferred method of building up capital is through retained earnings. So when new risk-based capital requirements are adopted, banks have a choice if they find that they do not have sufficient equity capital to be in compliance. They can either go and raise new equity capital or they can shed assets and make the balance sheet lighter so they need less capital. In the short run, given their aversion to raising new capital in the market—an option that is costlier for privately held banks than for publicly held banks—sometimes banks will sell assets to achieve short-term compliance with capital requirements,[18] and then over time add these assets back as capital levels are refurbished through earnings retentions.

The new risk-based capital requirements provided a third alternative for banks—they could simply change the composition of their asset portfolios in order to be in compliance. This way, they could have the same size of asset portfolio without having to change their capital. When the Federal Reserve pumped liquidity into the system, it was easier for banks to use the liquidity to purchase government bonds rather than using the money to make loans.[19]

The empirical evidence that this is what happened suggests that an increase in capital *requirements* can lead to a reduction in bank lending.[20] Quite often discussions of this issue end up co-mingling higher capital levels with higher capital requirements. This can lead to erroneous conclusions.

So higher capital levels lead to more lending and greater liquidity creation by banks, but higher capital requirements lead to lower lending. Do we have a paradox here?

The answer is no. The effects of diminished bank lending in response to higher capital requirements are *transitory*—they fade over time.[21]

This makes economic sense. Because banks do not like issuing new equity, they initially shift from lending to holding government securities to comply with the higher capital requirements. Over time, their capital levels rise due to retained earnings, so they can lend more again while being in compliance with capital requirements.

It is reasonable to conjecture that the bigger the increase in capital requirements, the larger and longer-lasting these transitory effects will be. From a regulatory policy standpoint, this has an obvious implication—when capital requirements are increased, it is best to allow banks to come into compliance over time rather than right away. That is, phase the new requirements in over three or four years. This is essentially what US regulators did with various aspects of FDICIA in 1991. Thus, when it comes to bank capital requirements, the *how* (the way it is implemented) is just as important as the *how much* (the level of new capital requirements).

A final point. Bankers often warn regulators about how higher capital requirements will dampen lending and hurt the economy. Lost in the cacophony of voices on this is the simple fact that not all bank lending is good for society. The 2007–2009 subprime crisis and the earlier S&L crisis were preceded by significant amounts of *overlending* by banks. It is this over-lending that contributed to the asset price bubbles that burst when the crises broke.[22] So sometimes a decline in bank lending may actually be a good thing.

But Don't Higher Capital Requirements Hurt Bank Values?

Bankers—and even the Wall Street equity research analysts who follow banks—often complain that if regulators increase capital requirements, they will make capital-raising more expensive for banks and lead to lower bank values. I was once at a conference for academics and bankers organized by the Bundesbank in Germany. A bank CEO repeated this oft-heard mantra: "Please don't raise capital requirements, because doing so will reduce shareholder value in banking." When I asked how this would happen, he said it is because higher capital means a lower return on equity (ROE). This is obviously true in a mechanical or formulaic sense—if you replace debt with equity and hold everything else constant, then ROE will fall. But basic finance tells us that a lower ROE by itself does *not* mean lower shareholder value. The reason is simple. Although ROE falls when equity replaces debt, so does the expected return demanded by shareholders, because their risk falls. If the bank's shareholders demand a 20 percent ROE to be adequately compensated for the time value of money and risk when the bank has 5 percent of its assets funded by equity, they may demand only 16 percent when the capital ratio rises to 10 percent.

Some years after my experience in Germany, I was presenting a paper at the Bank for International Settlements (BIS) in Basel, Switzerland. At the end of my talk, I said: "There may be sound reasons why we should not increase capital requirements in banking, but one of them should definitely *not* be that doing so will lower ROE in banking." The reaction from the BIS economists in the audience was: "But that is all we hear from the bankers."

To illustrate this point further, let me cite John Carney, a CNBC reporter who reported on Wednesday, August 24, 2011 on why Bank of America's stock price was rising. He starts out by stating:

> The going theory is that Bank of America must resist raising capital through an equity issuance at almost all costs.
> "The bull case for Bank of America is built on the idea that they do not need a capital round," one hedge fund manager told me.[23]

He then goes on to say that the argument is wrong and that he believes that the stock price rally was due to rumors that Bank of America was actually going to raise new equity capital. "Today's surge is very possibly built off of the prediction by J. P. Morgan analyst, Kabir Caprihan, that Bank of America will be forced to raise new capital," states Carney.

Carney states later in his report:

> This isn't just the case of anecdotal evidence. Recent studies have shown that the conventional wisdom on equity capitalization for banks is backwards. In a paper for the Review of Financial Studies called "Bank Capital and Value in the Cross-Section," scholars Hamid Mehran and Anjan Thakor looked at how equity capital effects the value of banks in merger contexts. What they found is that banks with more equity command higher prices. Yes, that's right: More equity capital raises the value of the bank and creates more value for shareholders.

Keeping more equity capital means a higher overall cost of capital, since equity costs more at the margin than deposits. But more capital means stronger incentives for the bank to monitor its relationship loans, which increases the value of those loans. Each bank makes its choice differently, with banks that have lower equity costs of capital choosing higher capital ratios. The model predicts that banks that have more equity capital will not only be more valuable but will also generate a higher net present value (NPV) on the investments their shareholders make in the bank.[24] That is, if we view the market value of the equity in the bank as the present value of all future cash flows going to the bank's shareholders and the book value of its equity as the investment in the bank made by the shareholders, then the difference between the market and book values of equity can be viewed as the NPV going to the shareholders. We showed that the higher the book value of equity in the bank, the higher the price an acquirer is willing to pay, and the wedge between the acquisition price and book value is bigger when the book value is higher. We then tested the predictions with data on bank holding company acquisitions and found support for the predictions of the model.

The magnitudes of the effects we found are striking. If the bank increases its equity-to-total-assets ratio by 1 percent, the ratio of the acquisition price the bank receives to its total assets increases by 1.4 percent to over 1.6 percent. If we think of the net present value (NPV) to the bank's shareholders as the price received by them when the bank is sold minus the amount the shareholders invested in the bank (measured by the book value of bank equity), then a 1 percent increase in the ratio of invested equity capital to total bank assets leads to a 0.4–0.6 percent increase in the ratio of NPV to total assets. In other words, the bank's shareholders are significantly better off when the bank has more equity capital.

The research finding that banks themselves (i.e., bank shareholders) benefit from higher capital presents us with a puzzle. Researchers understand well the idea that banks prefer to keep capital levels lower than what is good for society, because doing this increases the value of safety-net put options to banks, as was discussed earlier. In other words, the capital level that maximizes the wealth of the bank's shareholders is likely to be lower than what taxpayers want. But we have no rational explanation for why banks would operate with lower capital ratios than their own shareholders would like. One popular explanation is that the bonuses of bank executives depend on return on equity (ROE), so these executives take actions—like keeping lower capital—that increase ROE. Apart from the fact that this explanation leaves us with the puzzle of why bank shareholders would design executive compensation like this, the empirical evidence indicates that banks with higher capital actually have *higher* ROEs.[25] In other words, higher capital improves bank performance by so much that it more than offsets the direct mechanical effect of higher capital in decreasing ROE—hence the puzzle of why banks do not choose higher capital remains.

To sum up, the empirical evidence, well grounded in theory, debunks the myth that having higher capital in banks destroys shareholder value in banking. The fact that higher bank capital makes our banks more valuable is another nail in the coffin of the argument that we need to balance bank stability against economic growth. After all, more valuable banks are likely to make more and better loans, not fewer. This means higher bank capital eventually leads to more economic growth, not less.[26]

What about Systemic Risk?

Systemic risk—the risk that the entire financial system could melt down—is always the elephant in the room. It is not always visible, but it is there. So we should ask: How will higher capital in banking affect systemic risk?

It has been suggested that one benefit of debt in general, and demand deposits in particular, is that the threat of withdrawal (or non-renewal) of funding can discipline bank managers who might otherwise make bad asset choices.[27] Now imagine banks that make highly correlated asset portfolio choices, such as heavy concentrations in real estate or oil and gas lending. This is common in banking. Also imagine that while all creditors observe the *bank-specific* factors that influence the credit risks of the banks they have lent money to, only some creditors observe a signal about the quality of the correlated assets all banks are holding. For example, in the 2007–2009 crisis, some banks may have learned earlier than others that subprime mortgages were defaulting at a higher-than-expected rate and that the credit qualities of mortgage-backed securities had dipped well below those suggested by their credit ratings.

In such a world, imagine that the creditors of your bank decide to liquidate the bank. The creditors of my bank observe this. They do not know whether your bank was liquidated because of some bad news that was specific to your bank or because the creditors received a signal that the asset portfolio had declined precipitously in quality. There are circumstances in which the creditors of my bank may observe enough such liquidations that they decide to liquidate my bank, even though they did not see any bank-specific bad news about my bank. That is, they may refuse to renew the bank's short-term funding or ask for so much liquid collateral that the bank may be unable to comply. Moreover, they may do this and be wrong about it at times because your bank was liquidated for bank-specific bad news only, news that had no relevance for the health of my bank. Such contagious liquidations are obviously bad for society, because they involve erroneously shutting down healthy banks.

Now here is the punch line. The lower the capital in my bank, the worse the problem.[28] And the lower the capital in your bank, the worse the problem.

That is, lower capital in *your* bank can increase the odds of *my* bank being liquidated erroneously by my creditors. In other words, *lower capital in banking increases systemic risk in the financial system* through this mechanism of contagious liquidations. Increase bank capital and you lower systemic risk.

Summing It Up and Questions

Banks make many decisions that affect their risk, but none is more important than its capital structure. This decision affects a host of other decisions of the bank.

While there is much we do not know, on the issue of bank capital structure and how it affects financial stability and economic growth, we actually know more than apparent disagreements among researchers and between researchers and bankers might suggest. In particular, we know that higher bank capital leads to:

- higher bank values
- more bank lending
- higher bank liquidity creation
- lower systemic risk and greater financial stability

We also know that higher bank capital requirements lead to reduced lending in the short run, but that these transitory effects fade over time.

What has not been discussed in this chapter is how the bank's capital decision is affected by its higher purpose and its culture. These issues are taken up in the next chapter.

Notes

1. Miller 1995, 486.
2. Loosely put, the leverage ratio refers to the ratio of the bank's book equity to its total assets.
3. Tim Pawlenty, quoted in Touryalai 2013, 1.
4. The "few banks" Kelleher is referring to are the very large, systemically important institutions.
5. Dennis Kelleher, quoted in Touryalai 2013, 1.
6. Diamond and Dybvig 1983 develop a model in which depositors may run the bank simply because they believe others will. That is, in their model a bank run is triggered by "sunspots," not deteriorating economic fundamentals. Merton and Thakor

forthcoming argue that depositors wish to not be exposed to any of the bank's credit risk. If it is too costly for the bank to achieve this insulation for depositors on its own, deposit insurance may be desirable.

7. See Merton 1977.

8. Merton's logic applies to all firms, not just banks. However, the problem is more acute in banking because public safety nets like deposit insurance are essentially put options whose value increases as the bank's capital falls. Moreover, bank failures are often contagious and individual banks do not internalize the social costs of this contagion, inclining them to keep less capital than is good for society; see Thakor 2015, for example. Chan, Greenbaum, and Thakor 1992 provide an analysis of the ability of regulators to impose risk-based deposit insurance premia, and show that in a highly competitive banking system, it may not be feasible to implement risk-based deposit insurance premia.

9. The discussion below is based on Thakor 2014 and Thakor 2015.

10. This effect of reduced lending will show up if the bank is subjected to a higher liquidity or cash asset reserve requirement.

11. See Puri, Rocholl, and Steffen 2011.

12. These issues are discussed in depth in Thakor 2005.

13. See Haltenhof and Stebunovs 2014.

14. A widely used empirical measure of liquidity creation is the one developed by Berger and Bouwman (2009). Their research shows that higher capital is associated with more liquidity creation by large banks but less liquidity creation by small banks. Although there are more small banks than large banks, most of the liquidity is created by large banks.

15. A detailed discussion of these issues appears in Thakor 2014.

16. See Berger and Bouwman (2013), who document that capital improves large banks' performance during financial crises and small banks' performance during crises as well as normal times.

17. See Berger and Udell 1994, and Thakor 1996.

18. The aversion to raising capital may be due to adverse-selection costs and other informational frictions. But it is not always rational. See Thakor 2014 for an extensive discussion.

19. This suggests that how well monetary policy works in stimulating loan supply by banks depends on whether banks view capital requirements as binding. For an extended discussion, see Greenbaum, Thakor, and Boot 2015.

20. A similar decline in bank lending has been documented for French banks during the transition from Basel I to Basel II capital requirements. See Brun, Fraisse, and Thesmar 2013.

21. See the earlier-mentioned paper Brun, Fraisse, and Thesmar 2013.

22. Acharya and Naqvi (2012) make this point theoretically in the context of bank lending. Berger and Bouwman (2017) argue that excessive liquidity creation

by banks can lead to financial crises. Dong and Yen (2017) show that excessive injections of public liquidity during crises can reduce welfare.

23. Carney 2011.

24. See Mehran and Thakor 2011.

25. See Berger 1995

26. This is not a prescription for arbitrarily large increases in capital requirement. The evidence says that banks that have higher capital ratios are more valuable to their shareholders. But the evidence involves bank capital ratios we actually see in the data, which are mostly below 20 percent, i.e., equity capital as a percentage of total assets below 20 percent. Acharya, Mehran, Schuermann, and Thakor (2012) discuss how capital requirements should be designed in practice.

27. See Calomiris and Kahn 1991.

28. This theory is developed in Acharya and Thakor 2016. In addition, lower bank capital also exposes the bank's depositors to more bank-specific risk, which is inefficient, as shown by Merton and Thakor (forthcoming).

References

Acharya, Viral V., Hamid Mehran, Til Schuermann, and Anjan V. Thakor. 2012. "Robust Capital Regulation." *Federal Reserve Bank of New York Current Issues in Economics and Finance* 18 (4), https://www.newyorkfed.org/research/current_issues/ci18-4.html.

Acharya, Viral, and Hassan Naqvi. 2012. "The Seeds of a Crisis: A Theory of Bank Liquidity and Risk Taking over the Business Cycle." *Journal of Financial Economics* 106 (2): 349–366.

Acharya, Viral, and Anjan V. Thakor. 2016. "The Dark Side of Liquidity Creation: Leverage and Systemic Risk." *Journal of Financial Intermediation* 28:4–21.

Berger, Allen. 1995. "The Relationship between Capital and Earnings in Banking." *Journal of Money, Credit and Banking* 27:432–456.

Berger, Allen N., and Christa H. S. Bouwman. 2009. "Bank Liquidity Creation." *Review of Financial Studies* 22 (9): 3779–3837.

Berger, Allen, and Christa Bouwman. 2013. "How Does Bank Capital Affect Bank Performance During Financial Crises?" *Journal of Financial Economics* 109 (1): 146–176.

Berger, Allen, and Christa Bouwman. 2017. "Bank Liquidity Creation, Monetary Policy and Financial Crises." *Journal of Financial Stability* 30:139–155.

Berger, Allen, and Gregory F Udell. 1994. "Did Risk-Based Capital Allocate Bank Credit and Cause a 'Credit Crunch' in the United States?" *Journal of Money, Credit and Banking* 26:585–628.

Brun, Matthieu, Henri Fraisse, and David Thesmar. 2013. "The Real Effects of Bank Capital Requirements." Working Paper no. 988, HEC Paris.

Calomiris, Charles W., and Charles M. Kahn. 1991. "The Role of Demandable Debt in Structuring Optimal Banking Arrangements." *American Economic Review* 81 (3): 497–513.

Carney, John. 2011. "Practitioner Use of Mehran and Thakor: Why Are Bank of America's Shares Rallying?" CNBC, August 24.

Chan, Yuk-Shee, Stuart Greenbaum, and Anjan V. Thakor. 1992. "Is Fairly Priced Deposit Insurance Possible?" *Journal of Finance* 47 (1): 227–246.

Diamond, Douglas W., and Philip H. Dybvig. 1983. "Bank Runs, Deposit Insurance and Liquidity." *Journal of Political Economy* 91 (3): 401–419.

Dong, Feng, and Yi Wen. 2017. "Flight to What? Dissecting Quality Shortages in the Financial Crisis." Working Paper 2017-025B, Federal Reserve Bank of St. Louis, October.

Greenbaum, Stuart I., Anjan V. Thakor, and Arnoud Boot. 2015. *Contemporary Financial Intermediation*. 3rd ed. Amsterdam: Academic Press.

Haltenhof, S., S. Jung Lee, and Viktors Stebunovs. 2014. "The Credit Crunch and Fall in Employment during the Great Recession." *Journal of Economic Dynamics and Control* 43:31–57.

Mehran, Hamid, and Anjan V. Thakor. 2011. "Bank Capital and Value in the Cross-Section." *Review of Financial Studies* 24 (4): 1019–1067.

Merton, Robert C. 1977. "An Analytical Derivation of the Cost of Deposit Insurance and Other Guarantees: An Application of Modern Option Pricing Theory." *Journal of Banking and Finance* 1:3–11.

Merton, Robert C., and Richard T. Thakor. Forthcoming. "Customers and Investors: A Framework for Understanding the Evolution of Financial Institutions." *Journal of Financial Intermediation.*

Miller, Merton. 1995. "Do the M&M Propositions Apply to Banks?" *Journal of Banking and Finance* 19:483–489.

Puri, Manju, Jorg Rocholl, and Sasha Steffen. 2011. "Global Retail Lending in the Aftermath of the U.S. Financial Crisis: Distinguishing between Supply and Demand Effects." *Journal of Financial Economics* 100:556–578.

Thakor, Anjan, V. 1996. "Capital Requirements, Monetary Policy and Aggregate Bank Lending: Theory and Empirical Evidence." *Journal of Finance* 51 (1): 279–324.

Thakor, Anjan V. 2005. "Do Loan Commitments Cause Overlending?" *Journal of Money, Credit and Banking* 37 (6): 1067–1100.

Thakor, Anjan V. 2014. "Bank Capital and Financial Stability: An Economic Tradeoff or a Faustian Bargain?" *Annual Review of Financial Economics* 6:185–223.

Thakor, Anjan. 2015. "The Financial Crisis of 2007–09: Why Did It Happen and What Did We Learn?" *Review of Corporate Finance Studies* 4 (2): 155–205.

Touryalai, Halah. 2013. "Big Banks Warn Regulators: Tougher Capital Rules Will Hurt Everyone." *Forbes*, July 9.

5

Higher Purpose, Culture, and Capital

IS BANKING ON CULTURE A CAPITAL IDEA?

Introduction: A Game of Trust

Banking is a game of trust. You would never deposit your money in a bank if you thought the banker would run away with it. And since deposit warehousing and safekeeping represent the very origins of banking, it would be very difficult for banks to perform their core economic functions well if they lacked the trust of their customers, financiers, and other stakeholders. In many ways, banking requires greater trust than many other industries. Yet events of the past few decades have raised nettlesome questions about the honesty and ethics of bankers.

A recent study on the culture of banking uncovered some disturbing results.[1] In this study, 128 employees of an international bank were asked to participate in a coin-flipping game. The employees were randomly divided into two equal groups: the treatment group and the control group. Prior to playing the coin-flipping game, the subjects were asked "priming questions" in an online survey. Those in the treatment group were asked seven questions about their professional background, such as "What is your function at the bank?" The idea was to heighten their awareness of their own professional duties. Those in the control group were asked seven questions unrelated to their profession, such as "How many hours per week do you watch television on average?"

The two groups played the coin-flipping game after answering the priming questions. Each group had to anonymously flip a coin ten times and report the outcomes online. In advance of the coin flips, each group knew that one outcome (heads or tails) would fetch a $20 prize and the other would fetch nothing. There was an additional catch designed to introduce an element of competition. The subjects were told that their earnings would only be paid out if they exceeded those of a randomly drawn subject from a pilot study.

Because each group observed its own coin flips privately, there was ample opportunity to cheat and report exaggerated earnings. What the researcher found is that the control group—whose members had *not* been primed to have a heightened awareness of their professional identify as bankers—did not cheat—at least not in a statistically discernible way. On average, they reported successful coin flips in 51.6 percent of the cases, statistically indistinguishable from 50 percent. But the treatment group did cheat, reporting 58.2 percent successful coin flips on average, statistically significantly higher than 50 percent.

Reacting to the study, Duke University behavioral economist, Dan Ariely, who was not one of the authors involved in the study, stated:

> In some sense, it's pessimistic because it says it's the culture that's so corrosive. . . . Bankers do think of themselves as dishonest—not in a conscious way necessarily, but in an unconscious way. Because otherwise this priming would not work.[2]

In light of this, we should perhaps not be surprised that bank regulators in the United States and Europe are turning their attention to *bank culture*. The general counsel of the Federal Reserve Bank of New York said in March 2017 that everyone "should be concerned with culture in financial services."[3]

In the past few years, the Federal Reserve Bank of New York has organized numerous conferences to bring together academic researchers, bankers, and regulators to discuss issues related to bank culture. It reflects a growing recognition that paying greater attention to the issue is much needed because of the compelling importance of restoring public trust in the banking system. Everything we know about banking and what we have discussed in this book so far tells us that without trust in banking, there is no financial stability. Absent trust, deposits would flow out of banks, and alternative sources of financing would spring up for borrowers. If the very culture of banking is corrupted by the absence of an appropriate ethical code, then the ethical lapses for which hundreds of billions of dollars in fines were levied on major banks after the 2007–2009 crisis cannot be viewed merely as due to the actions of a few rogue traders, a few "bad apples." Rather, they would be reflections of systemic weaknesses in the banking system.

Why are regulators so interested in bank culture? To understand this, let us step back and discuss *prudential regulation* in banking, which is designed to ensure there is not an excessive or imprudent amount of risk in the system. There are two types of prudential regulation: microprudential and macroprudential. Microprudential regulation focuses on individual banks—their capital, their asset portfolios, their risk management, and so on. Macroprudential regulation focuses on more system-wide risk issues like financial crises, systemic risks, and so on. Prior to the 2007–2009 crisis, these two types of regulation were viewed in somewhat distinct silos. But now we understand they are connected. Hence, issues that affect microprudential regulation are also viewed as being of interest for macroprudential regulation.

The interest of regulators in culture is because of the view that culture could perhaps become a component of microprudential regulation. Since we have discussed bank capital as an essential tool of microprudential regulation, our discussion in this chapter will also focus on the *interaction* between the bank's higher purpose, its culture, and capital. The discussion will thus allow us to address some questions raised in previous chapters.

So fasten your seat belt. We are about to explore bank culture to see how far it takes us in understanding the answers to these questions.

What Is Culture, and How Is It Influenced by the Bank's Higher Purpose?

An organization's culture is the collective assumptions, expectations, and values that reflect the explicit and implicit rules determining how employees think and behave within the organization.[4] Culture includes not only explicit instruments to influence behavior like compensation contracts but also implicit contracts that enable the organization to delegate more effectively. Simply put, culture determines how employees behave without being told what to do when they are not being watched. The former president of the Federal Reserve Bank of New York William Dudley described culture as "a gentle breeze. You cannot see it, but you can feel it."[5]

The bank's higher purpose has a huge impact on its culture. Purpose is not the same as mission. An organization's mission is typically expressed in terms of creating long-term value for stakeholders—it is about acquiring resources to produce output that affects economic outcomes. Just go and look up any organization's website and you can read its mission statement. For example, Citi states: "Citi's mission is to serve as a trusted partner to our clients by responsibly providing financial services that enable growth and economic progress."

A higher purpose is different. It is not about the *acquisition* of resources. Rather, it is about the *contribution* the organization can make. It is about the resources the organization can create and give to society. My co-author Bob Quinn and I described it as "a reflection of higher intent. It's the most meaningful thing—beyond economic transactions and outcomes—that an organization has to give."[6]

Because purpose has been on my mind a lot, I was struck by an episode of *Shark Tank*—the addictive TV show in which entrepreneurs come to a group of billionaires, or "sharks," for funding—that I watched on February 19, 2018. One entrepreneur was seeking money in exchange for equity ownership in the company by one of the sharks. The business would sell real Christmas trees (that could be replanted) to people, and then after Christmas the customers could either have the tree planted in their own backyard or the company would take it away and plant it somewhere else. The higher purpose is to prevent the deforestation that accompanies the current practice of cutting evergreens down at Christmas and then throwing them away. Another part of the purpose is to employ veterans, giving them not just good jobs but employment with purpose.

One after the other, the sharks turned the entrepreneur down. The reasons made good economic sense. Too capital intensive. Only a two-month period over which sales could occur. Trees that would be so much more expensive than plastic trees that would look the same from a distance, so why would the customer buy your real trees? And on and on.

The entrepreneur pleaded his case—"But this business can do so much good for society. And I am employing veterans, giving them work with purpose." The response of the sharks was: "Great. But how will you make lots of money?" Their views mirrored those of economics Nobel Prize winner Milton Friedman (1970), who famously wrote:

> But the doctrine of "social responsibility" taken seriously would extend the scope of the political mechanism to every human activity. It does not differ in philosophy from the most explicitly collectivist doctrine. It differs only by professing to believe that collectivist ends can be attained without collectivist means. That is why, in my book *Capitalism and Freedom*, I have called it a "fundamentally subversive doctrine" in a free society, and have said that in such a society, "there is

one and only one social responsibility of business—to use its resources and engage in activities designed to increase its profits so long as it stays within the rules of the game, which is to say, engages in open and free competition without deception or fraud."

The entrepreneur was down to one shark, Mark Cuban, who had been observing the proceedings quietly. Finally, he spoke up. Shockingly, he was willing to fund the entrepreneur. He said he was doing it because he believed in the purpose of the organization and because he could help the business to "sell" its story and make money. "Each tree will have its own story—the veterans behind the tree and their lives," he proclaimed. He said they would sell the stories with the trees. He also explained how he would help to scale the business up into a nationwide company and make it highly profitable.

This is precisely what I mean by authentic higher purpose. Like Cuban's investment, the pursuit of higher purpose is not charity. Rather, it is the intersection of the organization's highest intent with its business strategy. A way to make money and contribute to society in the process.

Was Friedman wrong and Cuban right? No. Friedman, like the other sharks, recognized that the goal of an organization should be to produce the most long-term value for its owners. Nothing wrong with that. But what that point of view misses is that adopting an authentic higher purpose is not necessarily an "either-or" proposition when it comes to the pursuit of usual business goals. In fact, you can do both. And if the higher purpose is authentic and communicated with clarity, it can inspire employees, attract talent, and produce powerful results that are unattainable otherwise.[7]

But it is crucial that employees believe that the higher purpose is authentic and affects business decisions as well as how employees are judged. Absent this, research has shown that it can actually have no effect or even counterproductive effects on employee behavior.[8]

Banks have been accused of being detached from any such higher purpose. In fact, it has often been suggested that they take pride in not being influenced by such "soft" ideas. But an organization's sense of higher purpose significantly affects its culture and hence how it makes decisions.

One bank that has articulated its higher purpose in a way that intersects its business goals is JP Morgan Chase. It is now investing $250 million per year in community-building activities like small-business development, job-skills training, and neighborhood revitalization, and it is deploying a "service corps" of advisers to facilitate the success of these investments.[9] This higher purpose transcends the bank's usual goals, but it also intersects with these goals, since bank profits do not grow when the economy is not doing well. Helping local communities develop and flourish economically eventually helps banks in general do more business. It also appears that cooperatives (e.g., Farm Credit System institutions) and credit unions may have done a better job than banks in connecting organizational higher purpose to business strategy.

Community banks in the United States also have a higher purpose. It is to improve the standards of living in their communities.

It is also worth re-emphasizing that the pursuit of higher purpose is not charity. If the bank is not profitable and creating shareholder value, it will not be able to survive in a competitive marketplace and give anything back to society. Banks that are on the verge of being bailed out and whose employees are hanging on to their jobs by their fingernails are often too worried about survival to serve a higher purpose.[10] It is essential for the bank to ensure its continued financial viability, which is why it is the *intersection* of higher purpose and a shareholder-value-maximizing strategy that should guide the bank's decisions. This means decisions that are good for the bank in the sense of enhancing its profitability and also good for society—keeping sufficiently high levels of capital, avoiding excessively risky investments, not exploiting the deposit insurance safety net, not mis-selling products to customers, and so on.

How Does Bank Culture Affect Bank Behavior?

Research has shown the following:[11]

- A strong culture ensures that there is a "sorting effect" so that employees have shared beliefs that are alike. This allows decision-making rules to be simplified, and it makes delegation easier. By a "strong culture," I mean one in which there is less tolerance for deviations from the behavior prescribed by the culture.
- When culture is aligned with strategy, execution of the strategy improves and value creation is facilitated.

I have not met any organizational leader who denies the importance of culture. But culture is such a nebulous concept that it is often difficult for leaders to think about it in tangible terms, so the notion of culture sometimes ends up being blended into the organization's statement of values or ethical behavior. While the values of the organization do affect its culture, this comingling of ethical behavior guidelines and culture into a single expanded statement of values is often counterproductive. Most employees in these circumstances end up viewing culture merely as a guideline to avoid unethical behavior. Something nice to put on posters and banners on walls, but distinct from the things that determine day-to-day decision-making. When this happens, culture has little effect on strategy.

Culture is more than just a set of guidelines that define ethical behavior. As the *Economist* noted: "The overall culture of the organization matters as much as the experience of the top brass, particularly when it comes to risk management."[12] However, to make culture an integral part of the DNA of the organization, care must be taken to ensure the following:

- The culture of the organization must support the execution of the organization's growth strategy.
- The strategy must specify how human and financial resources will be allocated to different activities.
- Leadership capabilities of employees should be assessed based on their practice of the values embedded in the culture.

In other words, culture must be "practiced." But how do we practice culture if we cannot clearly articulate what it is? Leaders need to identify the culture of the organization and then clearly and succinctly communicate it up and down the line. Simplicity is paramount. A fundamental responsibility of leadership is to define, communicate, and model the sanctioned behaviors of the culture.

Whatever culture is chosen by the leaders of the organization, it has three salient effects: (1) a sorting effect, (2) a peer sanctions effect, and (3) an identity-shaping effect.[13] The sorting effect means that the chosen culture attracts employees who share the beliefs that underlie the culture, and this alignment encourages productive delegation. The peer sanctions effect is that an employee whose actions deviate from what the culture demands will be sanctioned by peers, so there is behavioral alignment beyond what is possible with compensation contracts. Finally, the identity-shaping effect means that the culture actually shapes the identity of the employee, making the employee more in conformity with the values of the culture.

Because culture can often be a complex concept, one must seek the help of a "master" rather than an "expert."[14] Let me explain. An expert understands the complexity of a phenomenon and is aware of all of its complicated elements. So the expert explains things in elaborate detail. Everything is captured, but not in simple terms. A master, on the other hand, achieves profound simplicity in explaining the concept. The essence of what matters is communicated, and distracting details are avoided.

So what we need for bank culture is a workable framework, something that leaders can use to not only diagnose culture but also to communicate it. In the most effective organizations, culture is communicated with remarkable clarity. Every employee, including blue-collar workers on the factory shop floor, can tell you what it is. Let me describe for you an organizational culture framework that has been widely used to diagnose, communicate, and proactively change culture.

The Competing Values Framework

The *competing values framework* (CVF), shown in figure 5.1, provides a way to characterize organizational culture in simple, easy-to-communicate terms. Developed in the organizational behavior literature,[15] this framework is widely used by organizations.[16]

The CVF begins with the observation that organizations engage in countless activities to create value, but most fall into one of the four categories, or quadrants, shown in figure 5.1: *collaborate, control, compete,* and *create.*

Collaborate: Activities in this quadrant deal with building human competencies, developing people, and encouraging a collaborative environment. The approach to change in this quadrant relies on consensual and cooperative processes. Leadership development, employee satisfaction and morale, the creation of cross-functional work groups, employee retention, teamwork, and decentralized decision-making are all areas of focus in this quadrant. Organizational effectiveness is associated with human capital development and high levels of employee engagement.

Control: Activities in this quadrant include improving efficiency through better processes. The goal is to make things better, at lower cost, and with less risk, achieving a high degree of statistical predictability in outcomes. Organizational effectiveness is associated with capable processes, measurement, and control. Examples of activities include risk management, auditing, planning, statistical process control, Six Sigma and Lean Six Sigma techniques

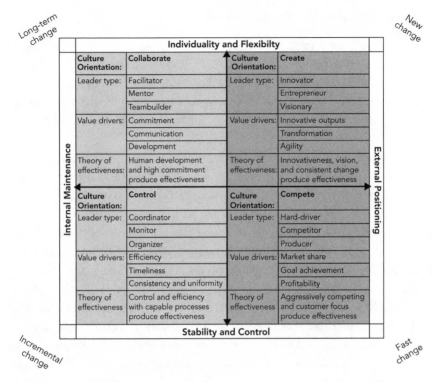

Long-term change

New change

Individuality and Flexibilty			
Culture Orientation:	**Collaborate**	**Culture Orientation:**	**Create**
Leader type:	Facilitator	Leader type:	Innovator
	Mentor		Entrepreneur
	Teambuilder		Visionary
Value drivers:	Commitment	Value drivers:	Innovative outputs
	Communication		Transformation
	Development		Agility
Theory of effectiveness:	Human development and high commitment produce effectiveness	Theory of effectiveness:	Innovativeness, vision, and consistent change produce effectiveness
Culture Orientation:	**Control**	**Culture Orientation:**	**Compete**
Leader type:	Coordinator	Leader type:	Hard-driver
	Monitor		Competitor
	Organizer		Producer
Value drivers:	Efficiency	Value drivers:	Market share
	Timeliness		Goal achievement
	Consistency and uniformity		Profitability
Theory of effectiveness	Control and efficiency with capable processes produce effectiveness	Theory of effectiveness	Aggressively competing and customer focus produce effectiveness
Stability and Control			

Internal Maintenance

External Positioning

Incremental change

Fast change

FIGURE 5.1 The Competing Values Framework.

for improving manufacturing processes, and so on. These activities make the organization function more smoothly and efficiently.

Compete: Activities in this quadrant involve being aggressive in the pursuit of competitiveness. These activities involve monitoring market signals and competitors. Interactions with external stakeholders and customers, are emphasized. The focus is on customer satisfaction and delivering shareholder value. Firms that excel compete hard, move fast, and play to win. Organizational effectiveness means growing profits, market share, and shareholder value—with speed. Market domination is a goal.

Create: Activities in this quadrant involve innovation in the organization's products and services. Firms that excel create, innovate, and envision the future, effectively handling discontinuity, change, and risk. They allow freedom of thought and action among employees, so thoughtful "rule breaking" and stretching beyond the existing boundaries are commonplace. Entrepreneurship, vision, new ideas, and constant change abound in organizations that are effective in this quadrant.

Tensions within the Framework

To understand the CVF, one must examine the similarities and differences between the quadrants. Consider first the *collaborate* and *control* quadrants, both of which are internally focused. *Collaborate* focuses on the "human capital" within the organization. *Control* focuses on the "process capital" within the organization—the manner in which internal processes are used to achieve efficiency and predictability of outcomes.

By contrast, the *compete* and *create* quadrants are outwardly focused. *Compete* is focused on the customers, competitors, markets, and opportunities that exist today, while *create* is focused on the customers, competitors, markets, and opportunities that will exist tomorrow.

So one dimension of similarity and difference is whether there is an internal or external focus. In this dichotomy, *collaborate* and *control* are similar in that they share an internal focus, and *compete* and *create* are similar in that they share an external focus.

A second dimension along which one can compare the quadrants is in the degree of their focus on stability and control as against individuality and flexibility. On this dimension, *control* and *compete* share an emphasis on stability and control. These quadrants place importance on tangible and measurable outputs, as well as the use of well-established best practices. Leadership style tends to be prescriptive, and organizations often have detailed manuals describing how things should be done. The time horizon for achieving results is typically short. By contrast, *collaborate* and *create* involve more individuality and flexibility. The rules of success are not as well defined, and more experimentation is encouraged. Leadership style is more participative than prescriptive, and the time horizon for achieving results is typically longer.

A key insight of the CVF is that diagonally opposite quadrants have nothing in common. That is, *collaborate* shares no similarity with *compete*, and *control* shares nothing with *create*. Indeed, one can make an even stronger statement: at the margin, these quadrants pull the organization in opposite directions. Any resources allocated to one quadrant pull the organization away from its diagonal opposite. In a sense, the quadrants represent competing forms of value creation. This split creates inherent tensions within the organization, as stakeholders at opposite ends engage in a veritable tug of war as they compete for resources to devote to the activities they believe will create the most value.[17]

When an organization chooses its culture, it is effectively deciding its relative degrees of emphasis on the four quadrants in figure 5.2. This picture of culture would typically be constructed on the basis of a survey of employees in the organization, using a diagnostic instrument that has been validated in organization behavior research.[18] The usefulness of such a picture of culture is that:

- it can communicate the organization's culture to all key stakeholders in a simple, visual way
- it clarifies how the organization will allocate resources to execute its growth strategy
- it becomes a guide for the organization's hiring, development, and retention processes, and
- it serves as a mechanism to coordinate beliefs and guide day-to-day decision-making.

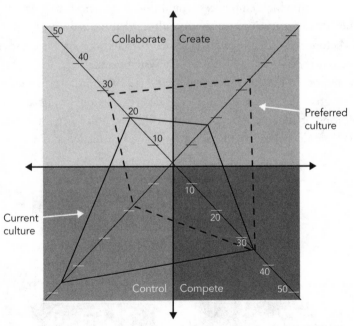

FIGURE 5.2 A Depiction of Hypothetical Existing and Preferred CVF Corporate Culture Profiles.

The figure has both a current and a preferred culture profile. The current culture reflects the state of the organization as it exists, whereas the preferred culture refers to the culture the employees would like the organization to move to in order to better support the execution of the strategy. In most organizations, these two culture profiles are different. Typically, both culture profiles are generated through surveys of employees in the organization.

Adapting the CVF to Analyze Credit Culture in a Bank

Not only can the CVF help to analyze the culture that supports the overall growth strategy of the organization, it can also analyze specific aspects of the overall culture, such as the credit risk-management of the bank. Figure 5.3 shows what the four quadrants of the CVF would translate into when it comes to credit culture (which reflects the values, norms, and formal and informal practices that pertain to how the organization makes credit decisions and manages credit risk).

A credit culture that emphasizes *collaborate* would be a partnership culture, one in which employees would find it beneficial to work in cross-functional teams, reminiscent of the culture that existed in US investment banks before they became publicly traded corporations, and it is the culture that currently exists among Farm Credit System banks.

A credit culture that emphasizes *control* is a risk-minimization culture, in which a great deal of importance is placed on rigorous credit analysis and monitoring of adherence to covenants, with a low tolerance for default risk. Growth would be sacrificed in the interest of prudence and safety. There

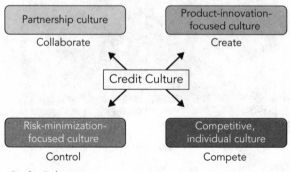

FIGURE 5.3 Credit Culture.

would be tight controls, and violations of process guidelines would not be tolerated.

A credit culture that emphasizes *compete* is a competitive, individual-performance-oriented culture, in which employee bonuses depend on exceeding performance targets; the ratio of bonus to base pay would be high. Organizational targets emphasize market share gains and revenue growth. Such firms will grow through acquisitions and will value decisive, fast-moving, and aggressive employees.

A credit culture that emphasizes *create* is focused on product innovation and organic growth. Experimentation with new products is encouraged. Firms with this culture would extend securitization to new asset classes, devise new contracts providing an expanding array of individuals and firms with access to the credit market, design new instruments for hedging and transferring risk, and so on. The investment banking industry in the United States has been a leader in financial innovation through its emphasis on this quadrant.[19]

A key message of the CVF is that while most banks will have an organizational culture that spans all four quadrants, each bank will typically be strongest in one quadrant, and this strength will influence how the bank operates, where it is most successful, and what it finds most challenging. For example, a bank with a *create* culture will consistently come out with new financial products and achieve a high level of organic growth but will have difficulty maintaining consistent risk-control standards and eliminating regulatory compliance errors. Similarly, a bank with a *compete* credit culture will be very competitive in the marketplace and will grow aggressively through acquisitions. Its biggest challenges will be creating trust among employees within the organization and achieving collaboration.

There is empirical evidence that a bank's credit culture affects measurable outcomes.[20] For example, using textual analysis to develop a measure of risk culture, an empirical analysis of European banks during 2004–2014 found that a sounder risk culture is associated with higher-quality loan portfolios, lower expected defaults, and higher bank stock returns.[21]

Levers for Changing Culture Using CVF

There are mainly four levers that must be pulled in order to change culture: performance metrics for judging individuals, projects, and business units; compensation; processes for decision-making and resource allocation; and behaviors to encourage, tolerate, and punish.

Consider performance metrics. Many organizations want their executives to develop the leadership abilities of their subordinates. However, mentoring and coaching take time, so quite often not enough is done. One organization that attaches high value to this activity altered performance metrics to encourage more effort in this activity. Specifically, every leader, in collaboration with his or her supervisor, is asked annually to evaluate all direct reports on their readiness to replace their boss. The mantra is: "The more easily replaceable you are, the better the job you have done in developing your direct report." Those who have done a better job of developing their direct reports to replace them are viewed more favorably for promotions. Just as criteria can be set for promotion, they can also be prescribed for dismissal.[22]

Compensation design has an obvious impact on how employees behave. In banking, there is a greater emphasis on return on equity (ROE) for calculating executive bonuses than in any other industry. It is not surprising, then, that bankers are averse to higher capital requirements, since holding higher capital leads to a lower ROE, other things being equal. Similarly, if loan officers are compensated for growth in loan volume, then they will have incentives to grow loan volume with far less emphasis on credit quality.[23] A culture that emphasizes *collaborate* and *create* will rely more on deferred compensation, perhaps imposing a longer compensation "duration."[24] This means that compensation design—not only for top executives but all the way down to loan officers and credit committee members—ought to be part of what regulators examine in connection with microprudential regulation.

Key Takeaways: Implications for Banks, Regulators, and Supervisors

I now summarize the key lessons from the research on culture and the CVF, discuss what leaders of banks and other financial services organizations can learn, and conclude with some takeaways for bank regulators and supervisors.

Summary of Insights

- A bank's higher purpose will influence its culture.
- A bank's culture must support the execution of its strategy, so that the culture affects all aspects of decision-making.
- A strong culture can act as a coordination mechanism and can help to achieve (desirable) outcomes that cannot be reached with formal contracts (such as incentive-based compensation) alone.

- It is more challenging to have a strong culture that operates effectively and consistently in a large and complex bank, since subcultures are likely to emerge, leading employees to identify first with their business unit and then with the bank. Size creates the potential for more intrabank competition and behavior that is at odds with the bank's preferred culture.
- A strong culture can change an employee's identity in a positive way and allow the bank to rely less on incentive compensation to induce the desired behavior.
- There is no such thing as a uniquely best culture. Both culture and strategy are codetermined, but culture must support the bank's growth strategy. Since banks have different strategies, there is likely to be a distinct preferred culture for each bank.

Lessons for Bank Executives

First, leaders should clearly articulate a sense of higher purpose for the bank that transcends business goals but also intersects with these goals.[25] Usually, a higher purpose is customer-centric, employee-centric, or designed to serve society. For example, Zingerman's, a deli in Ann Arbor, Michigan, states its higher purpose as developing its employees as entrepreneurs and giving customers the best restaurant experience possible. A higher purpose for Edward Jones, a financial services firm, is to help its clients manage their finances so that they can "provide better lives for their children and grandchildren." Howard Schultz, chairman and CEO of Starbucks, articulated a purpose for the coffee company of offering a "third place between work and home." Whatever a bank's stated objective, if it looks for the intersection of its growth strategy with that higher purpose and then ties its culture to it, the effect can be significantly positive. Research has shown that when a higher purpose has been communicated clearly so employees truly believe that the organization is driven by an authentic higher purpose that transcends the usual business goals, and that this higher purpose actually affects business decisions of the organization, employees are more engaged and productive.

Second, leaders should do a diagnostic survey to get a sense of the bank's existing and preferred cultures. This should be done at many different levels of the organization, not just the top.

Third, leaders can engage in a cultural-change exercise using the levers discussed in the previous section.

Fourth, leaders should be cognizant of the tensions and tradeoffs between the bank's growth strategy and preferred culture.

Finally, before finalizing a merger, leaders should consider the compatibility of the cultures of the merging banks, based on a cultural diagnosis.

Takeaways for Bank Regulators and Supervisors

Currently, much of the focus of bank regulators appears to be on ensuring ethical behavior and curtailing risk taking in banks. While this is understandable, the CVF provides a word of caution—an excessive focus on *control* can kill *create*. So the key takeaways for bank supervisors are the following:

First, it may be valuable to examine the practices of promotion and compensation to improve understanding of an organization; the criteria for both will be quite informative about a bank's culture.

Second, while it is not surprising that bank supervisors emphasize the *control* quadrant of the CVF more than banks themselves will, it would nonetheless be useful to consider the fact that an excessive focus on goals like predictability can hurt financial innovation, with negative consequences for growth. Thus, a balanced and nuanced approach is needed.

Third, in addition to focusing on deferred compensation as a way to encourage more long-term thinking, it may be valuable to consider formulating guidelines based on the compensation duration measure recently developed in the literature.[26]

Fourth, large and complex banks are likely to find it more challenging to implement a single overarching culture, so subcultures are likely to emerge. It will be important to understand the characteristics of these subcultures.

Finally, in the case of bank mergers, the cultural compatibility of the two banks is an important determinant of success. Large mergers—like Daimler-Chrysler and Citi-Travelers—have often failed owing to cultural incompatibility.[27]

What Is the Interaction between Bank Culture and Capital?

Bank culture is influenced by a bank's capital ratio.[28] Suppose the bank can choose between a safety-oriented culture and a growth-oriented culture. A safety-oriented culture emphasizes the *control* quadrant, whereas a growth-oriented culture emphasizes *compete* and *create*. It is shown that this choice of culture affects the organization's choice of:

- managerial compensation contracts
- resources allocated to loan prospecting versus credit analysis and risk control, and
- the kinds of people recruited to work for the bank.

A safety-oriented culture emphasizes growth less and the minimization of various risks more in designing its compensation contracts, compared to a growth-oriented culture. A safety-oriented culture also allocates more resources to credit analysis and risk control and less to loan prospecting than a growth-oriented culture. Moreover, a bank with a safety-oriented culture recruits people who tend to be more risk averse and attach greater importance to managing risk than to growing fast.

A key insight of the analysis is that when banks have more capital, they exhibit a stronger preference for a safety-oriented culture. The reason is simple. If banks are managed to maximize the wealth of their shareholders, then the shareholders have more skin in the game when more of their money is at stake. There are also other important findings:

- Whereas higher capital ratios push banks toward safety-oriented cultures, a higher probability of being bailed out by the government has the opposite effect—it pushes banks toward growth-oriented cultures.
- Higher competition between banks pushes banks to choose growth-oriented cultures at the expense of safety.
- Culture is contagious. Banks will tend to follow each other in their choices of culture. If some banks choose growth-oriented cultures, so will their competitors. Likewise, if some banks choose safety-oriented cultures, so will their competitors.

Monetary Policy, Culture, and the Reactive Regulatory Dynamic

We can see now how monetary policy also enters the picture. Easy monetary policy that includes low interest rates and "quantitative easing" feeds asset price bubbles, such as the real estate bubble that we saw prior to the

2007–2009 crisis. When asset prices are inflating, the importance of credit analysis declines for banks.[29] Why? Think of mortgage lending in the years before the crisis. A bank may be willing to lend me 105 percent of the price of the house I am buying without spending much time verifying my income or ability to repay the loan from income, because if I default, the bank can simply take possession of my house and sell it at a higher price than the loan it gave me. So why worry? Moreover, even if banks continue to emphasize rigorous credit analysis, the "institutional memory hypothesis" suggests that the longer things go well, the more difficult it becomes for loan officers to discern bad loans from good. The idea is that institutions are made up of individuals who make lending decisions, so institutions have "memories," just like individuals. When things go well, the institutional memory is dominated by good outcomes, which leads to an easing of credit standards.[30]

In such an environment, the diminished effectiveness and importance of credit analysis make growth-oriented cultures (*create* and *compete*) more attractive for banks. The combination of herding incentives and low capital ratios induced by safety nets, including bailouts, exacerbates this propensity—they lead most banks to prefer growth-oriented cultures. Of course, a higher purpose that emphasizes continuity of service to society can temper the propensity to focus excessively on growth. Nonetheless, the allure of growth may prove irresistible for some banks.

Culture thus suggests a way to avoid the reactive regulatory dynamic in which regulation is a spasmodic reaction to crises. Very simply, regulators should take actions that encourage a stronger emphasis on safety-oriented cultures during good times.

Capital and Culture as Distinguishing Features of Market-Integrated Banks

Apart from being cautious about reliance on easy monetary policies that feed asset price bubbles, regulators should focus on higher capital ratios and minimize bailouts of distressed institutions to induce banks to choose safety-oriented cultures. Some economic growth may be sacrificed, but this may well be a reduction of excessive lending. Not all lending is good for sustained economic growth and stability, as we discovered in the last financial crisis. Avoiding some growth may be worthwhile. Easy monetary policy and inflated asset prices may warrant higher bank capital requirements and a lower perceived bailout probability.

Stronger-safety-oriented bank cultures will also strengthen public trust in banking. And as non-bank, market-based alternatives to banks—like P2P lending platforms—grow in importance and banks become more integrated with markets, what will truly distinguish banks will be their culture and the public trust in banks.

Summing Up and Questions

This chapter touched upon issues that are typically not dealt with in banking research. Few people, if any, talk about higher purpose in banking. And there are many who believe that the recent regulatory focus on culture in banking is misplaced—regulators ought to focus on strengthening the traditional tools of prudential regulation. This is not a view that I share. Identifying an authentic higher purpose and strengthening bank culture can generate more trust in banking and complement the traditional tools of microprudential regulation—that is, regulators should seriously consider making bank culture a part of microprudential regulation. Many believe that culture is too nebulous to be useful for regulation. But the research shows that regulators can use traditional tools like capital requirements, limiting interbank competition, and reducing bailouts to strengthen banks' incentives to adopt a safety-oriented culture.

This chapter has addressed many of the questions that were raised in the previous chapter, but a few still remain. Specifically, banks are just one component of the financial system, along with other institutions and financial markets.

This raises the following questions:

1. Where do banks fit within the overall financial system?
2. Is it better to focus on banks or on the financial market to achieve economic stability and growth?
3. What is the nature of the interaction between banks and markets, and how does it affect the stability-growth tradeoff?

In the next chapter, I will take on these questions.

Notes

1. See Cohn, Fehr, and Maréchal 2014.
2. See Mohan 2014.

3. See Zaring 2017.

4. See Thakor 2016. My discussion in this chapter relies heavily on that paper.

5. William Dudley, "Enhancing Financial Stability by Improving Culture in the Financial Services Industry," remarks at the Workshop on Reforming Culture and Behavior in the Financial Services Industry, October 2014.

6. See Quinn and Thakor 2018, where organizational higher purpose is discussed along with steps organizations can take to identify an authentic higher purpose and infuse the organization with it.

7. See Quinn and Thakor 2018, for examples.

8. For example, Keenan 2018 reports the findings of field experiments in which employees avoided activities that had prosocial incentives attached to them, compared to "standard" incentives. One of the field experiments involved recycling as a prosocial incentive. This shows that when employees think that a prosocial higher purpose is a PR gimmick tacked on to the activities of the organization, they do not embrace it.

9. See Fry and Chew 2017, who report that these initiatives have created 1,700 jobs and helped start more than one hundred new businesses in Detroit since 2014.

10. However, as Bob Quinn and I point out, it is an organizational crisis that often triggers a discovery of higher purpose (see Quinn and Thakor 2018). So in some organizations, a crisis becomes a fight for survival, whereas in some it also creates an opportunity to discover purpose.

11. See Thakor 2016. My discussion in this chapter relies heavily on that paper.

12. "Tightrope Artists" 2008.

13. For a formal analysis of these effects, see Song and Thakor 2017. The notion of "identity shaping" was introduced by Akerlof and Kranton 2011.

14. See Cameron, DeGraff, Quinn, and Thakor 2014.

15. See, for example, Quinn and Cameron 1983; Quinn and Rohrbaugh 1983; Quinn 1988; and Cameron and Quinn 2011.

16. See, for example, Cameron, DeGraff, Quinn, and Thakor (2014).

17. The fact that these are competing views and beliefs about what creates value is similar to the disagreement stemming from heterogeneity described by Van den Steen 2010a, 2010b.

18. See Cameron and Quinn 2011 for a complete discussion of the diagnostic instrument, and Cameron, DeGraff, Quinn, and Thakor 2014 for a rebuttal for some of the criticisms of the CVF.

19. Boot and Thakor 1997 develop a theory that explains why US investment banks have been more successful in financial innovation than investment banks in Europe. Thakor (2012) develops a theory of how financial innovation can increase the likelihood of a financial crisis.

20. See Carretta, Fiordelisi, and Schwizer 2017 and Ellul and Yerramilli 2013.

21. See Bianchi, Farina, and Fiordelisi 2016.

22. As Jack Welch, former chairman and chief executive officer of General Electric, said in an interview with Stuart Varney on CEO Exchange in 2001, any organization

that fails to root out and dismiss those who deliver great results but behave in a manner inconsistent with the culture cannot talk credibly about values.

23. See Acharya and Naqvi 2012 for a theory of how such compensation incentives for loan officers sow the seeds of crises. Udell 1989 also shows empirically that banks that compensate loan officers more for growth also tend to invest more in loan reviews in order to monitor loan officers.

24. See Gopalan, Milbourn, Song, and Thakor 2014 for a definition of and empirical evidence on compensation duration.

25. See Thakor and Quinn 2014 for a discussion of the economics of higher purpose.

26. See, for example, Gopalan, Milbourn, Song, and Thakor 2014.

27. Bouwman 2013 discusses numerous case studies of mergers that failed due to lack of cultural compatibility. Fiordelisi and Martelli 2011 empirically examine the impact of culture on the success of mergers in US and European banking.

28. See Song and Thakor forthcoming.

29. The theory that explains this appears in Goel, Song, and Thakor 2014. They refer to banks' diluted incentives to engage in credit analysis as "intermediation thinning."

30. Evidence on this provided by Berger and Udell 2004, who use data on individual US banks over the 1980–2000 time period.

References

Acharya, Viral, and Hassan Naqvi. 2012. "The Seeds of a Crisis: A Theory of Bank Liquidity and Risk Taking over the Business Cycle." *Journal of Financial Economics* 106 (2): 349–366.

Akerlof, George, and Rachel E. Kranton. 2011. *Identity Economics: How Our Identities Shape Our Work, Wages, and Well-Being*. Princeton, NJ: Princeton University Press.

Berger, Allen, and Gregory Udell. 2004. "The Institutional Memory Hypothesis and the Procyclicality of Bank Lending Behavior." *Journal of Financial Intermediation* 13:458–495.

Bianchi, Nicola, Vincenzo Farina, and Franco Fiordelisi. 2016. "Risk Culture in Banks: Just Words?" Working Paper, University of Rome, November.

Boot, Arnoud, and Anjan V. Thakor. 1997. "Banking Scope and Financial Innovation." *Review of Financial Studies*, 10 (4): 1099–1131.

Bouwman, Christa. 2013. "The Role of Corporate Culture in Mergers and Acquisitions." In *Mergers and Acquisitions: Practices, Performance, and Perspectives*, edited by E. Perrault, 109–132. New York: Nova Science.

Cameron, Kim S., and Robert E. Quinn. 2011. *Diagnosing and Changing Organizational Culture*. San Francisco: John Wiley & Sons.

Cameron, Kim S., Robert Quinn, Jeff DeGraff, and Anjan V. Thakor. 2014. *Competing Values Leadership*. Northampton, MA: Edward Elgar.

Carretta, Alessandro, Franco Fiordelisi, and Paola Schwizer. 2017. *Risk Culture in Banking*. Palgrave Macmillan Studies in Banking and Financial Institutions. Cham, Switzerland: Palgrave Macmillan.

Cohn, Alain, Ernst Fehr, and Michel André Maréchal. 2014. "Business Culture and Dishonesty in the Banking Industry." *Nature* 516: 86–89.

Dudley, William C. 2014. "Enhancing Financial Stability by Improving Culture in the Financial Services Industry." Remarks delivered at the Federal Reserve Bank of New York's Workshop on Reforming Culture and Behavior in the Financial Services Industry, New York City, October 20. Available online at https://www.newyorkfed.org/newsevents/speeches/2014/dud141020a.html.

Ellul, Andrew, and Vijay Yerramilli. 2013. "Stronger Risk Controls, Lower Risk: Evidence from U.S. Bank Holding Companies." *Journal of Finance* 68 (5): 1757–1803.

Fiordelisi, Franco, and Duccio Martelli. 2011. Corporate Culture and M&A Results in Banking. March 9. Available at SSRN: https://ssrn.com/abstract=1784016 or http://dx.doi.org/10.2139/ssrn.1784016.

Fry, Erika, and Jonathan Chew. 2017. "Change the World." *Fortune*, September 15, 75–123.

Goel, Anand M., Fenghua Song, and Anjan V. Thakor. 2014. "Correlated Leverage and Its Ramifications." *Journal of Financial Intermediation* 23 (4): 471–503.

Gopalan, Radhakrishnan, Todd Milbourn, Fenghua Song, and Anjan V. Thakor. 2014. "Duration of Executive Compensation." *Journal of Finance* 69 (6): 2777–2817.

Keenan, Elizabeth. 2018. "Opting in to Prosocial Incentives." Working Paper, Harvard Business School, May.

Friedman, Milton. 1970. "The Social Responsibility of Business Is to Increase its Profits." *New York Times Magazine*, September 13.

Mohan, Geoffrey. 2014. "Banking Industry Culture Primes for Cheating, Study Suggests." *Los Angeles Times*, November 21.

Quinn, Robert E. 1988. *Beyond Rational Management: Mastering the Paradoxes and Competing Demands of High Performance*. San Francisco: Jossey-Bass.

Quinn, Robert E., and Kim Cameron. 1983. "Organizational Life Cycles and Shifting Criteria for Effectiveness." *Management Science* 29 (1): 33–51.

Quinn, Robert E., and John Rohrbaugh. 1983. "A Spatial Model of Effectiveness Criteria: Towards a Competing Values Approach to Organizational Analysis." *Management Science* 29 (3): 363–377.

Quinn, Robert, and Anjan V. Thakor. 2018. "Creating a Purpose-Driven Organization." *Harvard Business Review,* July–August, 2–9.

Song, Fenghua, and Anjan V. Thakor. Forthcoming. "Bank Culture." *Journal of Financial Intermediation*.

Thakor, Anjan V. 2012. "Incentives to Innovate and Financial Crises." *Journal of Financial Economics* 103 (1): 130–148.

Thakor, Anjan V. 2016. "Corporate Culture in Banking." In "Behavioral Risk Management in the Financial Services Industry—The Role of Culture, Governance and Financial Reporting," special issue, *Economic Policy Review, Federal Reserve Bank of New York* 22 (1): 1–12.

Thakor, Anjan V., and Robert E. Quinn. 2014. "The Economics of Higher Purpose." Working paper, Washington University in St. Louis and University of Michigan.

"Tightrope Artists." 2008. *The Economist*. May 15.

Udell, Gregory. 1989. "Loan Quality, Commercial Loan Review and Loan Officer Contracting." *Journal of Banking and Finance* 13 (3): 367–382.

Van den Steen, Eric. 2010a. "Culture Clash: The Costs and Benefits of Homogeneity." *Management Science* 56 (10): 1718–1738.

Van den Steen, Eric. 2010b. "On the Origin of Shared Beliefs (and Corporate Culture)." *RAND Journal of Economics* 41 (4): 617–648.

Zaring, David. 2017. "Focus on Bank Culture Is an Odd Regulatory Strategy." *New York Times,* March 14.

Banks and Markets

Interactions That Affect Stability and Growth

6

Financial System Architecture

WHERE DO BANKS SIT IN THE FINANCIAL
SYSTEM?

Banks in the Financial System

From 1986 to 1990, Japan experienced an economic bubble as real estate and stock prices soared. Then came the crash as the bubble burst. The Nikkei stock index peaked in 1989, and by early 1992, it had plunged to half its peak value. By 1991, real estate prices began a downward spiral as well. The decline in real estate prices from their peak in 1990 was even bigger than the stock market decline.

These events had little direct impact on the US economy. But they did have an indirect effect. The precipitous declines in stock prices and real estate values caused the capital ratios of Japanese banks to fall sharply. This caused these banks to significantly cut back on their overseas lending. Many of these banks had large market shares in some US real estate markets.

This decline in the capital ratios of Japanese banks caused a reduction in their lending to US borrowers.[1] This was a credit supply shock. That is, the lower lending was not because credit demand by these US borrowers declined. What is interesting is that these US borrowers were unable to borrow enough from other sources to make up for the lower credit available from their Japanese banks. This highlights the importance of relationship lending.[2] Borrowers are often able to obtain credit from banks they have relationships with during times when de novo lenders may be unwilling to offer credit. This means that the loss of credit from a relationship lender is often difficult to make up for. It also makes another important point. If the Japanese banks had more capital to begin with, they would have been better

**Table 6.1   Relative Sizes of US Banks and
Markets End 2016 ($ trillions)**

Total bank assets	$16.10
Total bond markets	$6.87
Total stock market capitalization	$24.00

equipped to absorb the loss in capital when it occurred, and the borrowers who took relationship loans from them would have experienced less disruption in their credit supply.

So even in the most advanced financial system in the world, bank credit is not easy to replace, at least in the short run. This has ramifications for Main Street. Banks occupy a large and prominent room in the house we call the financial system, and the more financially sound (better capitalized) they are, the better it is for the financial system and Main Street.

The prominence of banks in the architecture of the financial system is apparent at a glance from the table showing relative sizes of banks and markets at the end of 2016 (table 6.1).

The upshot of this is simple. Having even deep and liquid financial markets does not replace banks. Markets not only compete with banks, they also need banks Moreover, banking is big, both in absolute terms and compared to markets. Note that even the magnitudes in table 6.1 underrepresent the importance of banks, since the total bank assets number does not include off-balance-sheet items for banks.

Banks and Markets: Is There a Development Hierarchy?

It is well known that India has a physical infrastructure that is badly in need of repair. Most people acknowledge that to fulfill its economic potential, the country needs to significantly upgrade its roads and bridges and address power supply issues. However, the rapid progress of telecommunications technology and cellular devices has diminished the hurdle to commerce posed by a creaky physical infrastructure. Sophisticated logistical systems have developed even in villages lacking paved roads, as people using laptops and cell phones are able to ride bicycles on dirt roads to deliver goods and services in ways previously unimaginable.

A lot of countries lack the infrastructure for an effective and robust banking system that fosters economic growth. Bankers need skills. Human capital is important in banking, and it takes time to develop it. Markets, by contrast, rely more on information technology and other infrastructure that can be purchased and readily assembled. Does this mean that countries without robust banking systems can engage in "infrastructure leapfrogging," analogous to what has happened in India, in this case bypassing investments in banking and focusing instead on developing capital markets?

The answer, reflected in my experience with the Romanian financial system, is a categorical no. The theoretical foundations for this can be found in the research on financial system architecture.

This research has made the point that a financial system in its infancy will be bank dominated, and then markets will grow in importance with increased financial market sophistication.[3] Access to the financial market requires the borrower to have a credit reputation, and this is usually acquired through bank borrowing. It is therefore not surprising that even new firms rely heavily on bank financing, in addition to "informal finance" from family and friends.[4]

Banks serve a "cleansing" function. They screen out uncreditworthy loan applicants, monitor borrowers, reduce verification costs of various sorts, and provide a host of relationship banking services to enhance their chances of success. These relationship banking services include the protection of confidential borrower information by trusted banks.[5] This helps these borrowers to establish credit reputations, so that by the time they access the financial market, the uncertainty about their creditworthiness has been reduced enough to enable them to finance at attractive terms. Absent the heavy lifting by banks and the certification role bank credit plays,[6] credit rating agencies and investors would have a much more challenging task of separating the wheat from the chaff.

Of course, a vibrant banking system will not arise organically. It has to be designed and developed. It requires appropriate laws that foster an economic environment that is conducive to lending. This requires, for example, the adoption of best practice laws on collateral.[7] And it requires minimizing the distorting influence of politics on banking.[8]

The traditional view had banks and markets competing, so the growth of financial markets would come at the expense of banks.[9] This view seemed to be borne out by events like the outflow of deposits from the banking system in the 1980s when mutual funds emerged to provide higher rates of return to savers.

More recent research has shown, however, that this is too narrow a view of banks and markets.[10] The relation between banks and financial markets is *three-dimensional*: they compete, they complement, and they coevolve. The *competition aspect* is the most obvious. For example, the asset-backed commercial paper market that emerged in the United States was directly in competition with bank lending to medium-sized firms that lacked access to commercial paper and hence relied primarily on bank loans. *Complementarity* arises because of developments like securitization. As banks improve their technology for screening borrowers, the credits they securitize are of higher quality. The resulting asset-backed securities issued and traded in the market are therefore subject to lower financing frictions. Capital market financing costs go down as a result. Finally, bank capital gives rise to *coevolution*. As the capital market develops, financing frictions for banks are diminished, which makes it easier and cheaper for banks to raise equity capital. Higher bank capital provides banks with stronger incentives to screen borrowers,[11] which then means higher-quality credits are securitized, and this in turn fosters market growth—a virtuous cycle.

So it is important to develop banking first and then markets. The existence of a robust banking system along with a well-developed financial market then leads to positive feedback effects that accelerate the development of both. This is the bright side of complementarity and coevolution.

But there is a dark side as well. If banking is buffeted by negative shocks, the effects spill over into markets as well. We saw this in spades during the 2007–2009 financial crisis. Mortgages originated and securitized by banks began to default, and the consequent impact on the prices of mortgage-backed securities reverberated through the entire global financial system. Increased banking fragility means increased financial market fragility.

Blurring Boundaries: Securitization and the Alphabet Soup of PEs, P2Ps, and CRAs

The idea that there is a positive feedback that goes back and forth between banks and markets is reinforced by research, which shows that while both bank and stock market development have positive effects on economic growth, the impact of bank development is smaller when the stock market is more developed.

These spillover effects are reinforced when the boundary between banks and markets becomes blurred, a development that has been underway for some time.[12] Securitization has been a major driver of this phenomenon, because it directly links banks as originators of credit instruments and creators and sellers of claims against these assets.

But there is also another force at work. As markets evolve and compete more aggressively with banks in areas that were traditional bank strongholds, banks have an incentive to create new products and services that blend the services provided by markets with those provided by banks. This allows banks to follow their customers to the market and avoid losing them.[13] For example, when a borrower goes to the market and issues commercial paper, the bank loses a loan it could have made, but the bank can still keep some of the borrower's business by providing a backup line of credit. Another example is securitization—banks not only originate, pool, and securitize loans, but they also purchase various securitized tranches to hold on their balance sheets. The inducement for such market-based activities grows as interbank competition pressures profit margins and improved capital market liquidity lowers funding costs for bank borrowers, further reducing the demand for bank credit. As a consequence, banks are increasingly integrated with markets. This intertwining not only complicates both monetary policy and prudential bank regulation, but it also has profound implications for how we view the relationship between bank stability and economic growth. Moreover, the increasing integration of banks and markets has also influenced the organization structures and corporate cultures of banks.[14] For example, major investment banks like Goldman Sachs converted from partnerships to publicly traded firms, and many believe that this changed their cultures to encourage more risk-taking. That is, the cultures shifted to emphasize *compete* at the expense of *collaborate*.

When we mention banks, we typically think of depositories. But there are non-depository institutions that are also part of the architecture of the financial system. Many of these institutions—like investment banks, insurance companies, and the like—are in the shadow banking sector and perform "maturity transformation" services, just like banks. Maturity transformation refers to a bank taking in deposits that have very short maturities and making loans with much longer maturities. In general, maturity transformation occurs whenever an institution finances itself with liabilities that have a different maturity compared to the maturity of the assets the institution invests in. A particularly interesting institution is the private equity (PE) firm. These firms provide financing to firms too, but more often in the form of equity rather than debt. That is, these are "equity intermediaries." Even setting aside the Glass-Steagall restrictions that prevented US banks from holding equity, research has shown that it may not even be a good idea for the same institution to provide a firm with both debt and equity. The most popular argument for this is called the "timely intervention" effect. If the bank has both equity and debt claims on the borrower, it may not have the incentive that a pure creditor would have to intervene in a timely manner and pull the plug when things are going badly. The reason is that a shareholder would much rather gamble on a low-probability future upside than go for a surer low payoff to pay off all creditors now. This may be one reason why equity intermediation has largely been in the hands of PE firms and bulge-bracket investment banks.[15]

As PE firms gain deeper penetration into the market with equity intermediation, there are economic benefits to banks in partnering with them. That is, banks may engage in developing relationships with the PE firms rather than directly with the firms that obtain financing from PE firms. To the extent that PE firms are an integral part of the capital market, this development further deepens the involvement of banks in the capital market.

Also competing with banks are fintech lenders like peer-to-peer (P2P) lending platforms. These involve investors directly lending to borrowers through technology platforms, without an intermediating bank. With this arrangement, the lending platform charges borrowers a fee that covers its costs, and borrowers pay interest on a monthly basis that is passed along to investors. While unsecured lending dominates, secured P2P loans are on the rise. Although currently a small fraction of total lending in the economy, P2P lending is growing rapidly. It is worth noting, however, that while P2P lending was originally "peers" lending to "peers," it is no longer—investors in these platforms now are mostly institutional investors like hedge funds.

Facilitating market financing and other forms of non-bank credit are credit rating agencies (CRAs) that screen borrowers and assign ratings that are indicators of default probabilities.[16] The certification they provide acts as a partial substitute for bank screening. But as players in the capital market, CRAs also provide another connection between banks and markets. This happens in many ways. First, asset-backed securities issued by banks are rated by CRAs, thereby providing third-party verification of credit quality. The rating improves the banks' ability to sell these securities. Second, the book equity capital a bank has may depend on the ratings assigned by CRAs to the debt securities the bank holds. This is because changes in ratings induce changes in the market values of these securities, thereby resulting in changes in the book value of the bank's equity capital. For example, suppose a bank holds mortgage-backed securities on its balance sheet, and the credit ratings for these securities deteriorate, causing a drop in the market values of these securities. The bank will need to mark these holdings to market. The write-down will be a negative charge against the bank's book equity, and it may need to offset this dissipation by raising equity capital. Third, if the bank has contracts on its books that have "ratings triggers," there will be an added effect. For example, suppose the bank or perhaps an insurance company has sold credit default swaps. A decrease in the equity of the institution can cause a decline in the institution's credit ratings. This can trigger an increase in the cash or capital the institution has to set aside to secure the credit default swaps. This is what happened to AIG during the 2007–2009 crisis when its credit rating fell.

Consequently, as the boundaries between banks and markets blur, problems in the financial market can adversely affect banks and their ability to create liquidity—think of the plight of Japanese banks when their stock market bubble burst—and problems in banking can adversely influence markets. In other words, greater banking stability means greater market continuity and liquidity. The safer banks are, the safer the whole economic system is.

What Distinguishes Banks as the Boundaries Blur?

The blurring of boundaries between banks and markets raises important questions about the need for banks. If P2P lending platforms can provide consumer credit, why do we need banks that finance such credit with deposits that then have to be insured by the taxpayers? If money market mutual funds can replicate deposit accounts, do we need banks to provide the safekeeping services they provide?

Many view the emergence of capital market substitutes for banking services as a threat to banks. However, what truly distinguishes banks is that they can adopt a higher purpose and develop a culture that generates trust in a way that these market alternatives cannot. Whether banks will choose to do so remains to be seen.[17] But the opportunity is there. If they take advantage of the opportunity, then banks can coevolve with and complement the capital market, instead of merely competing with it.

Summing Up

As banks and markets become more integrated, greater subtlety is required in our thinking about how to achieve financial and economic stability without sacrificing economic growth. For example, markets expand the set of opportunities for banks to engage in nontraditional activities. Banks that distinguish themselves with an authentic higher purpose and a culture that supports it will be best equipped to benefit from these opportunities.

Notes

1. See Peek and Rosengren 2000.
2. For papers that discuss the benefits of relationship lending, see Berger and Udell 1995, Boot and Thakor 2000, and Petersen and Rajan 1994.
3. See Boot and Thakor 1997.
4. See Berger and Udell 1995 and Robb and Robinson 2014.
5. Merton and Thakor 2018 have developed a theory of banks as "trusted lenders."
6. See James 1987 and Lummer and McConnell 1989.
7. See Calomiris, Larrain, and Sturgess 2017.
8. There is substantial academic research on how politics distorts banking. See, for example, Huang and Thakor 2018, who document that directives to banks to make politically favored loans cause banks to become more fragile by reducing their capital ratios. More on this later.
9. See Allen and Gale 1995 and Boot and Thakor 1997.
10. See Song and Thakor 2010.
11. See Purnanandam 2011 for empirical evidence.
12. See Boot and Thakor 2018.
13. Boot and Thakor (2018) provide an extensive discussion of this.
14. In part this is because the increasing integration calls for different skills in employees and different compensation structures.
15. A "bulge-bracket" bank is a very large, multinational investment bank. Examples are Goldman Sachs, Barclays Capital, Credit Suisse, Deutsche Bank, JP Morgan Chase, Citigroup, Morgan Stanley, and UBS. Although debt and equity financiers have traditionally been distinct, there are instances in which the same lender provides both debt and equity financing to borrowers. In these cases, lenders react differently to covenant violations by borrowers, with a higher likelihood of providing waivers when there are violations. See Chava, Wang, and Zhou, forthcoming.
16. These are coarse indicators. Default probabilities lie in a continuum, whereas there are under twenty-five rating categories. See Goel and Thakor 2015 for a theory of coarse credit ratings that explains why it is economically rational for there to be far fewer ratings than there are default probabilities of debt issues.
17. As Song and Thakor (forthcoming) point out, bank culture choices are shaped by their growth strategy choices.

References

Allen, Franklin, and Douglas Gale. 1995. "A Welfare Comparison of Intermediaries and Financial Markets in Germany and the U.S." *European Economic Review* 39:179–209.

Berger, Allen, and Gregory F. Udell. 1995. "Relationship Lending and Lines of Credit in Small Firm Finance." *Journal of Banking and Finance* 68:351–382.

Boot, Arnoud, and Anjan V. Thakor. 1997. "Financial System Architecture." *Review of Financial Studies* 10 (3): 693–733.

Boot, Arnoud, and Anjan V. Thakor. 2000. "Can Relationship Banking Survive Competition?" *Journal of Finance* 55 (2): 679–714, April.

Boot, Arnoud, and Anjan V. Thakor. 2018. "Commercial Banking and Shadow Banking: The Accelerating Integration of Banks and Markets and Its Implications for Regulation." In *The Oxford Handbook in Banking*, 3rd ed., edited by Allen Berger, Phil Mullineaux, and John Wilson, 47–76. New York: Oxford University Press.

Calomiris, Charles W., Mauricio Larrain, José Liberti, and Jason Sturgess. 2017. "How Collateral Laws Shape Lending and Sectoral Activity." *Journal of Financial Economics* 123 (1): 163–188.

Chava, Sudheer, Rui Wang, and Hong Zhou. Forthcoming. "Covenants, Creditors' Simultaneous Equity Holdings, and Firm Investment Policy." *Journal of Financial and Quantitative Analysis*.

Goel, Anand, and Anjan V. Thakor. 2015. "Information Reliability and Welfare: A Theory of Coarse Credit Ratings." *Journal of Financial Economics* 115 (3): 541–557.

Huang, Shen, and Anjan Thakor. 2018. "Political Influence on Bank Credit Allocation: Bank Capital Responses, Consumption and Systemic Risk." Working Paper, Washington University in St. Louis, April.

James, Christopher. 1987. "Some Evidence on the Uniqueness of Bank Loans." *Journal of Financial Economics* 19:217–235.

Lummer, Scott L., and John J. McConnell. 1989. "Further Evidence on the Bank Lending Process and the Capital-Market Response to Bank Loan Agreements." *Journal of Financial Economics* 25:99–122.

Merton, Robert C., and Richard Thakor. 2018. "Trust in Lending." Working paper, MIT Sloan, January.

Peek, Joe, and Eric S. Rosengren. 2000. "Collateral Damage: The Effects of the Japanese Bank Crisis on Real Activity in the United States." *American Economic Review* 90 (1); 30–34.

Petersen, Mitchell, and Rajan Raghuram. 1994. "The Benefits of Lending Relationships: Evidence from Small Business Data." *Journal of Finance* 49 (1): 3–37.

Purnanandam, Amiyatosh. 2011. "Originate-to-Distribute Model and the Subprime Mortgage Crisis." *Review of Financial Studies* 24:1881–1915.

Robb, Alicia, and David Robinson. 2014. "The Capital Structure Decisions of New Firms." *Review of Financial Studies* 27 (1): 153–179.

Song, Fenghua, and Anjan V. Thakor. 2010. "Financial System Architecture and the Co-evolution of Banks and Markets." *Economic Journal* 120 (547): 1021–1255.

Song, Fenghua, and Anjan V. Thakor. Forthcoming. "Bank Culture." *Journal of Financial Intermediation*.

7

Changes in Banking over Time

Introduction

Banks are where the money is. This fact about banking has not changed in all the centuries that banks have been around. This is why there have been so many movies about bank robberies. In the typical bank robbery movie, the robber steals money from the bank's vault or a stagecoach delivering money to the vault. For example, in *The Invisible Man*, made in 1933, James Whale adapts H. G. Wells's concept of an invisible man to depict an invisible bank robber who makes money seemingly float out of the bank. But while most of these movies focus on robbers stealing the bank's liabilities (cash deposits), one clever movie focused on the asset side of the bank's balance sheet—its loans. In *Wisdom*, made in 1987, Emilio Estevez and Demi Moore play modern-day Robin Hoods during the 1980s farm debt crisis in the United States. Rather than robbing cash from banks, they burned the banks' mortgage records. Reducing a farmer's debt back then was just as useful to the farmer as receiving cash.

Changes in banking have occurred on both the liability side and the asset side of bank balance sheets. While bank liabilities still consist largely of deposits, they also include funds borrowed from other banks and capital market instruments. Assets are no longer limited to loans—they also include a host of asset-backed securities created by securitization and other capital market instruments. These changes are attributable to both how banking was initially configured in the United States and the market forces that buffeted banking subsequently.

Let's begin our story with how US banking was initially configured. While engaged in the rather simple business of taking in deposits and making loans, banks have always been viewed as powerful institutions that "control the purse strings of society." Populists tend to look askance at banks, suspicious of what they might do with the enormous wealth and power they can amass.[1] This view of banks resulted in regulations that created a highly fragmented banking industry in the United States with thousands of geographically restricted banks, so that a few large institutions would not dominate the country. Moreover, because banks were viewed as being more interested in serving the interests of corporations than the average household, savings and loan (S&L) institutions were chartered to provide mortgages for people to buy houses. Until it imploded in the crisis of the 1980s, the S&L industry grew alongside banking, taking in deposits, making loans, and functioning very much like specialized banks. Moreover, many organizations thought they could provide better banking services to their employees if they opened their own banks and limited them to serving their employees. After all, the common bond of employment that binds the employees together should lessen the likelihood of borrower default, so such banks should have an advantage over commercial banks that serve a wider clientele. These institutions are called "credit unions."

The Great Depression beginning in 1929 eventually led to the adoption of federal deposit insurance for banks. But there were grave concerns about conflicts of interest, like banks using insured deposits to fund risky borrowers and then getting these borrowers off their books by underwriting their securities in the capital market to raise financing with which the bank loans are paid off. Or what if banks used insured deposits to gamble in the market, making speculative investments that would make the banks rich if they paid off and leave taxpayers holding the bag if they did not? These concerns led to the enactment of the Glass-Steagall Act, which legally separated commercial banking from investment banking and insurance. So banks made loans with depositors' money—and money they created on their own via "fake receipts"—whereas investment banks provided their clients with underwriting services to raise money in the capital market from investors. And the idea of Glass-Steagall was to draw a big red line between bank loans and capital market bonds. This worked well until securitization came along and obliterated the distinction between bank loans and capital market securities (bonds), primarily because bank loans were converted into capital market securities. The end result was a highly fragmented financial services industry with a mosaic of different types of institutions that served overlapping economic functions. It also had the unfortunate consequence of leading to what Nobel laureate Robert Merton refers to as "regulation by labels," as opposed to "regulation by functions." Merton adopts what he calls the "functional approach" to financial institutions and prescribes regulating these institutions based on what they do rather than what they are called.[2]

Over time, economic forces have blurred the boundaries not only between banks and markets but also between these different types of banks. In this chapter, we will see how this factor and some others have changed banking over the years.

The Forces That Have Changed Banking

Changes in regulation and advances in information technology have been the underlying factors that changed banking in the past century. These two fundamental forces have led to many other developments that have shaped the evolution of banks, as shown in figure 7.1.

Increased Competition

We saw earlier that banks excel as relationship lenders. Developing long-term relationships with borrowers is not only good for borrowers but also profitable for banks. This profitability invites competitive entry by other banks. Thus, the very nature of banking makes banking potentially competitive, as long as regulations prevent banks from coalescing into a giant natural monopoly.[3] Of course, such was the case in the United States, where a large number of small banks dotted the landscape. For much of the post–Great Depression era, the extent of competition among banks was limited by regulation. Banks were not allowed to branch across state lines, and in many states they could not even freely branch within the state. This severely limited competition until

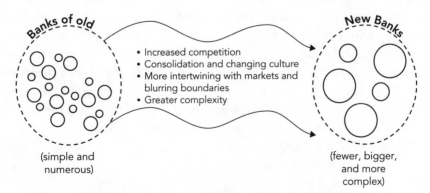

FIGURE 7.1 The Developments That Have Changed Banking.

1994, when the Riegle-Neal Act permitted nationwide branching for banks and opened the floodgates for banking consolidation.

How does competition affect relationship banking? Here theories give us two diametrically opposite answers. One theory says that greater competition among banks encourages borrowers to switch from one bank to another more readily, shortening the lifespan of bank-borrower relationships. In response, more competitive banks invest less in their relationships with borrowers and acquire less information about their borrowers, causing relationships to suffer.[4] There is empirical evidence that borrowers benefit from longer-duration relationships with banks in that they pay lower interest rates when they have longer relationships.[5] The shorter duration of the relationship may also make it more difficult for banks to use time as a contracting variable, say by subsidizing "young" (in terms of credit history) borrowers in the hope of making more profits later in the relationship.[6]

The opposite view is provided by a theory in which competition increases the importance of a relationship orientation as a competitive advantage. The idea is that competition erodes profit margins on existing credit products, forcing banks to seek competitive differentiation. A deeper relationship that adds more value for the borrower is one way to do this.[7] The empirical evidence supports this prediction, namely, that the orientation of relationship lending adapts to increasing interbank competition.[8]

Consolidation and Changing Culture

While fragmented in the decades after the Great Depression, the banking industries in the United States as well as in Europe have been consolidating. Natural economic forces always push banks to consolidate, so when deregulation in the 1980s and 1990s made consolidation possible, banks were eager to do it. In figure 7.2, we can see how consolidation has changed the US banking industry, with the number of commercial banks and savings institutions declining quite dramatically. US commercial banks declined in number from 14,495 in 1984 to 6,532 by the end of 2010. Similarly, savings institutions (S&Ls) that are insured by the Federal Deposit Insurance Corporation (FDIC) fell from 3,566 in 1984 to 1,128 by the end of 2010.[9] The five largest banks now hold more than 40 percent of total deposits in the United States. The populists who influenced the early banking laws in the United States must be turning in their graves!

What does this consolidation mean for relationship banking? One finding is that consolidation adversely affects the supply of loans to small

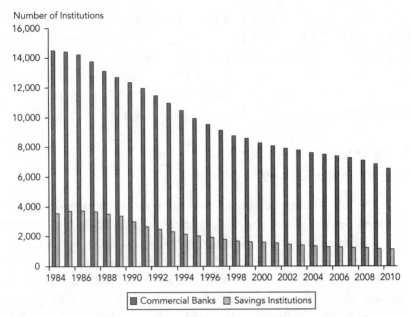

FIGURE 7.2 Number of U.S. Commercial Banks and Savings Institutions from 1984 to 2010.

Source: David C. Wheelock, "Banking Industry Consolidation and Market Structure: Impact of the Financial Crisis and Recession," *Federal Reserve Bank of St. Louis Review*, November/December 2011, 419–438.

businesses.[10] Perhaps one reason for this is that small banks tend to rely more on soft information—impressions formed through personal meetings, on-site visits to the borrower's business, subjective judgments about character, etc.—whereas large banks tend to rely more on hard, verifiable information like FICO scores and results of credit scoring models.[11] So when a large bank acquires a small bank, the reliance on soft information tends to diminish in the new bank. It turns out that small borrowers benefit more from soft information in getting loans. So the reduced reliance on soft information due to banking consolidation hurts them more.

Consolidation also changes bank culture. A relationship-banking-oriented culture is replaced by a more transaction-oriented culture as banks get bigger through mergers. Moreover, cultural mismatches be-tween merging partners lead to failed mergers. Because smaller banks tend to rely more on "soft" information about borrowers—information that can be gathered only via personal interactions[12]—they tend to adopt a more "people-oriented" (*collaborate*) culture. So if such a bank is acquired by a much larger bank with a more *compete*-oriented culture, there may be clash. The Citibank and Travelers merger is a case in point. It was a clash of Citi's relationship-oriented culture (*collaborate*) and Travelers' transaction-oriented (*compete* and *control*) culture, although the culture clash in this case was not due to differences in the sizes of the two institutions.

More Intertwining with Markets and Blurring Boundaries

Changes in the banking industry have also been affected by developments in the capital market. It has been shown both theoretically and empirically that both bank development and stock market development positively affect economic growth in the real sector. However, the growth impact of bank development is lower when the stock market is more developed.[13] That means that the Chinese economy gets a bigger bang for its buck when its banking system develops than the US economy when US banking develops.

Banks have become increasingly intertwined with markets in three ways: through their borrowers, through their non-lending investments, and through their liability (funding) activities. Consider bank borrowers first. In the old days, there was a clear borrowing hierarchy—borrowers first took bank loans and then went to the market after they had established a track record.[14] But this separation has become quite blurred, as borrowers often take bank loans and also issue debt in the capital market. In fact, research has shown that by simultaneously utilizing both bank debt and capital market debt, the borrower can lower its total funding cost.[15] The idea is that when a borrower takes a bank loan, the bank monitors the borrower's actions to control its credit risk. However, this monitoring does not just benefit the bank; it also benefits the capital market investors who bought the borrower's debt securities. This positive spillover effect lowers the cost of capital market debt for the borrower. So banks essentially become linked to the capital market through their borrowers, and increasingly so as the market develops.

Now consider banks' non-lending investments. The advent of securitization means that banks can invest in loans originated by other banks by buying asset-backed securities that represent debt claims against those loan portfolios. These asset-backed securities are traded in the capital market. In addition, banks trade in credit default swaps and a variety of derivative contracts, all of which intertwine banks with markets.

Finally, the funding activities of banks require them to interact with the capital market. Banks raise financing in the market by issuing subordinated debt and raising equity and through repurchase (repo) transaction that use capital market securities as collateral. This is all part of the blurring of boundaries between banks and markets. It is why banks and markets are joined at the hip and compete, complement, and coevolve with each other.[16]

Banking has thus changed from being a simple business of taking in deposits and making loans to being a financial services supermarket that changes constantly due to technological advances and regulatory changes that reshape financial markets. Peer-to-peer lending and cryptocurrencies are the latest examples of this reshaping, and both are changing banking in front of our eyes.

Greater Complexity

Partly because banks make money with the technology at their disposal and the smarts of the people who work for them, intelligence has always been highly valued in the industry.[17]

This viewpoint has shaped banking culture for decades. The cultural orientation goes something like this. The more complex the financial product, the smarter or more intelligent the person who designed it. So those who design more complex products should be paid more. And of course the products are more complex because they are designed to more precisely meet the needs of the customer, so customers should be willing to pay more for them.

Such a culture inevitably breeds a cascade of increasingly complex financial products. Some do make customers better off. But not all. However, the process of manufacturing increasingly complex products changes the banks themselves, particularly who they hire and how they compensate them. As a result, banks have become more and more opaque to their customers, regulators, and analysts over time.

Concluding Remarks

Technological advances and regulatory changes have been the main underlying drivers of changes in banking over the past few centuries. These drivers have manifested themselves through four forces that have reshaped banking over the years: increased competition among banks, consolidation in the banking industry, greater intertwining with capital markets, and increasing complexity in financial products and services. These changes have resulted in the industry going from a large number of relatively small and simple institutions to a smaller number of much bigger and more complex and opaque institutions. The culture of banking has also changed as a result. A relationship-oriented culture has been increasingly replaced by a more transaction-oriented culture. In light of this, it is more important than ever for banks to explicitly and clearly articulate a higher purpose that helps them get back to their roots as relationship lenders and revitalize their corporate cultures.

Did the forces that made banks more complex and less relationship-oriented contribute to the financial crisis of 2007–2009? This question is taken up in the next chapter.

Notes

1. Today we are asking the same questions about companies that control information—Google, Apple, Facebook, and so on.
2. See Merton 1995, for example.
3. The theories of banking we saw earlier (e.g., Ramakrishnan and Thakor 1984) suggest that economies of scale in banking are unbounded, i.e., banks are "natural monopolies."
4. See Boot and Thakor 2018 for a discussion of this.
5. See Brick and Palia 2007.
6. See Petersen and Rajan 1955.
7. Boot and Thakor (2000) develop this argument.
8. See Degryse and Ongena 2007.
9. See Wheelock 2011
10. See Sapienza 2002.
11. See Stein 2002, and Berger et al 2005.
12. The evidence indicates that both small and large banks engage in relationship lending, but smaller banks provide greater access to relationship loans to small firms, for which soft information may be more important due to a relative paucity of hard information. See Bonfim and Dai 2017.
13. See Deidda and Fattouh 2008.
14. See the discussions in Bhattacharya and Thakor 1993 and Boot and Thakor 2018.
15. See Hoshi, Kashyap, and Stein 1993 and Holmström and Tirole 1997.
16. As shown in the theory developed by Song and Thakor 2010.
17. Here including both commercial and investment banks.

References

Berger, Allen, Nathan Miller, Mitchell Petersen, Raghuram Rajan, and Jeremy Stein. 2005. "Does Function Follow Organizational Form? Evidence from the Lending Practices of Large and Small Banks." *Journal of Financial Economics* 76:237–269

Bhattacharya, Sudipto, and Anjan V. Thakor. 1993. "Contemporary Banking Theory." *Journal of Financial Intermediation* 3:2–50.

Bonfim, Diana, and Qinglei Dai. 2017. "Bank Size and Lending Specialization." *Economic Notes*, May 15.

Boot, Arnoud W. A. 2000. "Relationship Banking: What Do We Know?" *Journal of Financial Intermediation* 9:7–25.

Boot, Arnoud W. A., and Anjan V. Thakor. 2000. "Can Relationship Banking Survive Competition?" *Journal of Finance* 55:679–713.

Boot, Arnoud, and Anjan V. Thakor. 2018. "Commercial Banking and Shadow Banking: The Accelerating Integration of Banks and Markets and Its Implications for Regulation." In *The Oxford Handbook in Banking*, 3rd ed., edited by Allen Berger, Phil Mullineaux, and John Wilson. New York: Oxford University Press.

Brick, Ivan E., and Darius Palia. 2007. "Evidence of Jointness in the Terms of Relationship Lending." *Journal of Financial Intermediation* 16:452–476.

Degryse, Han, and Steven Ongena. 2007. "The Impact of Competition on Bank Orientation." *Journal of Financial Intermediation* 16:399–424.

Deidda, Luca, and Bassoum Fattouh. 2008. "Banks, Financial Markets and Growth." *Journal of Financial Intermediation* 17:6–36.

Holmström, Bengt, and Jean Tirole. 1997. "Financial Intermediation, Loanable Funds, and the Real Sector." *Quarterly Journal of Economics* 112 (3): 663–691.

Hoshi, Takeo, Anil Kashyap, and David Scharfstein. 1993. "The Choice between Public and Private Debt: An Analysis of Post-Deregulation Corporate Financing in Japan." National Bureau of Economic Research Working Paper no. 4421.

Merton, Robert C. 1995. "A Functional Perspective of Financial Intermediation." *Financial Management* 24 (2): 23–41.

Petersen, Mitchell, and Raghuram Rajan. 1995. "The Effect of Credit Market Competition on Lending Relationships." *Quarterly Journal of Economics* 110: 407–443.

Ramakrishnan, Ram, and Anjan V. Thakor. 1984. "Information Reliability and a Theory of Financial Intermediation." *Review of Economic Studies* 51:415–432.

Sapienza, Paola. 2002. "The Effects of Banking Mergers on Loan Contracts." *Journal of Finance* 57:329–367.

Song, Fenghua, and Anjan V. Thakor. 2010. "Financial System Architecture and the Co-evolution of Banks and Markets." *Economic Journal* 120:1021–1255.

Stein, Jeremy C. 2002. "Information Production and Capital Allocation: Decentralized versus Hierarchical Firms." *Journal of Finance* 57:1891–1921.

Wheelock, David C. 2011. "Banking Industry Consolidation and Market Structure: Impact of the Financial Crisis and Recession." *Federal Reserve Bank of St. Louis Review*, November/December, 419–438.

Financial Crises

Causes, Effects, and Cures

8

Financial Crises and Banks

WHAT CAUSED THE GREAT RECESSION, AND
WHAT WERE ITS EFFECTS?

Introduction: Personalizing Misery

In an article in *Smart Money*, Janna Herron (2013) reported the following story:

> Five years after the Great Recession, Jennifer Butz still makes out a
> weekly budget. She writes down how much she gets paid, subtracts her
> bills and leaves $50 for gas and groceries. She takes her lunch to work
> and never buys coffee or on-the-go breakfast.
>
> "It's worth the wait for things. I consider whether I really need or
> I really want something," says Butz, 35, who lost her job, her car, her
> house and filed for bankruptcy in the last four years.
>
> "I think I'm doing pretty good on my own now," she says.
>
> The financial scars of the longest post–World War II recession re-
> main etched in many Americans' everyday lives. Like Butz, many still
> hold on to the cost-cutting habits that kept them afloat after job losses,
> foreclosure and bankruptcy, as they regain financial security. Some
> are teaching younger generations these lessons. Still, some have yet to
> recover.

Jennifer Butz's story is that of many Americans who suffered economic
misery in the aftermath of the Great Recession. As house prices plunged and
unemployment peaked at 10 percent, countless homes were foreclosed upon.
The falling house prices also caused the prices of mortgage-backed securities
to fall, forcing financial institutions that were long in these securities to write

down the values of their holdings. This caused their equity capital to shrink, diminishing their capacity to lend. During the fourth quarter of 2008—the peak of the financial crisis—new bank loans to large borrowers fell by 79 percent compared with the peak of the credit boom (second quarter of 2007).[1] These developments are consistent with the patterns in the data show that when banks have less capital, they lend less.

The subprime crisis of 2007–2009 that led to the Great Recession was part of a trend. On a worldwide basis, there were thirty-eight financial crises between 1945 and 1971, but the frequency of crises picked up, and we had 139 financial crises between 1973 and 1997.[2] The consequences of crises are ugly, with significant drops in housing prices, stock prices, and GDP and substantial increases in unemployment.

But even in the context of financial crises, the 2007–2009 crisis was especially ugly. Between 2008 and 2010, over 250 banks failed, and Lehman Brothers, the fourth largest investment bank, filed for Chapter 11 bankruptcy—the largest bankruptcy filing ever in the United States. The US government spent a staggering $1.7 trillion to bail out investment banks, insurance companies, Fannie Mae, Freddie Mac, and so on.

What caused this crisis, and what were its effects? This is the question that will be explored in this chapter. It is an important question, because designing a banking system that fosters both stability and growth requires us to first understand how stability and growth are undermined. In this regard, the historical study of financial crises conducted by economists Carmen Reinhart and Kenneth Rogoff is instructive.[3] They studied eight hundred years of financial crises, and they point out that two factors show up in every crisis—some kind of asset price bubble (unsustainably high prices of some assets) and excessive leverage on the balance sheets of banks and/ or consumers. More recently, two additional "common causes" have been identified:[4] (1) financial innovation that creates new instruments whose returns rely on continued favorable economic conditions, and (2) financial liberalization/deregulation. These conditions were clearly evident prior to this crisis.[5]

The great mystery, then, is this; if we know all this, why do we not take steps to prevent financial crises and all the misery that accompanies them?

One possibility is that financial crises are often preceded by economic booms. The booms produce so many economic benefits that we are willing to put up with the excesses that follow. This is a bit like someone getting drunk knowing full well that the hangover the next morning will be awful. But the buzz from getting drunk seems so much fun that, in the fog of confusion accompanying inebriation, the person is willing to pay the price of the hangover.

In this chapter we will see there is another possibility that points the way to building a banking system that is far less crisis-prone.

What Happened, and When Did It Happen?

The roots of the 2007–2009 crisis were in the US housing market. The housing price crash was the culmination of a credit crunch that started in 2006 and continued into 2007. There was a housing price bubble in the United States that burst and precipitated a rash of mortgage defaults. In early 2007, Freddie Mac announced that it would no longer purchase high-risk mortgages, and New Financial Corporation, a leading mortgage lender to risky borrowers, filed for bankruptcy.

These were the early warning signs. The crisis began in earnest in August 2007. The indication that a crisis was afoot came in the form of short-term funding stresses experienced by many firms. Investors withdrew short-term funding in massive amounts. Issuers of asset-backed commercial paper had difficulty in issuing new paper. These stresses were triggered by a widespread decline in US house prices that increased the default risks of subprime mortgages. As a result, the rating agencies downgraded many mortgage-backed securities (MBS). The average downgrade in ratings was quite dramatic.[6]

The Federal Reserve provided liquidity in response to these stresses by establishing short-term lending facilities for various financial institutions. But this did not help much. In January 2008, mortgage lender Countrywide Financial, on the brink of collapse, was acquired by Bank of America. In March 2008, the sixth-largest investment bank in the country, Bear Stearns, found itself unable to renew its short-term funding due to losses in its hedge fund and the price declines in MBS. The bank was heavily reliant on thirty-day paper, so it faced significant "rollover risk" in its financing. The Federal Reserve arranged for an acquisition by JP Morgan Chase.

Then came the collapse of Indy Mac, the largest mortgage lender in the United States. It was taken over by the US government. Fannie Mae and Freddie Mac, which owned $5.1 trillion in US mortgages, were the next to fall and be acquired by the US government in September 2008. The biggest shock of all arrived when Lehman Brothers, a bigger investment bank than Bear Stearns, was not rescued by the government and filed for bankruptcy on September 15, 2008. The same day, AIG, the largest insurance company in the world, received $85 billion in government assistance. The next day, the

Reserve Primary Fund, a money market fund, "broke the buck," which caused a run on money market funds.[7]

All of a sudden, it wasn't just raining bad news; it was pouring. On September 25, 2008, Washington Mutual, the largest savings and loan company in the United States, collapsed due to runs on its deposits and was taken over by the FDIC, which later transferred most of its assets to JP Morgan Chase. By October, the crisis had spread to Europe, and global cooperation among central banks led to coordinated interest rate cuts and commitments to provide unlimited liquidity to financial institutions.

Central banks initially believed that this was a liquidity crisis, a belief that would be disproven by subsequent events. Eventually, central banks recognized that at its core this was really an insolvency or counterparty-risk crisis. This was reflected in the US government infusing equity capital into banks in exchange for ownership, a measure typically used to reduce insolvency risk. By mid-October 2008, the US Treasury had invested billions of dollars in eight major banks and Merrill Lynch. The crisis continued into 2009, and the US unemployment rate rose to 10 percent by October 2009.

Whodunnit? Cause and Effect

As with previous crises, this one had an asset price bubble and excessive leverage as preconditions to the crisis. To understand what happened, we need answers to three questions:

1. *What gave rise to the housing price bubble?*
   This is crucial to understand, because, absent the bubble, there is nothing to burst and hence no crisis.

2. *What caused households and institutions to tolerate such high financial leverage?*
   This is important too, because leverage affected both the incentives to take high risk and the inability to withstand the early shocks generated by the bursting of the asset price bubble.

3. *What caused the bubble to burst?*
   In the game of musical chairs, everyone knows that there aren't enough chairs for all the players, but as long as the music keeps playing, everyone keeps going. Of course, when the music stops, one person is chairless and

has to leave the game. So as long as house prices kept climbing, the music in the financial system kept playing. But what stopped the music?

Let us examine each of these three questions.

What Gave Rise to the Housing Price Bubble?

Let us now see each of the factors in figure 8.1.

Political Factors

Universal home ownership was touted by both major political parties in the United States as a laudable goal. After all, if more Americans owned homes, there would be more people who could build up wealth over time through appreciation in their home equity. The proposition was based on the assumption that, at least on average, house prices would keep rising over time. This building up of wealth would provide political stability, a goal that goes back to the 1930s when S&Ls were chartered. Moreover, it would help narrow the gap between the rich and the poor and deal with growing wealth inequality, an issue that was first highlighted in the 1980s. This led politicians to enact banking regulation that encouraged subprime mortgage origination and securitization. As liquidity flooded the market, demand for houses grew and drove prices up, eventually creating the bubble that burst during the crisis.

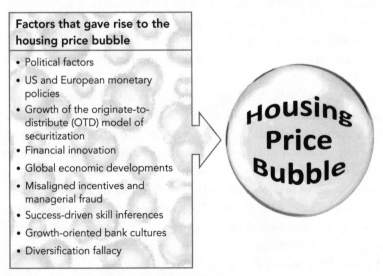

Factors that gave rise to the housing price bubble

- Political factors
- US and European monetary policies
- Growth of the originate-to-distribute (OTD) model of securitization
- Financial innovation
- Global economic developments
- Misaligned incentives and managerial fraud
- Success-driven skill inferences
- Growth-oriented bank cultures
- Diversification fallacy

Housing Price Bubble

FIGURE 8.1 Causes of the Housing Price Bubble.

One example of such a regulatory assist is the strengthening of the Community Reinvestment Act (CRA) during Bill Clinton's presidency, which essentially required banks to make more loans in low-income communities.[8] Another is the Bankruptcy Abuse Prevention and Consumer Protection Act (BAPCA) of 2005. BAPCA expanded the definition of repurchase agreements to include mortgage loans, mortgage-related securities, and interest from these loans and securities. This meant that repo contracts on MBS as collateral became exempt from automatic stays in bankruptcy.[9] This made MBS and other mortgage-related securities more liquid, increasing their demand and making it more attractive for banks to originate these securities.

Other political and regulatory factors that encouraged the origination of subprime mortgages and the creation of related MBS had to do with risk-based capital requirements and affordable housing mandates. On the issue of capital requirements, the Basel I Accord had a role to play. It called for a minimum ratio of total capital to risk-weighted assets of 8 percent, at least half of which had to be Tier 1 capital (mostly equity). The risk-weighted assets had to be computed using four risk buckets: 100 percent, 50 percent, 20 percent, and 0 percent. An asset in the 100 percent risk bucket would thus have an 8 percent capital requirement, whereas one in the 50 percent bucket would have a 50 percent × 8 percent = 4 percent capital requirement, and so on. US regulators assigned a 20 percent risk weight to AAA- and AA-rated MBS, lower than the 100 percent weight for loans. This encouraged banks to hold these MBS on their books. Many believe that assigning lower risk weights to mortgages than to other loans was done for political reasons (desire to encourage home ownership). Similarly, the capital requirements were close to zero for off-balance-sheet bank special investment vehicles and asset-backed commercial paper,[10] which provided encouragement for banks to engage in these activities.

Adding to this were the affordable housing mandates of the Department of Housing and Urban Development (HUD), which required that low-income and minority households be given access to affordable houses built in affluent neighborhoods that were "rich in opportunity" but consisted of homes that were priced beyond the reach of these households. Moreover, under the Soundness Act of 1992, as amended by the Housing and Economic Recovery Act of 2008, Fannie Mae and Freddie Mac were also made subject to affordable housing goals covering their purchases of single-family and multifamily mortgages. That is, the process for securitizing such mortgages and creating MBS from them was set in motion through legislation.

And although researchers disagree on the role played by subprime lending in causing the crisis, let us not forget the somewhat lax supervision of sub-prime lenders by regulators. Edward Gramlich, a Federal Reserve governor from 1997 to 2005, says that he was concerned about the "predatory lending" practices of subprime lenders,[11] and he suggested to Alan Greenspan, chairman of the Federal Reserve, that the Fed use its discretionary authority to send examiners into the offices of consumer finance lenders that were units of bank holding companies regulated by the Federal Reserve.[12] Gramlich said, "I would have liked the Fed to be a leader" in stopping predatory lending but that Greenspan was opposed to it, so he did not pursue it. There was also po-litical sensitivity at the Fed about cracking down on lenders who were making loans to "credit-constrained" borrowers.

When you combine political and regulatory encouragement to make more subprime loans that are securitized with the prevalence of (loosely supervised) predatory lending practices, you get a recipe for growing credit risks within the system. But if you are still skeptical of the role that politics and political ideologies played in this crisis, consider the Financial Crisis Inquiry Commission (FCIC) report on the causes of the financial crisis that was solicited by Congress. There are two noteworthy facts about this report. First, after authorizing the report, Congress decided to pass the Dodd-Frank Act, the most sweeping financial system regulatory reform in many decades, *before* the FCIC report actually came out. This raises the obvious question of why Congress bothered to authorize the report when it apparently had little interest in its findings about the causes of the crisis prior to voting on legislation to prevent future crises. Second, there were actually three versions of the FCIC report: the majority report (Democrats), the minority report (Republicans), and the Peter Wallison dissent.[13] Wallison, who believes that government-mandated subprime loans were the force behind the deteriora-tion in lending standards and eventually the financial crisis, writes:

> Like Congress and the Obama administration, the Commission's ma-jority erred in assuming that it knew the causes of the financial crisis. Instead of pursuing a thorough study, the Commission's majority used its extensive statutory, investigative authority to seek only the facts that supported its initial assumptions that the crisis was caused by "de-regulation" or lax regulation, greed and recklessness on Wall Street, predatory lending in the mortgage market, unregulated derivatives, and a financial system addicted to excessive risk taking.

Politics often interferes not only with reaching any sort of consensus on what the facts mean but even on what the facts are.

Thus, political considerations influenced regulations that caused the market for home mortgages to be flooded with liquidity, contributing to a housing price bubble. But, as we shall see shortly, it had another bad effect. It made leverage very attractive for households and banks, and it also made banks less diligent than they needed to be in screening borrowers. In short, the housing price bubble was caused by and also contributed to a massive failure of societal risk management.

US and European Monetary Policy

The easy-money monetary policy followed by the US Federal Reserve, especially in the seven or so years preceding the crisis, added considerable fuel to the housing price boom in the United States. The "Taylor rule," named after Stanford economist John Taylor, stipulates how much the central bank should change the nominal interest rate in response to changes in inflation, output, and other economic conditions. Empirical evidence suggests that monetary policy was too "loose" prior to and during the crisis in that interest rates were too low, and that this was a deliberate monetary policy choice by the Federal Reserve. Many European countries followed similar policies.[14]

Why did the Fed choose this easy-money policy for so long? One answer is that it was concerned about deflation.[15] Chairman Bernanke and others at the Fed had been chastened by Japan's experience with protracted deflation. In monetary policy, you increase interest rates if you are worried about inflation, and you decrease them if you are worried about deflation.

Taylor's research shows that the unusually low interest rates during 2001–2007 contributed positively to the housing price boom. Moreover, a simulation reveals that if the Taylor-rule interest rate policy had been followed, we would not have experienced the housing boom. And, of course, absent a housing boom, there would have been no asset price bubble and hence no crisis.

This effect of low interest rates on housing prices was amplified by the incentives that the politically driven regulatory environment created for lenders to make highly risky mortgage loans. When interest rates are kept low for so long, the net interest margins of banks—the difference between the rates at which banks lend and borrow—are crushed. This encourages banks to "pursue yields" by taking on more risk, which in the case of mortgages meant expanding the borrower pool to include previously unserved high-risk borrowers. This further accelerated the housing price boom. Indeed, there is evidence that there is an interaction between the easy-money monetary policy of the central bank and bank capital. When the central bank lowers short-term interest rates, banks with low capital increase lending to riskier borrowers and do so with lower collateral requirements. Thus, a lax monetary policy reinforces the effect of low bank capital in increasing risk in the banking system.[16] So there we are again—low capital in banking rears its head once more as a culprit in increasing risk in the system.

Taylor provides evidence that there seemed to be coordination among central banks to follow these easy-money policies. The European Central Bank and European nation central banks followed the lead of the Federal Reserve. Moreover, European countries that deviated the most from the Taylor-rule monetary policy experienced the biggest housing price booms.

Growth in the OTD Model of Banking

The easy-money monetary policy had another effect—it led to softer lending standards by banks. Moreover, this softening was amplified by the originate-to-distribute (OTD) model of banking[17] and weak supervision over bank capital.[18] This made it attractive for commercial banks to significantly expand their mortgage lending and for investment banks to engage in "warehouse lending" using non-bank mortgage lenders. Because the OTD model meant that banks could collect fees for originating loans and then not have to keep them on their books, they had little skin in the game and hence originated risky loans in ever-increasing volume. It is estimated that a one-standard-deviation increase in a bank's propensity to sell off its loans increases the default rate by about 0.45 percentage points, which represents an overall increase of 32 percent.[19] The fact that this was happening and credit standards were weakening is borne out by evidence that the quality of loans deteriorated for six consecutive years prior to the crisis.[20] And even though lenders may have underestimated the credit risks in their loans, they do seem to have been aware that they were making riskier loans.

There is also evidence that this was part of the "mass production" process of securitization. From the end of 2006 until the beginning of 2008, loan originators, sold loans, collected the proceeds, and then used them to make new loans.[21] This effect of originating riskier loans seemed to be more pronounced for banks with lower capital, which is another piece of evidence that higher capital leads to stronger screening incentives in banks.

Another factor that may have played a role is that there was ever-increasing demand for collateralizable assets for repurchase (repo) transactions, which then led to a "flash flood" of mortgage-backed securities that could serve as collateral for these transactions. Apparently, the precipitating event was the earlier-mentioned BAPCA of 2005. It expanded safe-harbor provisions in bankruptcy to MBS.[22] This meant that repo counterparties can avoid having their collateral frozen by the "automatic stay" restriction in bankruptcy. This significantly increased the demand for MBS, in turn making it more attractive for banks to originate even more mortgages that could be securitized.

The engine of mass-produced bank loans was really humming. Originations of new and refinanced loans went from $500 billion in 1990 to $2.4 trillion in 2007, only to fall off to $900 billion in the first half of 2008 as the crisis set in. Over this period, the total amount of mortgage loans outstanding grew from $2.6 trillion to $11.3 trillion. This credit supply propelled US house prices to new highs—as of early 2009, the US housing market was valued at about $19.3 trillion.[23] A significant portion of this growth came from subprime mortgages whose share of home mortgages grew from 8.5 percent in 1995 to 13.5 percent in 2005.[24]

Financial Innovation

Advances in information technology, coupled with the immense competitiveness of the financial system, led to an explosion of financial innovation in the two decades prior to the crisis. Because financial innovations cannot be patented, high profit margins from new financial products have a rather limited lifetime for the innovator. One way to reduce potential competition is to come up with new products that others may not agree are good ideas, that is, "non-standard" financial products that "break the mold" and are so new that historical data are of limited use in assessing their profit potential. Competitors may not rush in to introduce such products until they have seen "proof" that these products will indeed be successful. Thus, lack of unanimity about the investment worth of the new financial product can limit competition and allow the innovator to earn high initial profits.[25]

But this is a double-edged sword. The very lack of unanimity about the investment worth of the new product may also invite disagreement from investors that funding of the innovator should be renewed. Financial institutions rely heavily on short-term debt funding, so renewal of this funding must occur on a regular basis. The paucity of historical data associated with the innovation diminishes the ability of investors to come to agreement about the investment worth of the new product by analyzing such data. This then creates a potentially high likelihood that funding may not be renewed when some bad news arrives about the performance of the new product and investors are unable to agree on whether it is a temporary hiccup or a more ominous sign. Absent such a renewal, the innovating financial institutions as well as those that imitated it in offering the same (or similar) product will fail. In this way, a significantly high level of financial innovation can sow the seeds of a (funding) crisis.[26]

Global Economic Developments

In the two decades or so between 1985 and 2006, the global economy was transformed, with the rapid growth of emerging-market economies in India, China, Brazil, Russia, and other countries. This led to the accumulation of substantial savings in these countries. Lack of social safety nets encouraged the citizens of these countries not to significantly increase their consumption as they grew wealthier, at least not to the extent people in the West would have. These ever-increasing savings were then channeled into investments in relatively safe assets like US government Treasuries and AAA-rated mortgages. This huge influx of liquidity—referred to by Federal Reserve chairman Ben Bernanke as "the global savings glut"—did not cause inflation to rise in the US and Europe, because companies kept the prices of goods and services low by outsourcing production to emerging-market countries with low labor costs. But this flood of liquidity *did* cause "inflation" in the housing market, as it gave home buyers access to cheap credit and boosted home demand, lifting house prices to unsustainably high levels.

Misaligned Incentives and Managerial Fraud

A long period of low interest rates had crushed the net interest margins of banks, inducing them to pursue aggressive growth strategies to boost their profit margins. Aggressive growth, of course, comes with high risk, but banks were willing to take these risks because deposit insurance and other government safety nets (such as bailouts associated with too-big-to-fail policies) provided downside protection. Lax oversight by regulators, whose incentives were not aligned with those of taxpayers, may have facilitated this.[27] And aiding this process were the credit rating agencies that had skewed incentives to provide high ratings for securitized products.

An important element of growth strategies of banks was increased mortgage lending. This created increased "throughput" for investment banks to securitize their mortgages and create and sell securities that generated profits for the investment banks. Many claim that credit rating agencies were complicit in this process, because they assigned high ratings to the structured financial products that were being created by securitization. The consequence of this was to lower the cost of financing mortgages for banks, increase credit supply, and further boost house prices. As this was happening, commercial and investment banks also substantially increased their leverage, partly in order to magnify the impact of the profitable growth on the return on equity (ROE) for their shareholders. This made banks quite fragile.

Reputational concerns of banks and managerial fraud may have also exacerbated the damage caused by misaligned incentives. Banks that extend loan commitments tend to overlend during economic booms and periods of high stock prices.[28] This is because the average credit quality of borrowers is relatively high during such times, so refusing to lend under a commitment can damage the bank's reputation for being a reliable lender. This may have also accounted for some of the pre-crisis surge in bank credit supply. Adding fuel to this fire was managerial fraud. There is evidence that buyers of mortgages received false information about the true quality of assets in contractual disclosures made by selling intermediaries in the non-agency market.[29] These misrepresentation incentives got stronger as the housing market continued to boom, peaking in 2006. This meant that investors purchased mortgages that were of lower quality than they expected, so once they began to realize this, liquidity in the market dried up quickly. This is similar to the idea that investors ignored tail risks in new products when they purchased them and then dumped these products when they realized the true risks, except that in this version of events, investors were not irrationally exuberant. Rather, they were simply misled.

Having said this, it is worth noting that while politicians often refer to the misaligned incentives of "greedy bankers" as *the* cause of the crisis, in the overall scheme of things, this factor played a smaller role than many of the other factors I have discussed, and certainly a much smaller role than it did in the S&L crisis in the 1980.

Success-Driven Skill Inferences

While misaligned incentives at various levels definitely played a role in this crisis, it would be quite a stretch of logic to say that was the whole story. It is difficult to explain the timing of the crisis with misaligned incentives. After all, these incentives were in place long before the crisis, so why did this become such a big problem in 2007 and not before? Why was this crisis so unexpected for even the watchdogs of the financial system like the credit rating agencies and federal regulators, despite the fact that the warning signs were emerging at least as early as 2006? For example, federal bank examiners had noted that bank lending standards had been progressively becoming more lax for a number of years prior to the crisis, and it was evident to many that real estate prices were very high relative to historical valuations in many areas. Indeed, there is considerable empirical evidence that bank lending is procyclical, which means banks tend to lend "excessively" during economic booms, thereby feeding asset price bubbles.[30]

There is an alternative theory of what happened that operates even when incentives are completely aligned. Suppose there is a high probability that loan default outcomes are due to the skills of bankers in managing credit risk—the more skilled the bankers, the lower are default probabilities—and a low probability that these outcomes are just exogenous, that is, random chance. Moreover, there is uncertainty and learning about whether outcomes depend on the skills of bankers or are just pure luck.[31] Initially, banks make relatively safe loans because the cost of funding riskier loans is prohibitive. Over time these loans pay off consistently, so defaults are low during a fairly long economic boom. As this is happening, everybody—investors, rating agencies, regulators, and the banks themselves—rationally revise beliefs about the skills of bankers upward. The smarter bankers look, the more willing investors are to fund their loans at low interest rates, the more eager rating agencies are to give the credits they extend high ratings, and the more willing regulators are to appear "lax" in their oversight as they allow banks to make increasingly risky loans. Beliefs are driven by past experience, and as long as the experience continues to be good, why would anyone doubt the ability of bankers to continue to keep it that way?

Now maybe there were some clever skeptics—and there certainly were not too many of them before the crisis—who said: "Wait a minute, could this all not just be dumb luck? How do we know it is due to the skill of bankers? Why are we tolerating so much risk and leverage in the system? Should the risk premia not be higher?" But just like the proverbial boy who cried wolf once too often, the longer the boom went on, the less credible the skeptics' words became.

Before beliefs could change so that the skeptics were heeded, bad things had to happen. As Benjamin Franklin said: "You can give advice but not conduct. For experience keeps a dear school, but fools will learn in no other."[32] Well, it was not that the people involved were fools. What I showed in my theory is that even if they were (Bayesian) rational, they may have behaved exactly the way they did prior to the crisis. This approach explains the timing of the 2007–2009 crisis—it was the long boom that preceded it, followed by unexpectedly high mortgage defaults that forced a sudden change in beliefs that outcomes were driven by the skills of bankers to the belief that they were largely luck-driven. If people think that it is mostly luck, then the banker falls from his pedestal, and loans and structured products that may have looked low-risk yesterday suddenly seem excessively risky today.

Aggressive-Growth-Oriented Bank Cultures

The long period of tranquil success that banks experienced prior to the crisis also influenced their corporate cultures. In line with the theory of bank culture that Fenghua Song and I developed,[33] whenever banks perceive the credit quality of their borrower pool to be high, they have an incentive to lean toward a more growth-oriented corporate culture. After all, if 99.9 percent of your borrowers are excellent credit risks, why bother to divert valuable resources from loan prospecting to credit analysis? This meant that compensation contacts within banks were designed to incent the pursuit of growth much more than the pursuit of prudence. This too fed the aggressive overexpansion of bank credit.

Diversification Fallacy

There were two kinds of diversification fallacies at work. One was the idea that there was geographic diversification of house price risk. Even former Federal Reserve chairman Ben Bernanke said in a 2005 CNBC interview that high housing prices did not represent a huge threat to the economy, because geographic diversification would help dissipate this risk—loan defaults due to falling house prices in one region would be offset by lending profits for banks on loans in other regions where housing prices did not fall. The only reason to worry would be if there was a *national* house price decline. But we had not seen that since the Great Depression, so why worry? "Experience-based beliefs" again! Of course, this does not explain why we did not learn from the Japanese financial crisis in the 1990s, during which a real estate price bubble burst and caused solvency problems at Japanese banks.[34]

So what was the fallacy in terms of geographic diversification? It was in not fully recognizing the roles that two developments would play. One is that many of the subprime loans were to households with little prior experience with home ownership and relatively low net worth, with even less invested in the home. Many of them could barely afford the houses they were in, and many simply could not afford them. As long as house prices were rising, banks worried little about the possible inadequacy of the borrower's income to service the loan once the "teaser rates"—artificially low initial interest rates—were in the past and the borrower had to make higher monthly mortgage payments. This is because the bank could simply take possession of a house on which there was a loan default and sell it (at a higher price) to recover its loan. But the credit risks of these borrowers were highly sensitive to macroeconomic shocks. And their low net worth meant they had little capacity to absorb any income or employment shocks.[35] These people were deep in debt and low in income, and they owned houses they could not afford.[36] In that sense, their future prospects were highly correlated. There is evidence that higher-income borrowers also overextended themselves and defaulted on their mortgages, so the household over-leveraging phenomenon was possibly widespread.[37]

When some of these homeowners lost their jobs or suffered other forms of economic dislocation, mortgage defaults spiked. What happens in a neighborhood when banks foreclose on a couple of houses? The prices of all houses in the neighborhood are adversely affected. This downward pressure on house prices then left banks with losses on future defaults, since the game of recovering loans by selling the collateral of delinquent borrowers was coming to an end. Moreover, some borrowers who saw their house prices drop below their repayment obligations simply walked away from their "underwater" mortgages. That is, they engaged in "strategic default"—they stopped paying their mortgage interest and principal even though they had the income to do so. All of a sudden, everything was becoming correlated. The benefits of diversification were hard to find.

The other diversification fallacy was simply a regulatory failure, namely, the assumption made by many—including regulators—that risks were spread out *across* banks in the system. If true, this would imply that bank failures would be uncorrelated. However, counter to this assumption, commercial and investment banks had become highly interconnected. Many loan originators who had securitized their loans and sold MBS to other banks also held some of these MBS on their own balance sheets and additionally provided recourse to investors in these securities. Rather than risks being spread out across a large number of institutions in the financial system, they were concentrated on the balance sheets of large, systemically important institutions that were connected to each other in many ways—similar asset portfolios, correspondent banking and interbank trading relationships, and so on. My conversations with economists at the Federal Reserve suggest that the Fed simply did not realize until very late in the game just how much of housing credit risk was concentrated in large financial institutions. The desire of commercial banks to circumvent regulation led them to push activities into the less-regulated shadow banking system, which then concentrated risks in large institutions in that sector.[38] This risk concentration created an effect that was the *opposite* of diversification. It created the potential of transforming local shocks into systemic shocks. And as we saw in the previous chapter, the low levels of capital in banking also made bank failures more highly correlated, giving another boost to systemic risk.

The combined effect of all these factors was to create a housing price bubble as liquidity from highly leveraged banks flooded the housing market and consumers borrowed to the hilt to boost housing demand and house prices. The Case-Shiller house price index more than doubled between 1987 and 2005, with a significant portion of the appreciation coming after 1998.

What Caused Households and Institutions to Tolerate Such High Financial Leverage?

The answer to the household leverage question is simple—the desire to finance higher consumption. Low interest rates, easy credit, expanded government services, cheap goods, and rising house prices for well over a decade elevated confidence enough to induce households to go on a consumption binge. Per capita consumption of US households grew steadily at $1,994 per year during 1980–1999, but then jumped dramatically to $2,849 per year from 2001 to 2007.[39]

This higher consumption was financed partly through a reduction in savings—the US household savings rate dropped below 2 percent for the first time since the Great Depression—and partly from higher borrowing, much of it supported by rising house prices. People figured out that the simplest way to convert housing wealth into consumption was to borrow more. As house prices grew, mortgage borrowing grew even faster, causing home equity as a percentage of home value to drop from 58 percent in 1995 to 52 percent in 2007. See figure 8.2.

What was odd and alarming about these developments was that the biggest growth in borrowing was occurring in areas where there was *declining* income growth. The years 2002–2005 were the only period in almost two decades since 1987 during which personal income and mortgage credit growth were negatively correlated.[40]

What made the situation worse was that the increase in household leverage was accompanied by an increase in the leverage of financial institutions, especially investment banks and others in the shadow banking system,[41] which is where the effects of the crisis were most evident. This "correlated leverage" meant that these institutions were not well equipped to absorb the losses they incurred when borrowers began to default on their mortgages.[42]

So why were financial institutions so highly leveraged? An argument often advanced to address this question is that raising equity capital is very

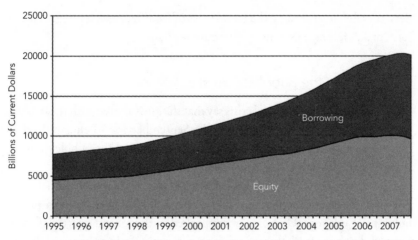

FIGURE 8.2 The Evolution of Household Equity and Borrowing in Residential Real Estate in the United States.

expensive for banks and other financial institutions. However, this argument does not hold much water for this time period, since banks were earning large profits and paying substantial dividends. If only these stock repurchases and dividends had been halted for a while, banks could have built up substantial amounts of equity capital simply through retained earnings and would not have had to raise this capital through equity issues.

A much more plausible explanation is that banks did not believe they needed the capital. This goes back to the "experience-based beliefs" hypothesis explained earlier. Capital is meant to protect the bank against unexpected negative outcomes. But if the good times have been rolling for a long time, few people believe that trouble may be around the corner. If there is never going to be a storm, why spend money to build a shelter? If negative shocks are unlikely—or perhaps are very low-probability tail risks or black-swan events—they may be easily ignored. This makes the argument for keeping more equity capital a hard one to sell, especially if the bonuses of bank executives depend on the bank's ROE. And even concerned bank regulators might have a challenge on their hands if they attempted to implement higher capital requirements. Banks are likely to push back through their elected representatives: "How do you justify this additional burden on banks when their loan portfolios have been doing so well?" And of course, de facto government safety nets exacerbate this problem, since they often protect even uninsured creditors from the losses they would experience absent these safety nets, thereby desensitizing the bank's cost of funding to its leverage. This, in turn, makes leverage even more attractive for banks.

What Caused the Bubble to Burst?

Most accounts of the financial crisis say that the crisis started with the bursting of the housing price bubble, and that the September 2008 Lehman Brothers failure led to a deepening of the crisis. But what caused the bubble to burst? People often gloss over this issue.

The answer lies in the dynamics of loan defaults in relation to initial house price declines and how this created a snowballing effect that led to further house price declines. US home prices peaked in the second quarter of 2006. Prices did not crash all of a sudden from this peak. Rather, the initial decline was only 2 percent from the second quarter of 2006 to the fourth quarter of 2006.[43]

If all mortgages were held by (creditworthy) prime borrowers, such a small decline would have had little effect, especially at the national level when one factors in the effect of geographic diversification. These borrowers typically have 20 percent or more of equity in their homes, so a small price drop does not trigger default by putting the mortgage "underwater."

But it is a different story with subprime mortgages. Many of these borrowers had loan-to-value ratios exceeding 100 percent.[44] Even a small decline in house prices creates a big "negative equity" hole for these borrowers, creating a strong incentive to simply stop making mortgage payments and let the bank take possession of the house. After all, the house is worth less than what you owe the bank, so why not do this? Foreclosure rates increased by 43 percent over the last two quarters in 2007 compared with 2006.[45] Many of the subprime borrowers had been enticed to buy homes they probably could not afford by the lure of "teaser rates" with adjustable rate mortgages—mortgage interest rates that were artificially low in the first year or so and then adjusted upward. So when these rates adjusted upward, these borrowers were even more hard-pressed to make their monthly payments. Add to this the fact that some of these mortgages were "negative amortization" loans in which part of the interest was added to the principal (in order to lower initial payments) so that the principal increased over time rather than going down.

All of this was part of the predatory lending discussed earlier. It is worth pointing out that there is a debate about the extent to which the problems were due to predatory lending or "predatory borrowing," where the latter refers to *borrowers* defrauding lenders by misrepresenting relevant information they provide to lenders.[46]

As these borrowers defaulted, credit rating agencies began to downgrade MBS. This caused credit markets to tighten and raised interest rates. Because house prices behave like bond prices—they go up when interest rates fall and down when interest rates rise—this accelerated the downward spiral in house prices. The key was that this began to financially constrain even the prime borrowers. The general economic tightening and loss of home equity caused households to cut back on spending, and this reduced demand for goods and services led to firms cutting back on production and laying people off. The labor market also did not work very smoothly in helping the laid-off workers find new jobs, because they were reluctant to sell their homes at big losses in order to take jobs elsewhere. Thus, what started as a subprime loan crisis now engulfed even prime borrowers. From the second quarter of 2006 to the end of 2007, foreclosure rates for fixed-rate mortgages increased by about 55 percent for prime borrowers and by about 80 percent for subprime borrowers. And the numbers were much worse for prime and subprime borrowers with variable-rate mortgages.[47]

But why did all this have such global ramifications? Why would even a national housing price decline, as unexpected as it was, lead to the global financial system being threatened with collapse?

The answer lies in three factors. One is that the easy-money policies were adopted not only in the United States but also in Europe. Hence, house price bubbles formed not only in the United States but also in European countries. For example, Spain, whose monetary policy deviated the most from the Taylor rule, had the biggest housing price bubble and hence the biggest crash.

The second factor was the *shadow banking system* and the role that MBS played in it. While commercial banks rely on insured deposits for much of their short-term funding, shadow banks—these are broker dealers, investment banks, insurance companies, and other non-depository financial intermediaries—rely heavily on commercial paper and repos.[48] This sector grew dramatically in the years leading up to the crisis. The International Monetary Fund estimates that total outstanding repo in US markets was between 20 percent and 30 percent of US GDP in each year from 2002 to 2007. And this number was even higher for the European Union (EU)—between 30 percent to 50 percent of EU GDP per year from 2002 to 2007.

Repo transactions need collateral. There is just so much collateral that is available in the form of US Treasury securities. MBS provided another source of collateral. But as news of mortgage defaults spread and the rating agencies significantly downgraded MBS, "haircuts" on MBS began to rise in repos. A haircut in a repo is essentially a "margin requirement." If you have an MBS worth $100 that you use as collateral in a repo and you can only borrow $90 against it, the haircut is 10 percent, meaning that is how much equity you need to put in. The worse the news got about mortgage defaults, the more haircuts spiked. An increase in these haircuts meant that for any given stock of securities available as collateral, the short-term borrowing capacity of those with that collateral declined.

The third factor for causing the US subprime crisis to spread to other countries was that many of them had adopted the Basel II capital requirements, and banks were thus faced with very low capital requirements on AAA-rated MBS. These banks thus held AAA-rated tranches of subprime MBS that originated in the United States, providing a global channel for the virus to spread.

What Was the Impact of the Crisis on the Real Sector?

The worst of the Great Recession, from an employment standpoint, was in 2010, when the economy was down 8.8 million jobs compared to three years earlier.[49] Merrill Lynch and JP Morgan Chase each laid off 35,000 people, and Bank of America topped them with 37,402 layoffs. Citigroup was even more aggressive, with 75,000 layoffs. And it wasn't just financial service companies. The layoffs affected every sector of the economy. Even the US Postal Service cut 30,000 jobs. Hewlett-Packard laid off 74,300 employees, and General Motors shed 77,100 jobs.

The crisis reverberated throughout the US economy. The effects on the real economy can be classified in three broad categories, as shown in figure 8.3.

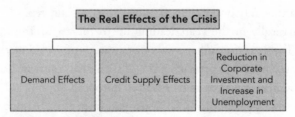

FIGURE 8.3 The Real Effects of the Crisis.

Demand Effects

The sequence of events went something like this.[50] Due to a variety of reasons—easy credit with relaxed underwriting standards, booming house prices, and low interest rates—household debt ballooned. Then the housing price bubble burst, depleting household net worth. The households that had significant leverage responded by reducing consumption, with the biggest decline in consumption occurring in the highest-leverage counties with the greatest reliance on housing as a source of wealth and the largest decreases in house prices. There was not an offsetting increase in consumption by less-levered households. So overall consumption fell.

When households reduced consumption, the demand for goods and services fell. Companies responded by reducing production, and they fired workers they no longer needed. Hence, unemployment went up.

Credit Supply Effects

The crisis also caused the supply of credit from banks to decline. For example, syndicated lending began to fall in mid-2007. By September 2008, the decline had gathered considerable momentum.[51] Syndicated lending volume was 47 percent lower in the fourth quarter of 2008 than in the prior quarter. And compared to the second quarter of 2007, which was the peak of the credit boom, the fourth-quarter 2008 syndicated lending volume was 79 percent lower.

Not only did the supply of credit decline, but its price also rose. Firms paid higher loan spreads during the crisis, and those that borrowed at banks that incurred larger losses paid even more.[52]

But how do we know that this lower supply of credit was not just a response to dampened loan demand in a recession? Economists are particularly interested in *causal effects*, not just correlations. There are two ways in which researchers have addressed this issue. One is with survey evidence. A survey of CFOs on three continents revealed that these CFOs believed they faced reduced availability of credit.[53] More systematic firm survey analyses, using the European Bank for Reconstruction and Development BEEPs survey and the European Commission's SAFE survey, also provide strong evidence of reductions in credit supply in cross-country studies.[54]

The second approach is to design clever empirical approaches to isolate credit supply effects. In one interesting study, the researchers examined German savings banks, which operate in specific geographies and are legally required to serve only local customers.[55] In each geography, there is a *Landesbank*, owned by the savings bank in that area. These Landesbanken had different exposures to US subprime mortgages and therefore suffered different levels of losses. This meant that the different Landesbanken required different levels of equity injections from their savings banks to repair their capital positions. The researchers document that the savings banks that were hit the hardest cut back on credit the most—they rejected loan applicants the most.

Reduction in Corporate Investment and Increase in Unemployment

For corporations, the crisis was a double whammy. There was diminished demand for their goods and services as households cut back on consumption, and there was reduced supply of credit from banks. So it was both more expensive to manufacture and more difficult to sell products in an environment of falling demand in which the higher cost of financing could not be readily passed along to consumers. Not surprisingly, companies cut back on investment and laid off workers.

As a consequence, the Great Recession began in the United States. Almost 9 million jobs were lost during 2008 and 2009, about 6 percent of the workforce. The labor participation rate also plunged as discouraged job seekers simply stopped looking for jobs. This meant that the measured unemployment rate understated the more relevant unemployment rate. By January 2009, the US unemployment rate had spiked to 7.6 percent. Average US house prices fell 30 percent, and the US stock market fell approximately 50 percent by mid-2009. US car sales were hit really hard—between September 2008 and October 2008, they fell 31.9 percent. Research has provided causal evidence that the reduction in credit supply to firms increased unemployment.[56]

Did Consumer Indebtedness Directly Affect Unemployment?

It seems reasonable that high consumer indebtedness contributed to an increase in unemployment via the demand channel, meaning that highly indebted households reduced their demand for goods and services when faced with diminished net worth due to falling house prices, and this caused companies to lay off workers and scale back operations. But there is also another channel that was at work, and that was the *labor supply channel*.

This channel works as follows.[57] How high the unemployment rate is depends on the search behavior of workers. Each worker can choose which labor submarket to explore. Some submarkets pay higher wages, so more people search for a job in those markets, lowering the likelihood that any given job seeker will land a job. To think of this concretely through an example, suppose you have an MBA and your major is finance. You could easily find a job as a financial analyst or a financial advisor at a local brokerage or financial advisory firm in your town that will pay $85,000 per year. Alternatively, you could choose to look for a Wall Street job with a renowned investment bank that will pay you $126,000. But a lot of MBAs are seeking the job you are seeking, so the probability of getting an offer is much lower than if you concentrated on a job in your town.

Now suppose you have no debt. No mortgage. No student loans to pay back. If the probability of finding a job with a local firm is, say, 0.9 and that of finding a job with a top Wall Street investment bank is 0.5, you would prefer to settle for a focused search in your local area rather than spending that time seeking a Wall Street job; this assumes you would have no income without a job.

But now imagine you have student loans and credit card debt that require an annual payment of $36,250. What will you do now? Simple calculations show that if you are risk neutral—you accept actuarially fair bets—then you will now prefer to search for a Wall Street job. The reason is that you don't just care about your wage. Rather, you care about your wage net of your debt obligation. The expected value of your wage net of your debt obligation is higher with the higher-paying job. The problem with the lower-paying job is that a large fraction of the wage is used simply to discharge your debt obligations. While the debt obligation is the same if you land the higher-paying job, it is a much smaller fraction of that wage. This makes you willing to risk a lower probability of successfully landing a job and focus your search efforts on finding the higher-paying job.

What is the implication of this for unemployment? It indicates that when households are highly levered, they are less likely to seek jobs in labor submarkets where the probability of finding a job is relatively high, and more likely to search in labor submarkets where the probability of finding a job is relatively low. This in turn will cause unemployment to rise through the (endogenous) search behavior of highly levered households. Simply put, when you have high leverage, you are more interested in the high-paying job you are less likely to get and less interested in the low-paying job that is a sure bet. When the economy has a lot of households with high leverage, it also has a lot of people who are unemployed.

But at this stage, you might say, "Wait a minute; if I don't find a job, the consequences could be far worse than if I find a low-paying job. How has this been factored into the analysis?" If so, you have noticed that I made an assumption that was not articulated—limited liability for households.[58] This means that if you do not find a job, you can simply walk away from your debts. In the argument above, limited liability simply means that not having a job is the same as having a zero wage.

In reality, of course, a zero wage can be painful if it means you starve. But this does not happen in practice because of a variety of safety nets, with unemployment insurance (UI) being a prominent member of this set. An obvious implication of this line of thinking is that the milder the pain associated with being unemployed, the more likely it is that you will prefer searching in the high-wage labor submarket when you are highly indebted. This means higher UI should go hand in hand with higher unemployment. This is clearly a testable prediction. It turns out there is empirical evidence that supports this prediction, based on analysis that exploits the cross-state heterogeneity in UI in the United States.[59] States that extend unemployment benefits experience an increase in unemployment. If benefits are extended from 26 to 99 weeks, the long-run average unemployment rate rises from 5 percent to 10.5 percent. During the financial crisis, the US government kept extending unemployment benefits, and this may have actually encouraged unemployment.

So one implication of this analysis is that there is an economic rationale for imposing caps on household leverage. A simple way to do this is to use loan-to-value restrictions on mortgage loans, where "loan" takes into account *all* of the debt of the household.[60]

We can stretch the argument further. Based on the discussions in the previous chapters, we know that banks that have higher capital ratios invest more resources in screening borrowers.[61] This means that when banks are more highly capitalized, the borrowers who are identified as creditworthy receive loans at lower interest rates, which reduces their indebtedness. Consequently, households are less highly leveraged, and by the logic outlined in this section, unemployment drops.

There is thus a labor-market-based argument for higher capital both at the household level and at the bank level. In other words, there is an economic justification for a combination of loan-to-value restrictions for households and minimum capital requirements for banks.

The Nature of the Beast: This Was an Insolvency Crisis, Not an Illiquidity Crisis

An *insolvency crisis* is essentially a "counterparty risk" crisis. Investors refuse to extend financing to institutions because they view the credit risk of the institutions as being excessive, given their asset portfolios and capital structure.[62] A *liquidity crisis* is one in which, for some reason, liquidity gets sucked out of the market, so that institutions that rely on short-term debt experience funding declines and may be forced to engage in fire sales during the crisis.[63] In both cases, liquidity dries up.

An important difference between the two types of crises is that an insolvency risk crisis is *bank specific*—it affects only banks that are viewed by investors as being excessively leveraged or excessively risky, or both—whereas a liquidity crisis more or less indiscriminately affects all banks, regardless of financial health.

Why do we care what kind of crisis this was? Because it determines what we learn from it and how it equips us to deal with similar crises in the future.

An analogy may help. When someone suffers a stroke, the doctor needs to know what kind of stroke it is before treatment can be administered. An ischemic stroke occurs as a result of an obstruction or a clot within a blood vessel supplying blood to the brain. A hemorrhagic stroke occurs when a weakened blood vessel ruptures. The treatments for the two are completely different. Ischemic strokes may be treated with medications that dissolve the clot. But if these medications are administered to a patient who has suffered a hemorrhagic stroke, the result would be death. Hemorrhagic strokes may be treated with medications that reduce intracranial pressure and blood transfusions that increase the amount of blood-clotting materials.

So it is with financial crises. A liquidity crisis would be dealt with by massive infusions of liquidity into the system. Essentially, the central bank would open up the liquidity spigot to one and all, giving institutions access to the short-term debt funding that is denied to them by the market. The liquidity infusion would be intended to "unfreeze" the market.

An insolvency crisis would be confronted very differently. Instead of opening its liquidity spigot, the central bank would ask banks to increase their capital ratios, and the riskier and more undercapitalized banks would be asked to infuse more capital. Dividends would be frozen in order to enable banks to build up capital levels. Regulators have a number of choices in dealing with banks that are unwilling or unable to do so: (1) arrange for them to be acquired by other banks or (2) allow them to fail, or (3) assist them with equity capital infusions by the government.

There are some who would say that distinguishing between liquidity and insolvency crises is virtually impossible. After all, if liquidity dries up, banks can only raise funding by selling assets. This can lead to fire sales and a plunge in bank equity values, leading to insolvency. Similarly, insolvency can cause a bank's access to liquidity to dry up. So illiquidity can cause insolvency, and insolvency can cause illiquidity. How can you tell them apart? It is tough. But we will see how next.

A Crisis That Looked Like a Liquidity Crisis

The early diagnoses of the Great Recession all seemed to scream "liquidity crisis!" The asset-backed commercial paper (ABCP) market fell by $350 billion in the second half of 2007. Many of these programs required support from their sponsors to cover the shortfall. As holders of ABCP, money market mutual funds (MMFs) took a hit, and when the Reserve Primary Fund "broke the buck," ABCP yields rose for outstanding paper. Issuers of commercial paper were unable to renew funding in many cases when a portion of the commercial paper matured. Some referred to this as a "run" on shadow banks,[64] conveniently borrowing the term from historical depositor runs. As figure 8.4 shows, things deteriorated in a hurry in this market beginning in August 2007.

The initial responses by the Federal Reserve and the European Central Bank both appeared to reflect the belief that this was a liquidity crisis. Beginning in August 2007, the governments of all developed countries undertook various policy interventions to deal with the financial crisis. There were forty-nine initiatives in the United States alone. Many of the initial initiatives were intended to make liquidity available to investors and institutions.

The Federal Reserve:

- *expanded its traditional role as a lender of last resort in providing short-term liquidity for depository institutions and access to short-term liquidity for*

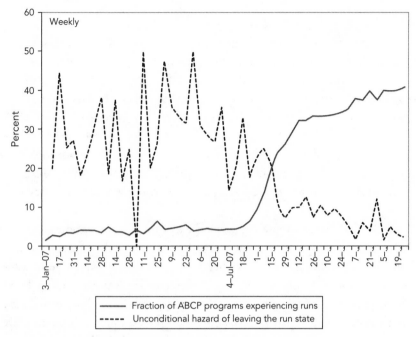

FIGURE 8.4 Runs on ABCP Programs.

Note: Loss of short-term borrowing capacity and large-scale withdrawals from MMFs commonly interpreted as liquidity crisis.

primary securities dealers; this also included the Term Auction Facility, which existed during 2007–2010 and gave depository institutions additional access to term credit;[65]

- *provided liquidity directly to borrowers and investors in key credit markets;* this involved purchases of commercial paper by the Fed directly from issuers, loans to depositories and bank holding companies to help them purchase high-quality ABCP from MMFs, the provision of liquidity to US money market investors, and the creation of a loan facility to facilitate the issuance of asset-backed securities collateralized by consumer and small-business loans; and

- *increased open market operations,* which involved purchases of longer-term securities by the Federal Reserve in order to support the credit markets and put downward pressure on long-term interest rates. This has been referred to as "Quantitative Easing" (QE), and it resulted in a huge expansion of the Fed's balance sheet.

A Crisis Misread

These initiatives notwithstanding, an impressive body of post-crisis research evidence indicates that this was an insolvency crisis, *not* a liquidity crisis.

First, as indicated earlier, if this was a liquidity crisis, it should have engulfed all institutions.[66] The empirical evidence, however, is that the majority of commercial and investment banks did not experience diminished funding during the crisis and did not engage in the fire sales predicted to accompany liquidity crises.[67] There is evidence that the institutions that did experience liquidity shortages during the crisis were those that had suffered deterioration in asset values, that is, those whose insolvency risk had gone up.

Second, there is also empirical evidence that the massive withdrawals from MMFs during 2008 were not due to a market-wide liquidity crunch that just caused a run on those funds. Rather, these withdrawals were due to asset risk and insolvency concerns, in part triggered by the Reserve Primary Fund announcing that it had suffered significant losses on its holdings of Lehman Brothers commercial paper.[68] This disclosure blew a hole in the commonly held belief that MMFs invested only in safe, almost-money-like assets.

Third, in direct contradiction to the liquidity crisis hypothesis, there is substantial evidence that banks with higher capital ratios were less adversely affected by the crisis. Banks that had higher pre-crisis capital ratios

- were more likely to survive the crisis and gained market share during it[69]
- took less risk prior to the crisis, and[70]
- had smaller contractions in lending during the crisis.[71]

Fourth, additional evidence that buttresses the evidence above is provided by economists John Taylor and John C. Williams.[72] They examined the LIBOR-OIS spread, which is the three-month LIBOR minus the three-month Overnight Index Swap (OIS) rate. Because the OIS involves a swapping of cash flows, there is no credit risk or liquidity risk reflected in the OIS. Further, because both are chosen for three-month maturities and one is subtracted from the other, expectations about future short-term interest rates are controlled for, so that risk and liquidity effects can be isolated. Figure 8.5 displays the behavior of this spread just before and after the crisis.

This figure shows that the spread increased sharply in early August 2007 and stayed high. This was a problem because the rates on loans and securities

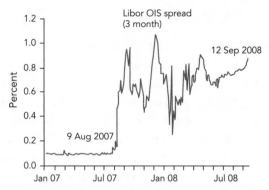

FIGURE 8.5 The LIBOR-OIS Spread during the First Year of the Crisis.
Note: LIBOR-OIS spread controls for interest rate expectations and isolates risk and liquidity effects.

are indexed to LIBOR, which means that an increase in the spread, holding the OIS fixed, increases borrowing costs. Policymakers thus have an interest in lowering the spread, which is what the Federal Reserve tried to do. However, despite huge liquidity injections during 2008, not only did the spread not decline, it actually increased. Since the spread reflects both liquidity and credit risks, the fact that huge liquidity injections did not cause the spread to fall suggests that liquidity risk was not the problem.

To further examine whether the spread went up due to heightened risk concerns or liquidity problems, Taylor and Williams measured the difference between the interest rates on unsecured and secured interbank loans of the same maturity, that is, the "unsecured-secured" spread. This spread is essentially a measure of credit risk. They then regressed the LIBOR-OIS spread against the unsecured-secured spread and found them to be highly and positively correlated. Their conclusion was that the LIBOR-OIS spread was driven mainly by insolvency risk concerns and that liquidity concerns did not play much of a role. There is also additional evidence supporting the Taylor and Williams conclusion, which is that a sharp reduction in the quality, not the liquidity, of private assets was responsible for the 2007–2009 crisis.[73]

Thus, the evidence we have until now suggests strongly that this was an insolvency risk crisis. This is something central banks eventually realized as well. So the interventions that came later in the crisis were explicitly designed to address insolvency risk, and they helped to varying degrees to bring the crisis to an end.

So What Eventually Worked?

The initiatives designed to address insolvency concerns included various programs. One of these was the Troubled Asset Repurchase Program (TARP), which was authorized in October 2008 and ended on October 3, 2010. The initial objective of TARP was for the US government to buy illiquid assets from financial institutions to "unfreeze" the market. The idea was that if the most troubled assets were removed from the market through government purchases, the adverse selection premium would decline and trade could resume in the remaining assets. However, for a variety of good reasons, this strategy was not actually pursued. Instead, the government purchased equity (the Capital Purchase Program) and took ownership stakes in various financial and non-financial firms, and also provided assistance to consumers to avoid home foreclosures.

In addition, dividend payments were halted at the banks receiving this capital assistance, and regulators demanded that banks recapitalize themselves through other means as well.[74] Failure to respond meant the only way out for the bank would be to rely on additional equity infusions by the government, a slippery slope to being nationalized. Since no bank wanted that fate, US banks recapitalized fairly quickly. With hindsight, this was probably the most effective policy response to the crisis.[75] Such aggressive recapitalization of banks did not occur in Europe, and the struggle of eurozone banks lasted much longer.

Following the crisis, the Federal Reserve also introduced stress tests of large banks, with the goal of determining their ability to withstand systemic shocks. The idea was to obtain early-warning signals to help regulators assess how much more capital or liquidity specific banks might need in order to withstand the kinds of stresses that crushed the financial system in 2007–2009. While the idea of using stress tests to determine how much capital banks need is worthwhile, I believe that using them to determine liquidity requirements is misguided. The 2007–2009 crisis was *not* a liquidity crisis, so imposing such requirements simply freezes loanable bank funds into immobility, sacrificing economic growth.[76]

Summing Up and Questions

A central message of this chapter is that the Great Recession was caused by a perfect storm. Among the multitude of factors, high leverage that was simultaneously on the balance sheets of banks as well as households played a central role.[77] It may have even contributed quite directly to the increase in unemployment, even apart from the fact that highly leveraged consumers, hit by declining home equity values, cut back on spending and contributed to unemployment.

This chapter has also discussed how the 2007–2009 financial crisis caused considerable pain in the real sector and that the crisis was an insolvency risk crisis that was easy to misread as a liquidity risk in the early phases. The crisis abated only when regulators recognized it as an insolvency risk crisis and took appropriate steps. This discussion sets the stage for what should be done in the future to avoid financial crises.

Notes

1. See Thakor 2015a and the references therein.
2. See Thakor 2015a.
3. See Reinhart and Rogoff 2010.
4. See Claessens and Kodres 2014.
5. My discussion in this chapter draws heavily from my paper Thakor 2015a. There are many sources one may go to in order to read about the crisis. For example, see Lo's (2012) excellent review of over twenty-one academic and non-academic books written on the subject. He concluded that the authors of these books disagree not only on what caused the crisis but also on the basic facts about the crisis.
6. The average downgrade was 5–6 rating notches. Compare this to the 2000–2001 recession, during which the average downgrade in ratings was two to three notches. See Benmelech and Dlugosz 2009.
7. Breaking the buck means that the net asset value of the money market fund falls below $1. This can happen when the fund's investment income cannot cover operating expenses and investment losses. It is a sign of financial distress.
8. The CRA first became US law in 1977. The extent to which the CRA played a role in the crisis has generated quite a bit of controversy. For example, former Federal governor Randall Kroszner asserts, "Only a small portion of subprime mortgage originations are related to the CRA" (see "Fed's Kroszner: Don't Blame the CRA" 2008). Agarwal, Benmelech, Bergman, and Seru 2012 provide evidence that the CRA led to riskier lending. Bhutta and Ringo 2015 disagree with idea that the CRA and subprime lending had much of a role to play in the crisis: "Overall, there appears to be little reason to believe that the CRA was an important factor in the subprime boom and the subsequent crash." Adelino, Schoar, and Severino 2017 document that the mortgage expansion was shared across the entire income distribution, i.e., the flow and stock of debt rose across the entire income distribution (except for the top 5 percent). Most significantly, post-crisis default rates went up the most in areas with the biggest housing price drops, especially for high-income and high-FICO-score borrowers.

9. See Acharya and Oncii 2011.

10. See Acharya and Richardson 2009.

11. This term "predatory lending" is used to refer to lenders aggressively marketing and making loans to borrowers who financially cannot afford them, with the lender often misrepresenting or withholding relevant information, which results in the lender "imposing unfair and abusive loan terms on borrowers."

12. See Ip 2007.

13. See Wallison 2011. Peter Wallison was a member of the FCIC.

14. See Taylor 2009. There is also other evidence that easy-money monetary policies encourage banks to make riskier loans. Paligorova and Santos 2017 provide a thorough empirical analysis that shows that loan spreads for borrowers become lower during periods of monetary policy easing and that this effect is driven by the increased risk appetite of banks.

15. Inflation rates were also underestimated, as revealed by subsequent evidence.

16. See Jimenez, Ongena, Peydró, and Saurina 2014 for this evidence.

17. See Maddaloni and Peydró 2011 for an empirical study of euro-area and US bank lending standards.

18. Many investment banks retained asset-backed securities they could not sell and financed them with increased leverage. This made these banks riskier.

19. See Purnanandam 2011 for this evidence.

20. See Demyanyk and Van Hemert 2011.

21. See Purnanandam 2011.

22. See Srinivasan 2016.

23. See Barth, Lice, Liu, Phumiwasana, and Yago 2009. Nonetheless, the evidence in Adelino, Schoar, and Severino 2017 indicates that the phenomenon was broader than subprime mortgages and low-income borrowers—it involved all but the top 5 percent of the income distribution.

24. See Barth, Caprio, and Levine 2008.

25. This argument was put forth in a theory developed by Thakor 2012.

26. Gennaioli, Shleifer, and Vishny 2012 provide a related but alternative view. In their model, investors simply ignore the tail risks in new securities, causing them to be overpriced and oversupplied. Eventual recognition of these risks causes investors to dump these securities, leaving financial institutions stuck with them.

27. This aspect of misaligned incentives was discussed by Boot and Thakor 1993 and Kane 1990. Lambert, Noth, and Schuwer (2017) provide causal empirical evidence on how deposit insurance safety nets increase risk taking by banks.

28. That is, they do not invoke the Material Adverse Change clause to deny credit to borrowers whose financial condition has worsened. Thakor 2005 develops a theory that predicts this.

29. See Piskorski, Seru, and Witkin 2015.

30. See Berger and Udell 2004, who provide evidence that this is caused in part by the loss of "institutional memory"—the longer it has been since the bank had to deal

with bad loans, the more difficult it becomes for loan officers to discern bad loans from good ones.

31. See Thakor 2015b, 2016 for related theories of financial crises along these lines.

32. See Franklin 1733–1758.

33. See Song and Thakor, forthcoming.

34. Indeed, that crisis makes one question the credibility of Alan Greenspan's assertion that this crisis was a "once in a hundred years" event.

35. This argument is based on a theory developed in Goel, Song, and Thakor 2014.

36. This toxic combination also had a pernicious effect on the labor market. I will develop this point in the next chapter.

37. See Adelino, Schoar, and Severino 2017.

38. See Acharya and Richardson 2009.

39. See Jagannathan, Kapoor, and Schaumburg 2013.

40. See Mian and Sufi 2009.

41. The term "shadow banking" refers to the collection of non-depository institutions that engage in "maturity transformation," meaning they have assets and liabilities of very different maturities. Examples are investment banks and insurance companies.

42. See Goel, Song, and Thakor 2014.

43. See Holt 2009 and Thakor 2015b.

44. There is now a great deal of interest in regulating loan-to-value ratios. See Jacome and Mitra 2015.

45. See Liebowitz 2008 and Thakor 2015b.

46. See Cowen 2013, for example.

47. See Liebowitz 2008.

48. Essentially a repo is a "collateralized" deposit—a short-term loan secured by a security as collateral. See Gorton and Metrick 2012.

49. See Fastenberg 2013. The material in this chapter also relies substantially on Thakor 2015b. Large-sample empirical evidence on the effect of the crisis on employment is provided by Haltenhof, Lee, and Stebunovs (2014).

50. This argument has been developed by Mian, Rao, and Sufi 2013.

51. See Ivashina and Scharfstein 2010.

52. See Santos 2011.

53. See Campello, Graham, and Harvey 2010.

54. See Ferrando, Popov, and Udell, forthcoming, and Popov and Udell 2012.

55. See Puri, Rocholl, and Steffen 2011.

56. See Thakor 2015b for a review of this evidence.

57. The theory on which this argument is based was developed by Donaldson, Piacentino, and Thakor Forthcoming.

58. Limited liability protection of some sort for households exists in every state in the United States, although the extent of the protection varies across states.

59. See Hagedorn, Manovskii, Mitman, and Karahan 2013. Donaldson, Piacentino, and Thakor, forthcoming, discuss a lot of other supporting evidence.

60. Caps on loan-to-value ratios represent an important component of macroprudential policies, and there is now a growing academic literature on this. See, for example, Claessens 2014.

61. The reason is that a bank that screens more carefully can have greater confidence that a borrower identified as creditworthy through its credit analysis is indeed creditworthy, so a lower default-risk premium can be charged.

62. Thakor 2012 develops a theory of financial crises in which a crisis results from investors perceiving counterparty risk in the banks they finance as being excessive, given the innovative financial products they hold as assets.

63. See Diamond and Rajan 2011.

64. See Covitz, Liang, and Suarez 2013. See also Gorton 2010.

65. Evidence on the effect of these facilities on bank lending is provided by Berger, Black, Bouwman, and Dlugosz 2017. Their evidence shows that banks that accessed those facilities ended up lending more. This indicates that the lower bank lending during the crisis was not just due to lower loan demand but also due to lower credit supply. However, it does not mean this was a liquidity crisis. The other evidence discussed earlier indicates that high-capital banks had little trouble getting access to funds for lending.

66. See Thakor 2015b for a discussion of this implication of a liquidity crisis.

67. See Boyson, Helwege, and Jindra 2014.

68. See Kacperczyk and Schnabl 2010.

69. See Berger and Bouwman 2013.

70. See Beltratti and Stulz 2012.

71. See Carlson, Shan, and Warusawitharana 2013 and Popov and Udell 2012.

72. See Taylor and Williams 2009.

73. See Dong and Wen 2017, who arrive at this conclusion by developing a model that they calibrate to match US aggregate output fluctuations and bond premia.

74. But they were not halted fast enough. Initially, when capital was infused into banks, the government did not halt dividends, leading to predictable behavior by banks, which passed along some of the public equity infusion to their shareholders as dividends. This inexplicable error by the Fed was later corrected with dividend halts.

75. The evidence suggests that banks that received equity infusions under the TARP also increased their own equity capital during the peak of the crisis (see Berger, Roman, and Sedunov 2017), but in some cases made riskier loans (e.g., Duchin and Sosyura 2014). Nonetheless, economic output and employment were boosted in the markets served by the TARP banks (Berger and Roman 2017).

76. I develop this point in detail in Thakor (2018) where I point out that the liquidity requirements of Basel III are misguided and hurt economic growth, and I provide a set of regulatory reform recommendations.

77. Goel, Song, and Thakor 2014 call this the problem of "correlated leverage" and develop a theory in which this arises in an equilibrium in which there are inflated house prices and high leverage on the balance sheets of both banks and households.

References

Acharya, Viral V., and Sabri Oncii. 2011. "The Repurchase Agreement (Repo) Market." In *Regulating Wall Street: The Dodd-Frank Act and the New Architecture of Global Finance*, edited by V. V. Acharya, J. F. Cooley, M. P. Richardson, and I. Walter, 319–347. Hoboken, NJ: John Wiley & Sons.

Acharya, Viral V., and Matthew P. Richardson. 2009. *Restoring Financial Stability: How to Repair a Failed System*. Hoboken, NJ: John Wiley & Sons.

Adelino, Manuel, Antoinette Schoar, and Felipe Severino. 2017. "Dynamics of Housing Debt in the Recent Boom and Great Recession." *NBER Macroeconomics Manual*.

Agarwal, Sumit, Efi Benmelech, Nittai Bergman, and Amit Seru. 2012. "Did the Community Reinvestment Act (CRA) Lead to Risky Lending?" *NBER Working Paper* no. 18609, December.

Barth, James, Gerald Caprio, and Ross Levine. 2008. *Rethinking Bank Regulation: Till Angels Govern*. New York: Cambridge University Press.

Barth, J., J. Lice, W. Liu, T. Phumiwasana, and G. Yago. 2009. *The Rise and Fall of the U.S. Mortgage and Credit Markets: A Comprehensive Analysis of the Meltdown*. Hoboken, NJ: John Wiley & Sons.

Beltratti, Andrea, and René Stulz. 2012. "The Credit Crisis around the Globe: Why Did Some Banks Perform Better?" *Journal of Financial Economics* 105 (1): 1–17.

Benmedech, Efrain, and Jennifer Dlugosz. 2009. "The Great Rating Crisis." *NBER Macroeconomics Annual* 24:161–207.

Berger, Allen, Lamont Black, Christa Bouwman, and Jennifer Dlugosz. 2017. "Bank Loan Supply Response to Federal Reserve Emergency Liquidity Facilities." *Journal of Financial Intermediation* 32:1–15.

Berger, Allen N., and Christa H. S. Bouwman. 2013. "How Does Capital Affect Bank Performance during Financial Crises?" *Journal of Financial Economics* 109 (1): 146–176.

Berger, Allen, and Raluca A. Roman. 2017. "Did Saving Wall Street Really Save Main Street? The Real Effects of TARP on Local Business Conditions." *Journal of Financial and Quantitative Analysis* 52:1827–1867.

Berger, Allen, Raluca A. Roman, and John Sedunov. 2017. "Do Bank Bailouts Reduce or Increase Systemic Risk? The Effects of TARP on Financial System Stability." Working Paper, University of South Carolina.

Berger, Allen, and Gregory Udell. 2004. "The Institutional Memory Hypothesis and the Procyclicality of Bank Lending Behavior." *Journal of Financial Intermediation* 13:458–495.

Bhutta, Neil, and Daniel Ringo. 2015. "Assessing the Community Reinvestment Act's Role in the Financial Crisis." *FEDs Notes*, May 26.

Boot, Arnoud, and Anjan V. Thakor. 1993. "Self-Interested Bank Regulation." *American Economic Review* 83:206–212.

Boyson, Nicole, Jean Helwege, and Jan Jindra. 2014. "Crises Liquidity Shocks and Fire Sales at Financial Institutions." *Financial Management* 43 (4): 857–884.

Campello, Murillo, John R. Graham, and Campbell Harvey. 2010. "The Real Effects of Financial Constraints: Evidence from a Financial Crisis." *Journal of Financial Economics* 97 (3): 470–487.

Carlson, Mark, Hui Shan, and Missaka Warusawitharana. 2013. "Capital Ratios and Bank Lending: A Matched Bank Approach." *Journal of Financial Intermediation* 22:663–687.

Claessens, Stijn. 2014. "An Overview of Macroprudential Policy Tools." IMF Working Paper WP/14/214, December.

Claessens, Stijn, and Laura Kodres. 2014. "The Regulatory Responses to the Global Financial Crisis: Some Uncomfortable Questions." IMF Working Paper WP/14/46.

Covitz, Daniel, Nellie Liang, and Gustavo A. Suarez. 2013. "The Evolution of a Financial Crisis: Collapse of Asset-Backed Commercial Paper." *Journal of Finance* 68 (3): 815–848.

Cowen, Tyler. 2013. "Predatory Borrowing?" *Marginal Revolution*, January 30.

Demyanyk, Y., and O. Van Hemert. 2011. "Understanding the Subprime Mortgage Crisis." *Review of Financial Studies* 24:1848–1880.

Diamond, Douglas and Raghuram Rajan. 2011. "Fear of Fire Sales, Illiquidity Seeking and Fire Sales." *Quarterly Journal of Economics* 126 (2):557–591.

Donaldson, Jason, Giorgia Piacentino, and Anjan V. Thakor. Forthcoming. "Household Debt, and Unemployment." *Journal of Finance*.

Dong, Feng, and Yi Wen. 2017. "Flight to What? Dissecting Liquidity Shortages in the Financial Crisis." Working Paper 2017-025B, Federal Reserve Bank of St. Louis.

Duchin, Ran, and Denis Sosyura. 2014. "Safer Ratios, Riskier Portfolios: Banks' Response to Government Aid." *Journal of Financial Economics* 113 (1): 1–28.

Fastenberg, Dan. 2013. "Employers That Cut the Most Jobs Since the Financial Crisis." *AOL Finance*, September 13.

"Fed's Kroszner: Don't Blame the CRA." 2008. *Wall Street Journal*. December 3.

Ferrando, Annalisa, Alexander Popov, and Gregory F. Udell. Forthcoming. "Sovereign Stress, Unconventional Monetary Policy, and SME Access to Finance." *Journal of Banking and Finance*.

Franklin, Benjamin. *Poor Richard's Almanack for the Years 1733-1758*. Norwalk, CT: Easton Press, 2004.

Gennaioli, Nicolai, Andrei Shleifer, and Robert Vishny. 2012. "Neglected Risks, Financial Innovation and Financial Fragility." *Journal of Financial Economics* 104:452–468.

Goel, Anand, Fenghua Song, and Anjan V. Thakor. 2014. "Correlated Leverage and Its Ramifications." *Journal of Financial Intermediation* 23 (4): 471–503.

Gorton, Gary. 2010. *Slapped by the Invisible Hand: The Panic of 2007*. Oxford: Oxford University Press.

Gorton, Gary, and Andrew Metrick. 2012. "Getting Up to Speed on the Financial Crisis: A One-Weekend Reader's Guide." *Journal of Economic Literature* 50:128–150.

Hagedorn, Marcus, Iourii Manovskii, Kurt Mitman, and Fatih Karahan. 2013. "Unemployment Benefits and Unemployment in the Great Recession: The Role of Macro Effects." *NBER* Working Paper.

Haltenhof, Samuel, Seung Jung Lee, and Viktors Stebunovs. 2014. "The Credit Crunch and Fall in Employment during the Great Recession." *Journal of Economic Dynamics and Control* 43 (C): 31–57.

Herron, Janna. 2013. "4 Personal Stories of the Great Recession." *Smart Money*, September 27.

Holt, J. 2009. "A Summary of the Primary Causes of the Housing Bubble and the Resulting Credit Crisis: A Non-technical Paper." *Journal of Business Enquiry* 8:120–129.

Ip, Greg. 2007. "Did Greenspan Add to Subprime Woes?" *Wall Street Journal*, June 9.

Ivashina, Victoria, and David Scharfstein. 2010. "Bank Lending during the Financial Crisis." *Journal of Financial Economics* 97 (3): 319–338.

Jacome, Luis, and Srobana Mitra. 2015. "LTV and DTI Limits—Going Granular." IMF Working Paper WP/15/154, July.

Jagannathan, Ravi, Mudit Kapoor, and Ernst Schaumburg. 2013. "Causes of the Great Recession of 2007-2009: The Financial Crisis Was the Symptom Not the Disease!" *Journal of Financial Intermediation* 22:4–29.

Jimenez, Gabriel, Steven Ongena, Jose-Luis Peydró, and Jesus Saurina. 2014. "Hazardous Times for Monetary Policy: What Do Twenty-Three Million Bank Loans Say about the Effects of Monetary Policy on Credit Risk Taking?" *Econometrica* 82 (2): 463–505.

Kacperczyk, Marcin, and Philipp Schnabl. 2010. "When Safe Proved Risky: Commercial Paper during the Financial Crisis of 2007-2009." *Journal of Economic Perspectives* 24 (1): 29–50.

Kane, Edward. 1990. "Principal-Agent Problems in S&L Salvage." *Journal of Finance* 45:755–764.

Lambert, Claudia, Felix Noth, and Ulrich Schüwer. 2017. "How Do Insured Deposits Affect Bank Risk? Evidence from the 2008 Emergency Economic Stabilization Act." *Journal of Financial Intermediation* 29:81–102.

Liebowitz, S. 2008. "Anatomy of a Train Wreck: Causes of the Mortgage Meltdown." Independent Policy Report, available online at http://www.independent.org/pdf/policy_reports/2008-10-03-trainwreck.pdf.

Lo, Andrew. 2012. "Reading about the Financial Crisis: A Twenty-One Book Review." *Journal of Economic Literature* 50:151–178.

Maddaloni, A., and J. Peydró. 2011. "Bank Risk-Taking, Securitization, Supervision and Low Interest Rates: Evidence from the Euro Area and the U.S. Lending Standards." *Review of Financial Studies* 24:2121–2165.

Mian, Atif, Kamalesh Rao, and Amir Sufi. 2013. "Household Balance Sheets, Consumption and the Economic Slump." *Quarterly Journal of Economics* 124:1687–1726.

Mian, Atif, and Amir Sufi. 2009. "The Consequences of Mortgage Credit Expansion: Evidence from the U.S. Mortgage Default Crisis." *Quarterly Journal of Economics* 124:1449–1496.

Paligorova, Teodora, and Joao A. C. Santos. 2017. "Monetary Policy and Bank Risk Taking: Evidence from the Corporate Loan Market." *Journal of Financial Intermediation* 30:35–49.

Piskorski, Tomas, Amit Seru, and J. Witkin. 2015. "Asset Quality Misrepresentation by Financial Intermediaries: Evidence from the RMBS Market." *Journal of Finance* 70 (6): 2635–2678.

Popov, Alexander, and Gregory F. Udell. 2012. "Cross-Border Banking, Credit Access and the Financial Crisis." *Journal of International Economics* 87:147–161.

Puri, Manju, Jörg Rocholl, and Sascha Steffen. 2011. "Global Retail Lending in the Aftermath of the U.S. Financial Crisis: Distinguishing between Supply and Demand Effects." *Journal of Financial Economics* 100:556–578.

Purnanandam, Amiyatosh. 2011. "Originate-to-Distribute Model and the Subprime Mortgage Crisis." *Review of Financial Studies* 100 (5): 1881–1915.

Reinhart, Carmen, and Kenneth Rogoff. 2010. "Growth in a Time of Debt." *American Economic Review: Papers & Proceedings* 100: 573–578.

Santos, João A. C. 2011. "Bank Corporate Loan Pricing Following the Subprime Crisis." *Review of Financial Studies* 24 (6): 1916–1943.

Song, Fenghua, and Anjan V. Thakor. Forthcoming. "Bank Culture." *Journal of Financial Intermediation*.

Srinivasan, Kandarp. 2016. "The Securitization Flash Flood." Working Paper, Washington University in St. Louis, November.

Taylor, John B. 2009. "Economic Policy and the Financial Crisis: An Empirical Analysis of What Went Wrong." *Critical Review: A Journal of Politics and Society* 21:341–364.

Taylor, John B., and John C. Williams. 2009. "A Black Swan in the Money Market." *American Economic Journal: Macroeconomics* 1 (1): 58–83.

Thakor, Anjan V. 2005. "Do Loan Commitments Cause Overlending?" *Journal of Money, Credit and Banking* 37:1067–1099.

Thakor, Anjan V. 2012. "Incentives to Innovate and Financial Crises." *Journal of Financial Economics* 103:130–148.

Thakor, Anjan V. 2015a. "The Financial Crisis of 2007-09: Why Did It Happen and What Did We Learn? *Review of Corporate Finance Studies* 4 (2): 115–205.

Thakor, Anjan V. 2015b. "Lending Booms, Smart Bankers and Financial Crises." *American Economic Review* 105 (5): 305–309.

Thakor, Anjan V. 2016. "The Highs and the Lows: A Theory of Credit Risk Assessment and Pricing through the Business Cycle." *Journal of Financial Intermediation* 25 (1): 1–29.

Thakor, Anjan V. 2018. "Post-Crisis Regulatory Reform in Banking: Focus on Insolvency, Not Illiquidity!" Working Paper, Washington University in St. Louis, January.

Wallison, Peter, J. 2011. "Dissent from the Majority Report of the Financial Crisis Inquiry Commission." *American Enterprise Institute*, January 26.

Reforming Banking and Looking Ahead

Improving Banking and the Potential Interactions with Fintech

9

The Final Frontier

AN IMPROVED BANKING SYSTEM TO ACHIEVE
FINANCIAL STABILITY AND ECONOMIC GROWTH

Introduction

"You can't have your cake and eat it too" perhaps best describes what economists like to claim when it comes to discussions about economic stability and growth, namely that there is a tradeoff. You can either have relatively safe banks that provide stability, as in Canada, for example, or you can have banks that take risks in support of economic growth but are embroiled in occasional financial crises as in the United States. This choice implies that you can't have both stability and growth. Sounds reasonable, right?

I believe, however, that it is a false tradeoff. Like the old joke about the "rational" economist not picking up the $100 bill lying on the street because in an efficient market it would have already been picked up if it was really there, it has been difficult for some people to accept the truth that research has established.[1] That is, in the long run, we get more economic growth *with* greater financial stability if we avoid long periods of loose monetary policy—which lead to asset price bubbles—and weak microprudential regulation that lets banks get away with low levels of equity capital.

An Improved Banking System: The Case for Safer, Not More Fragile, Banks to Promote Both Stability and Growth

In the old *Star Trek* episodes, Captain Kirk would refer to space as "the final frontier" and direct his crew to take the starship *Enterprise* to strange new worlds. In many episodes, the behavior of the people on the planet they were visiting would reflect some social issue on earth, typically some repugnant behavior magnified many times and leading to planetary disaster. In some cases, Captain Kirk would violate the "prime directive" not to intervene and at least offer advice on what to do.

In that spirit, I made up my own episode of *Star Trek*. The *Enterprise* visits a planet where young adults borrow extensively using their credit cards to support consumption beyond their earning capacity and the legal requirement is for their parents to cover half their repayment obligations every month. If the young adults ever got to the point at which they were on the verge of declaring bankruptcy, the government required their parents to bail them out and pay off their creditors. For this, the parents received big tax breaks. Captain Kirk happens to meet some of the parents who like the tax breaks but despise the mandatory bailout obligation and want the government to change it. So Captain Kirk talks to the head of the planetary government council. She is sympathetic to the demand for change, because the huge tax breaks have almost bankrupted the planet and the planetary infrastructure is crumbling. But she says that the government has had economists do research on the issue, and these economists have advised that dire consequences will ensue if this kind of debt support is eliminated:

- The young adults will be depressed by the lack of mandated parental support and work less hard,
- they will have less money to invest in the education of their own children, and
- they will be less willing to accept entrepreneurial risks.

Her question to Captain Kirk is, "Do you really want us to have a society of depressed young adults with ill-educated children?" Befuddled by all this, Captain Kirk invokes the prime directive and decides to leave things alone.

If you have read the previous chapters, you obviously recognize the thinly veiled analogy to banking on earth. We have created a system in which there are structural incentives for banks to prefer more leverage to less.[2] While we have produced theories that say that there might be societal benefits from this, we also have theories that say the opposite, and the empirical evidence overwhelmingly supports the latter. In a nutshell, more highly capitalized banks support higher liquidity creation and economic growth, and also are safer and less crisis-prone.

Thus, despite the dire warnings of doom and gloom from bankers—who have the same incentives to justify their high leverage that the young adults in my *Star Trek* episode have to justify legal parental support for their excessive borrowing—*a more highly capitalized banking system will, in the long run, provide us with both higher economic growth and greater financial stability.* Thus, we need a safer banking system not just for greater financial stability but also for long-run economic growth.

So How Do We Do It?

I will discuss the measures in advance of crises in this section and measures during crises in the next. The reason why it is important to distinguish between these two is that measures in advance are *preventive* measures, whereas those during the crisis are *cures* designed to end the crisis. While both are important, the old adage "An ounce of prevention is worth a pound of cure" applies.[3]

Higher Capital Requirements for Depository Institutions and Shadow Banks

As we saw earlier, when things go well for a long time, it is easy to develop a false sense of security, which then leads financial institutions to become excessively leveraged and fragile. It is thus useful to consider higher capital requirements in both depository institutions and shadow banks. The reason to include shadow banks is to minimize "regulatory arbitrage," whereby regulated depositories shift activities to the shadow banking sector to escape "regulatory taxes" like capital requirements.[4] Regulatory-mandated "haircuts" in repo transactions and "skin in the game" requirements for securitized mortgages (requiring originating banks to hold some of the equity tranche in securitizations) are some of the ways in which capital requirements can be implemented in shadow banking (see figure 9.1).

Higher capital requirements for financial institutions will not eliminate all future financial crises. But they will help in many ways. They will:

- lead banks to lend more and create more liquidity[5]
- create safer banks that are more likely to survive financial crises[6]
- generate fewer contagion-related bank failures[7]
- cause banks to exercise greater due diligence in screening and monitoring loan applications[8]

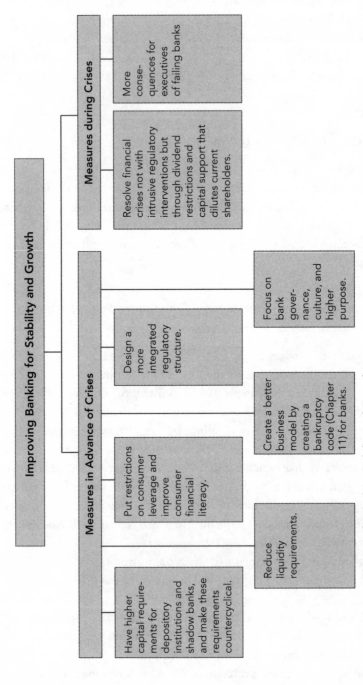

FIGURE 9.1 A Blueprint for Banking Stability and Growth.

- cause banks to contract lending less during crises[9]
- create banks that are more valuable to their depository customers[10]
- create banks that are more valuable to their shareholders[11]
- lead banks to develop stronger safety-oriented cultures[12]
- maintain/increase access to short-term (uninsured) funding (and hence liquidity) during periods of stress[13]
- create less systemic risk[14]
- reduce the probability of ad hoc expansions of the government safety net, expansions that bring with them increased moral hazard
- reduce the likelihood of fire sales, since highly capitalized institutions will be able to hold on to assets longer without having to engage in fire sales
- reduce incentives of banks to take more risks[15]
- reduce the extent to which a looser monetary policy that lowers short-term interest rates will cause banks to make riskier loans.[16]

Absent fire sales, market liquidity will also improve,[17] without institutions having to burden their balance sheets with a lot of lazy (low-return) liquid assets.

You might wonder at this point about *how high* capital requirements should be set. At one level, the answer to this question is really simple—why not just go back to the capital ratios that were common in banking before the advent of deposit insurance? But that would mean capital ratios (equity capital as a percentage of total assets) in the 25–30 percent range.[18] That is unlikely to be a palatable solution for most constituencies. The arguments against it are legion—this is not 1925, capital markets are much more developed, banks have access to far more opportunities to manage their risks, very high capital ratios will deter uninsured creditor monitoring and disciplining of banks, there will be regulatory arbitrage as banks will eschew activities that entail capital requirements and migrate to those that do not carry capital requirements, and so on. So the issue is more complex now. We will see that the issue of how high capital requirements should be is quite nuanced and depends, in part, on bank culture and higher purpose. For now, it suffices to note that there is overwhelming evidence that increases in capital levels from current levels will benefit bank shareholders, enhance financial stability, and facilitate economic growth, but we cannot say for sure *how much* they should be increased.

One of the most important theoretical objections to raising capital requirements is that if we raise them too high, we may reduce market discipline imposed on the bank by its uninsured creditors (including depositors).[19] Now you might say: "Wait a minute. Did we not just conclude that the empirical evidence supports the idea that more capital in banking is better? So this theoretical possibility should not be a worry, right?" Not quite. The empirical evidence refers to the effects of increasing capital by a little bit from the present levels. It does not say that the market-discipline argument can be disregarded if capital requirements were raised substantially, say to close to the pre-deposit-insurance levels of 25–30 percent. So if we want to propose something like "leverage ratios" (equity as a percentage of total assets, including adjustments to the denominator for off-balance-sheet claims) in the range of 15–20 percent, we do need to worry about the possible loss of market discipline from uninsured creditors.[20] The question is: Can you increase capital requirements without diluting the monitoring incentives of uninsured creditors and thereby weakening market discipline on banks?

The issue is that we would like more equity capital in the bank for all of the reasons we have discussed. And yet by doing so, we run the risk of losing market discipline from uninsured creditors. This is like the sailors in ancient Greek mythology who had to navigate between two sea monsters on opposite sides of the Strait of Messina between Sicily and the Italian mainland. Scylla was a six-headed sea monster on the mainland side of the strait, and Charybdis was a whirlpool off the coast of Sicily. Avoiding one monster meant passing too close to the other. See figure 9.2.

So are banks really trapped between the Scylla of bad incentives and fragility due to low capital and the Charybdis of weak market discipline due to high capital (and hence low leverage)? Or can we increase bank capital requirements without diluting market discipline?

We can; it turns out that we can have our cake and eat it too. I describe in figure 9.2 a scheme that achieves this.[21]

The scheme calls for having two kinds of capital requirements. One is what we call a "normal capital requirement," which can be specified as a leverage ratio the way it is specified under the Basel III requirements—equity as a percentage of total assets (i.e., loans, cash, investments in securities, etc.), roughly speaking (with an adjustment for off-balance-sheet items). In addition, there would be a "special capital account" (SCA). This is equity capital that is invested in very liquid securities (like US Treasuries, for example) and belongs to the bank's shareholders as long as the bank is solvent, but it goes to the *regulator* in case the bank is insolvent and is not bailed out. That is, if the bank experiences idiosyncratic failure, neither the bank's shareholders nor its creditors have access to the SCA. Of course, if there is a systemic failure and many banks fail together, the regulator may decide to bail them all out,

FIGURE 9.2 Caught between Scylla and Charybdis?

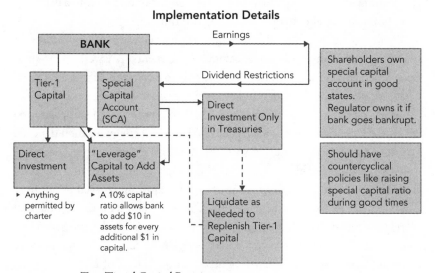

FIGURE 9.3 Two-Tiered Capital Requirements.

in which case the bank effectively does not lose the assets in the special capital account. But keeping the SCA invested in a segregated set of assets means that the regulator can readily seize these assets in the event of an idiosyncratic failure of the bank. See figure 9.3 for a schematic.

How does this solve the problem? Note that the purpose of equity capital in the bank is to create skin in the game for the shareholders so they will not take excessive risks. The SCA represents skin in the game, since the shareholders own the assets in the bank as long as the bank is solvent. However, the SCA does not dilute the creditors' incentives to monitor the bank, since they do not get the assets in the SCA when the bank fails.

If the bank experiences asset write-downs (due to marking its assets to market) or has losses that deplete its book equity capital, its normal capital will fall. In this case, a transfer will be made from the SCA to the normal capital account to replenish it and bring it back up above the required level. Of course, now the SCA will decline, so it will need to be built back up. During the time that the SCA is below the regulatory requirement, dividend payments by the bank would be halted, and stock buybacks would be prohibited.[22] More Treasury securities would be purchased with the retained earnings, and the SCA would be refurbished. It may even be necessary to require (at least some) banks to maintain a buffer above the minimum SCA.

Both the normal capital requirement and the SCA should have buffers that are countercyclical. This means the buffers should be larger when the economy is booming and banks are doing well and smaller when the economy is not doing well. Consequently, banks can save capital for a rainy day during good times and be able to operate during bad times.

Finally, on this point, the question regulators want to see addressed is: Exactly how high should we set capital requirements? Answering this question requires a careful calibration exercise. We do not have a definitive answer, but figure 9.4 shows the different factors that impact this determination.

In this figure, E_A is the minimum level of capital the bank needs to keep to ensure that it has the trust of its depositors that it will safeguard their deposits (safekeeping) and not abscond with the money.[23] Point B represents additional bank services that will typically be associated with funding liquidity creation, including borrower screening and monitoring, as well as lending, and the corresponding capital level is E_B.[24] Thus, E_B represents the capital level corresponding to all of the economic service banks provide that we covered in chapter 2. Inducing banks to create a safety-oriented culture that has positive contagion effects (point C) corresponds to a capital level of E_C.[25] Finally, insulating depository customers from the bank's credit risk and providing them an information-insensitive claim (point D) requires capital E_D.[26]

So what numerical value should we give E_D? Here I must confess I do not have a definitive answer, but I can venture a reasonable conjecture. Based on the calibration research done so far,[27] the kinds of numbers that are popping up are in the neighborhood of a 10 percent "leverage ratio"

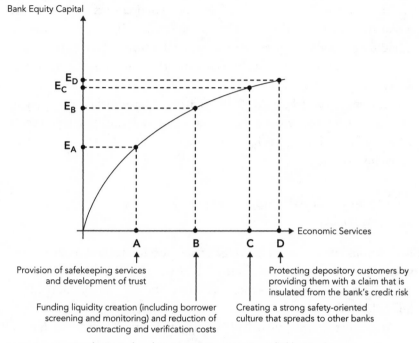

FIGURE 9.4 Bank Capital and Economic Services Provided by Banks.

and a 20 percent risk-weighted-assets capital ratio. But these studies do not account for all of the factors depicted in the figure above. That is, because they focus on just some—but not all—of the benefits of capital, they understate the desired level of bank capital. My own view is that a 15–18 percent leverage ratio (including stress-test-based capital buffers and the SCA considered earlier) and a risk-weighted-assets ratio around 23–28 percent are appropriate. Banks should be allowed to operate with *no less*. Note that by equity I just mean common equity capital, which is the highest-quality risk-absorbing capital. And unlike current practice (at least in terms of observed capital ratios), I would want the larger banks to be at the higher end of this range, given the bigger "culture contagion" and systemic risk implications associated with them.[28]

Reduce Liquidity Requirements

I believe the adoption of liquidity requirements under Basel III was misguided.[29] It stemmed in part from the mistaken belief that the 2007–2009 crisis was a liquidity crisis. It was not. Rather, it was an insolvency (or counterparty risk) crisis. In fact, research has shown that even if we want to prevent future liquidity crises, having liquidity requirements may be counter-productive in that they may worsen the future crisis.[30] This is particularly true if imposing liquidity requirements somehow leads to a "compromise" with banks that involves lower capital requirements. Moreover, because of high liquidity requirements, banks earn lower overall returns on their investments—cash is a lazy asset—which then induces them to "chase yield" by seeking out risky investments to overcome the low returns on cash and other liquid assets. Thus, paradoxically, higher liquidity requirements can cause banks to make riskier investments.

Restrictions on Consumer Leverage and Improving Financial Literacy

Restrictions on consumer leverage are important to ensure that excessive consumer leverage does not lead to the two pernicious outcomes we discussed previously—increased fragility of banks and higher unemployment.

As discussed earlier, there is now ample theoretical foundation for, and empirical evidence in support of, the idea that consumer leverage ought to be capped. This can be done in a variety of ways. Perhaps the simplest is on a *transaction* basis. That is, loan-to-value (LTV) ratios in mortgages can be restricted, taking into account total indebtedness, to ensure sufficient equity in the home.[31] Another would be to impose substantially higher capital requirements on banks making high-LTV loans.

Additionally, it would be helpful if banks collaborated with universities to launch extensive programs in improving the financial literacy of consumers. Many consumers borrowed excessively during the crisis because they did not fully understand the implications of the variable rate mortgages they were taking, especially the fact that the low initial "teaser" rates would eventually rise and impose a bigger debt burden. They did not comprehend what prudent financial leverage means and how leverage amplifies both gains and losses on an investment. Improved financial literacy may have helped in keeping consumer financial leverage in check.[32]

But this has to be part of the higher purpose of banks. Not another government program. Universities and community colleges can join in the effort, and this can be buoyed by private-sector support from banks.

Refine and Strengthen Process for Resolving Failing Banks

Until the Dodd-Frank Act, passed in the aftermath of the 2007–2009 financial crisis, merger with a healthy institution or liquidation by the government were the only failure options for a bank not bailed out. The lack of an orderly bankruptcy like Chapter 11 of the Bankruptcy Code was a serious shortcoming in dealing with bank failure. Title II of the Dodd-Frank Act attempts to improve things by stipulating a process to quickly and efficiently liquidate a large and complex financial company that is on the verge of failure. It is an alternative to bankruptcy. Under Title II, the FDIC is given certain powers as receiver and a time period of three to five years within which to complete the liquidation process.

Once the treasury secretary determines, based on a multitude of factors, that a financial company should be liquidated, the FDIC takes control of the assets, obligations, and operations of the company as receiver. There is a fund created by the US Treasury called the Orderly Liquidation Fund that covers the administrative cost of liquidation.[33] There are a series of rules to allow for liquidation of assets and the payment of claims to claimholders based on a priority list. The executives, directors, and shareholders of the institutions are at the bottom of this priority list.

The goal of Title II is to maintain the financial stability of the system as a whole, rather than to merely address the needs of the failing company. It gives the FDIC power to fire the management and board members of the company, but the FDIC cannot take an equity interest in the financial company.

While Title II is an improvement on what we had before, it needs to be complemented with a financial-institutions analog of Chapter 11 bankruptcy for non-financials. Financial institutions differ in many respects from non-financials, most notably due to the presence of public safety nets, so the bankruptcy process for them would need to be different too. But we should have a resolution process that is an alternative to liquidation.

Design a More Integrated Regulatory Structure

The 2007–2009 crisis exposed serious weaknesses in the way the financial system is regulated. Insurance companies, commercial banks, investment banks, securities broker-dealers, and other institutions are all highly interconnected, and yet they were regulated by distinct regulatory entities that did not communicate effectively and coordinate across regulatory silos. Consequently, prior to the crisis, there was little attention paid to the growth of the repo market and its increasing importance in the short-term funding of shadow banks. Adding to this inattention was inconsistent and often conflicting regulation. This facilitated regulatory arbitrage and risks that were carefully regulated and monitored in one sector migrated in an amplified form to a less-regulated sector.

We have learned now that we need a more integrated approach to the regulation of depositories and shadow banks. The creation of the Financial Stability Oversight Council under the Dodd-Frank Act is intended to help regulators more effectively see the early warning signs and coordinate across jurisdictional boundaries.

Unfortunately, Dodd-Frank has not done enough. Little has been done to deal effectively with possible future occurrences of insolvency-driven stresses in the repo market or the liquidity evaporation that may accompany such stresses.[34] As we discovered in the last crisis, if the repo market gets into trouble, the whole economy becomes exposed. In other words, the risk is potentially *systemic*. Much more research is needed on the optimal design of regulatory agencies.[35]

The balkanized and complex regulatory structure that still remains not only leads to uneven implementation of regulations[36] but also increases regulatory costs for banks and makes them less competitive vis-à-vis shadow banks, P2P lending platforms, and other non-depositories.

Focus on Bank Governance, Culture, and Higher Purpose

One of the arguments against higher capital requirements in banking is that they would weaken the incentives of uninsured creditors to monitor the bank and impose market discipline. A more highly capitalized bank provides creditors with more of a cushion against losses, so their claims become less risky. This makes their tradeoff shift in favor of expending less resources on monitoring the bank.

At this point, you should be smelling something fishy about this reasoning. If the bank has more equity on its balance sheet, don't the shareholders have more skin in the game? Why don't they now monitor more to pick up the slack created by a decrease in bank creditor monitoring?

A partial answer is that equity governance in banking is viewed as not being as effective as it is in non-financial corporations, at least not in the United States. One reason for this is that ownership of banks is restricted by law. Non-financial companies are not allowed to take ownership positions in US banks. An investor with more than 10 percent ownership in a bank is considered a "controlling shareholder" and thus must become a bank holding company (BHC). A BHC is not permitted to invest in non-bank activities. This means that ownership of banks is out of reach for many firms that specialize in creating value through more effective governance, such as private equity firms. The constraint on bank ownership means that equity governance in banking is likely to be weaker than in non-financials.

Governance is affected by corporate culture. The culture of an organization is defined by the explicit and implicit contracts that govern how employees behave. Culture, as we discussed earlier, can influence behavior beyond what is possible using explicit wage contracts and other incentive mechanisms.[37] Whether governance is effective or not will be strongly influenced by the bank's culture. And since the bank's equity capital also determines its governance, and higher capital leads to a more safety-oriented culture, we can expect the overall effect of higher bank capital to be to strengthen governance and reduce risk.

Finally, there is the issue of the purpose of the bank. Or to be more precise, what is the bank's higher purpose for existing? How does the bank perceive it, and how does this perception influence its business strategy and day-to-day decisions?

As we discussed earlier, when an organization has an authentic higher purpose, its decisions are not driven solely by the usual business goals, but also by the desire to serve a purpose that transcends usual business goals. When employees believe in the bank's higher purpose, they are more inclined to act in the interest of the organization, rather pursuing selfish goals. Governance becomes easier and more effective,

Measures During the Crisis
Resolve Financial Crises by Capital Support, Rather Than Intrusive Interventions

When banks become financially distressed, there are two approaches that are used commonly. One is regulatory interventions that revoke bank charters, fire executives, and so on. The other is capital support through injections of equity capital. Recent research has shown that regulatory interventions reduce liquidity creation by the affected banks, whereas capital support does not.[38] There is also evidence that when capital injections are sufficiently large to reestablish compliance with bank capital requirements, they lead to an increase in the supply of credit and higher investment. But if the capital injections are too small, not only do they fail to increase the supply of credit, but they also encourage the evergreening of non-performing loans and encourage bad investments by "zombie" firms.[39]

Capital support by the government should be followed by dividend halts that lead to the affected banks building up their capital levels over time. At some point, the bank's shareholders can buy back the government's equity stake.

More Consequences for Executives of Failing Banks

There are various ways in which the executives of failed banks can be made more accountable. One is compensation "clawbacks" that would require executives to return some of their past bonuses. Another is fines on executives if they took undue risks. In extreme cases, if criminal behavior is discovered, there may be more severe sanctions like imprisonment. A word of caution, though: these sorts of measures can too easily become politicized.

Another word of caution: if we go too far in punishing bank executives for bank failures, we will create strong disincentives for honest risk-taking and damage liquidity creation and economic growth. I once met an investment banker who had joined a Wall Street firm and had been required to sign an agreement (as part of the employment contract) that he would be held personally liable if a decision he made went wrong, even if that decision had been endorsed by his boss or a committee. He said he signed the document but became instantly more risk averse. He said, "I will walk away from risky deals even when it means leaving money on the table that the bank could have made, if the deals create personal liability for me."

Summing Up and Questions

Self-inflicted wounds are often the hardest to bear. Allowing banks to operate with low capital ratios, not strengthening equity governance in banking, ignoring issues related to bank culture and higher purpose, and persisting with long periods of a loose-money monetary policy all combined to inflict a wound on the banking system that was avoidable. This chapter has discussed a variety of measures that can enable a banking system that is both growth-friendly and stable. These measures arise naturally from the vast body of research is available.

While this chapter has discussed ways in which the existing banking system can be improved, it takes the existing system as a given. But what if we could design the system from scratch? How would we do it? Let us take up these questions in our next chapter.

Notes

1. See the discussions of the research in Thakor 2014a, 2014b.
2. Thakor 2014a discusses the various factors that contribute to this preference.
3. Figure 9.1 and the ensuing discussion are based in part on Thakor 2014b.
4. There is quite a bit of evidence on this. See, for example, Acharya and Oncii 2011. This is one of the drawbacks of "regulating by product/institutional label" rather than "regulating by function" as advocated by Merton 1993, 1995.
5. See Berger and Bouwman 2009, Peek and Rosengren 2000, and Puri, Rocholl, and Steffen 2011.
6. See Berger and Bouwman 2013.
7. See Acharya and Thakor 2016.
8. Beltratti and Stulz 2012 and Purnanandam 2011.
9. See Carlson, Shan, and Warusawitharana 2013.
10. See Merton and Thakor, forthcoming.
11. See Mehran and Thakor 2011 and Bouwman, Kim, and Shin 2017.
12. See Song and Thakor, forthcoming.
13. See Perignon, Thesmar, and Vuillemey 2018 for empirical evidence.
14. See Acharya and Thakor 2016 for a theory, and Laeven, Ratnovski, and Tong 2014 for international evidence that systemic risk in the economy is inversely related to bank capital.
15. Lambert, Noth, and Schüwer 2017 provide evidence that an increase in insured deposits causes banks to become more risky and that this effect is stronger for banks with lower capital. See also Beltrati and Stulz 2012.
16. Jimenez, Ongena, Peydró, and Saurina 2014 provide evidence that when the short-term (overnight) rate falls due to a looser monetary policy, banks with low capital grant more loans to risky firms with lower collateral requirements and a higher ex post likelihood of default.
17. See Brunnermeier and Pedersen 2009.
18. In the Basel III framework, these are called "leverage ratios." Basel III specifies a minimum leverage ratio of 3 percent. US regulators have stipulated a 5 percent minimum.
19. See Calomiris and Kahn 1991 for the original version of this argument.
20. Of course, some of this lost discipline may be made up with greater equity discipline on the bank.
21. The discussion below is based on Acharya and Thakor 2016.
22. Usually firms experience stock price declines when they cut dividends, because that signals bad news about future earnings. But that will not be a problem here, because

investors will know that the reason for the dividend halt is not lower expected future earnings.

23. This follows from the theory developed in Donaldson, Piacentino, and Thakor 2018.

24. The funding liquidity creation part of this is linked to the theory in Donaldson, Piacentino, and Thakor 2018. Coval and Thakor 2005 provide an analysis of the capital needed to support the bank's (pre-lending) screening or credit analysis incentives. Mehran and Thakor 2011 analyze the capital needed to provide the appropriate monitoring incentives for the bank.

25. This is based on the theory developed in Song and Thakor forthcoming.

26. This is based on Dang, Gorton, Holmström, and Ordoñez 2017 and Merton and Thakor, forthcoming.

27. See Thakor 2014 for a discussion of this research.

28. In this sense my proposal is somewhat similar to the "Minneapolis plan" (see Kashkari 2016), which asks for equity as a percentage of risk-weighted assets to be 23.5 percent for banks with assets above $250 billion. However, my proposal calls for less capital for banks not certified as "too big to fail" by the US Treasury than the Minneapolis plan, which asks for a 38 percent capital ratio. My proposal also calls for less capital than prescribed in Admati and Hellwig 2013.

29. See Thakor 2018, where I develop this point in great detail.

30. Malherbe 2014 develops a theoretical model in which holding cash reserves worsens future adverse selection for long-term assets, impeding the ability of banks to get out of a liquidity crisis.

31. There is now an emerging literature on macroprudential regulation that emphasizes LTV ratios.

32. There is a growing body of economic research on the importance of financial literacy. See, for example, Lusardi and Mitchell 2014.

33. For broker-dealers, in addition to the FDIC, the Securities Investor Protection Corporation (SIPC) is appointed as a trustee that will take over managing any assets that are transferred to a bridge company by the FDIC.

34. See Acharya and Oncii 2011 for a discussion of this.

35. There is a great deal of heterogeneity across countries in terms of the extent of integration in bank regulatory structure. See Barth, Caprio, and Levine 2008.

36. Agarwal, Luca, Seru, and Trebbi 2014.

37. For a theoretical model of bank culture, see Song and Thakor, forthcoming.

38. This evidence appears in Berger, Bouwman, Kick, and Schaeck 2016.

39. That is, firms that are economically insolvent and have nothing to lose by "gambling for resurrection." See Giannetti and Simonov 2011.

References

Acharya, Viral, and T. Sabri Oncii. 2011. "The Repurchase Agreement (Repo) Market." In *Regulating Wall Street: The Dodd-Frank Act and the New Architecture of Global*

Finance, edited by V. V. Acharya, F. Cooley, M. P. Richardson, and I. Walterm 319–350. Hoboken, NJ: John Wiley & Sons.

Acharya, V., and Anjan Thakor. 2016. "The Dark Side of Liquidity Creation: Leverage Induced Systemic Risk and Implications for the Lender of Last Resort." *Journal of Financial Intermediation* 28: 4–21.

Admati, Anat, and Martin Hellwig. 2013. *The Bankers' New Clothes: What's Wrong with Banking and What to Do about It*. Princeton, NJ: Princeton University Press.

Agarwal, Sumit, David Lucca, Amit Seru, and Francesco Trebbi. 2014. "Inconsistent Regulators: Evidence from Banking." *Quarterly Journal of Economics* 129:889–938.

Barth, James, Gerald Caprio, and Ross Levine. 2008. *Rethinking Bank Regulation: Till Angels Govern*. New York: Cambridge University Press.

Beltratti, Andrea, and René Stulz. 2012. "The Credit Crisis around the Globe: Why Did Some Banks Perform Better?" *Journal of Financial Economics* 105 (1): 1–17.

Berger, Allen, and Christa Bouwman. 2009. "Bank Liquidity Creation." *Review of Financial Studies* 22 (9): 3779–3837.

Berger, Allen N., and Christa H. S. Bouwman. 2013. "How Does Capital Affect Bank Performance during Financial Crises?" *Journal of Financial Economics* 109 (1): 146–176.

Berger, Allen, Christa H. S. Bouwman, Thomas Kick, and Klaus Schaeck. 2016. "Bank Liquidity Creation Following Regulatory Interventions and Capital Support." *Journal of Financial Intermediation* 26: 115–144.

Bouwman, Christa, Hwagyun Kim, and Sang-Ook Shin. 2017. "Bank Capital and Bank Stock Performance." Working paper, Texas A&M University, July.

Brunnermeier, Markus K., and Lasse Heje Pedersen. 2009. "Market Liquidity and Funding Liquidity." *Review of Financial Studies* 22 (6): 2201–2238.

Calomiris, Charles, and Charles Kahn. 1991. "The Role of Demandable Debt in Structuring Optimal Banking Arrangements." *American Economic Review* 81 (3): 497–513.

Carlson, Mark, Hui Shan, and Missaka Warusawitharana. 2013. "Capital Ratios and Bank Lending: A Matched Bank Approach." *Journal of Financial Intermediation* 22 (4): 663–687.

Coval, Joshua, and Anjan V. Thakor. 2005. "Financial Intermediation as a Beliefs-Bridge between Optimists and Pessimists." *Journal of Financial Economics* 75 (3): 535–569.

Dang, Tri Vi, Gary Gorton, Bengt Holmström, and Guillermo Ordoñez. 2017. "Banks as Secret Keepers." *American Economic Review* 107 (4): 1005–1029.

Donaldson, Jason, Giorgia Piacentino, and Anjan V. Thakor. 2018. "Warehouse Banking." *Journal of Financial Economics* 129:250–267.

Giannetti, Mariassunta, and Andrei Simonov. 2011. "On the Real Effects of Bank Bailouts: Micro-Evidence from Japan." Working paper, Stockholm School of Economics, September.

Jimenez, Gabriel, Steven Ongena, Jose-Luis Peydró, and Jesus Saurina. 2014. "Hazardous Times for Monetary Policy: What Do Twenty-Three Million Bank Loans Say About the Effects of Monetary Policy on Credit Risk Taking?" *Econometrica* 82 (2): 463–505.

Kashkari, Neel. 2016. "The Minneapolis Plan to End Too Big to Fail." Speech delivered at the Economic Club of New York, November 18.

Laeven, Luc, Lev Ratnovski, and Hui Tong. 2014. "Bank Size, Capital Requirements and Systemic Risk: Some International Evidence." IMF working paper, March 31.

Lambert, Claudia, Felix Noth, and Ulrich Schüwer. 2017. "How Do Insured Deposits Affect Bank Risk? Evidence from the 2008 Emergency Economic Stabilization Act." *Journal of Financial Intermediation* 29:81–102.

Lusardi, Annamaria, and Olivia S. Smitchell. 2014. "The Economic Importance of Financial Literacy: Theory and Evidence." *Journal of Economic Literature* 52 (1): 5–44.

Malherbe, Frederic. 2014. "Self-Fulfilling Liquidity Dry-Ups." *Journal of Finance* 69 (2): 947–970.

Mehran, Hamid, and Anjan Thakor. 2011. "Bank Capital and Value in the Cross-Section." *Review of Financial Studies* 15 (2): 277–300.

Merton, Robert C. 1993. "Operation and Regulation in Financial Intermediation: A Functional Perspective." In *Operation and Regulation of Financial Markets*, edited by Peter Englund, 17–67. Stockholm: The Economic Council.

Merton, Robert C. 1995. "A Functional Perspective of Financial Intermediation." *Financial Management* 24 (2): 23–41.

Merton, Robert, and Richard Thakor. Forthcoming. "Customers and Investors: A Framework for Understanding the Evolution of Financial Institutions." NBER Working Paper no. 21258.

Peek, Joel, and Eric Rosengren. 2000. "Collateral Damage: Effects of the Japanese Banking Crisis on Real Activity in the United States." *American Economic Review* 90 (1): 30–45.

Perignon, Christophe, David Thesmar, and Guillaume Vuillemey. 2018. "Wholesale Funding Dry-Ups." *Journal of Finance* 73 (2): 575–617.

Puri, Manju, Jorg Rocholl, and Sascha Steffen. 2011. "Global Retail Lending in the Aftermath of the U.S. Financial Crisis: Distinguishing Between Supply and Demand Effects." *Journal of Financial Economics* 100:556–578.

Purnanandam, Amiyatosh. 2011. "Originate-to-Distribute Model and the Subprime Crisis." *Review of Financial Studies* 100 (5): 1881–1915.

Song, Fenghua and Anjan Thakor. Forthcoming. "Bank Culture." *Journal of Financial Intermediation*.

Thakor, Anjan. 2018. "Post-Crisis Regulatory Reform in Banking: Address Insolvency Risk, Not Illiquidity!" *Journal of Financial Stability* 37:107–111.

Thakor, Anjan V. 2014a. "Bank Capital and Financial Stability: An Economic Tradeoff or a Faustian Bargain?" *Annual Review of Financial Economics* 6:185–223.

Thakor, Anjan V. 2014b. "Leverage, Systemic Risk and Financial Health: How Do We Develop a Healthy Financial System?" In *Governance, Regulation and Bank Stability*, edited by Ted Lindblom, S. Sjogren, and M. Willesson, 9–19. Basingstoke, UK: Palgrave MacMillan.

10

Closing Curtain

SHOULD BANKING BE FUNDAMENTALLY REDESIGNED?

Introduction

Single-minute exchange of die (SMED) is a manufacturing process designed to improve efficiency by permitting a quick and seamless transition from manufacturing one product to the next. It has had a profound effect on automobile manufacturing. Until the SMED transformed automobile manufacturing in the 1970s, it took car makers between two and eight hours to change from making one model of a car to another in the same manufacturing facility. The longer the changeover time, the greater the production time lost, so the higher is the cost of manufacturing. Losing up to one whole shift every day was very expensive. This was a big problem for car manufacturers like Toyota.

One of Toyota's consultants, Shigeo Shingo, came up with the SMED innovation, leading to just-in-time manufacturing that reduced changeover time from many hours to just three minutes by the 1970s. This was not just an improvement in the manufacturing process—it was a revolution.

So it is with banking. We can either talk about improving banking for stability and growth or we can talk about transforming banking. Recently, there was an attempt in Switzerland to achieve such a transformation.

The *Wall Street Journal* of June 2–3, 2018, reported:

A Shocking Challenge to the Banking System
A decade after the collapse of Lehman Brothers, the world is still debating the causes of the financial crisis—down to the meaning of money itself.

In buttoned-down Switzerland, the debate is taking the form of a nationwide referendum set for June 10. Voters are being asked to consider fundamental questions rooted in the crisis: What is money; who creates it; and how safe is it? And they'll have a chance to blow up one of the foundational features of global finance: the ability of banks to create money with just a few keystrokes.

That's right: now, if a bank gives you a loan, it can pretty much create the money on the spot. It's something that banks do every day around the world.

But if the Swiss referendum passes, all money creation there would have to be done directly by the country's central bank.

Under the current system, when a borrower is approved for a mortgage, the bank doesn't take existing money from a vault. Instead, it creates an electronic deposit for the borrower, which the borrower transfers to the seller's bank account. Much of the growth in money in circulation is through bank-created deposits. . . .

Of the 645 billion Swiss francs (about $652 billion) in circulation, only about 85 billion francs are notes and coins.[1]

The referendum was defeated, so those who were shocked by the idea of money creation being taken away from banks breathed a sigh of relief. Recall our earlier discussion of the evolution of the goldsmith into a bank via the creation of fake receipts. Banks create money simply by lending what they do not have as cash in their vaults, in a manner similar to the goldsmith issuing fake warehouse receipts. The Swiss referendum was an attempt to take away banks' ability to create money through this mechanism. The quote above sheds light on how big this mechanism is—out of the 645 billion francs of Swiss money in circulation, 540 billion Swiss francs is money generated by bank-created deposits or fake receipts. So why was there interest in Switzerland in putting an end to money creation by banks?

To understand the Swiss motivation, let us briefly revisit the history of money-creating banks. For as long as people can remember, banks have taken in deposits and made loans. A large fraction of the deposits can be withdrawn on demand, which allows deposits to serve the transaction and liquidity needs of individuals and businesses, permits checks to be written against bank deposits, and makes banks an integral part of the payments system. However, the ability of demand depositors to withdraw at a moment's notice also renders banks inherently fragile. Either sunspots or (more realistically) the slightest whiff of insolvency-related trouble can cause a sharp decline in the bank's deposit base due to a bank run.[2] The failure of an individual bank can lead to possibly erroneous inferences by the depositors of other banks, generating contagion in bank runs and failures.[3] This poses an unacceptable threat to the payments system, so it typically invites federal intervention in the form of deposit insurance and bailouts that protect even the interests of de jure uninsured creditors of the bank. In turn, this creates moral hazard, as banks have incentives to pursue risk and have correlated asset choices and high leverage,[4] which then makes financial crises more likely. As researchers have noted,[5] over the past eight hundred years financial crises have been recurring and have had a disturbingly familiar look—asset price bubbles and highly leveraged banks that fail when the price bubble bursts. And the cost to taxpayers of these financial crises has been growing exponentially. As discussed earlier, the 2007–2009 subprime crisis cost US taxpayers an estimated \$6–14 trillion in direct costs,[6] and about \$22 trillion overall.

Banks are at the heart of most financial crises, and it is the collective actions of banks—endogenous choices rather than "acts of God"—that generate these crises. The approach to solving the problem thus far has been to create an increasingly complex system of regulations that limit, proscribe, and direct banking activities to reduce the probability of banks making decisions that increase the likelihood of crises. A major problem with this approach is that the net private benefits to banks from such regulations are typically smaller than the social benefits, so banks have incentives to innovate and come up with ways to circumvent the restrictions imposed on them. Absent a clear prosocial higher purpose and a culture that helps to make this higher purpose the arbitrator of all decisions, these incentives to circumvent regulation and take more risk dominate bank behavior. Like organisms responding to environmental constraints, banks evolve, but it is evolution designed to make regulation less binding. Eventually, another crisis occurs, regulators respond with a wider and more complex web of regulations, and the endless game of cat-and-mouse goes on. The result is a highly complex regulatory structure that is costly to administer, and an opaque banking industry that few understand. Even bank directors and stock analysts who follow banks admit that the complexity and opacity of large banks make it difficult to assess the implications of new information that emerges about these banks.

The Swiss proposal was an attempt to overcome these problems. In the next section, I will describe what a new banking system that has elements of the Swiss proposal would look like, how it compares to the existing system, and what its economic rationale might be. The reason for this deep dive is that variants of the Swiss proposal have been discussed elsewhere (e.g., Iceland),

and I suspect they will resurface in the future. The stakes are high—banks are even more important to us than the electronic devices we are addicted to—so I believe attempts to change the system for greater stability will continue.

Preview of a New Design

One not-so-publicized implication of the existing research that focuses on the role of liquidity risk in banking crises is that the role of individual banks as gatherers of deposits should be eliminated entirely, since this is the root cause of banking instability. If banks do not have deposits, presto—no more bank runs! Instead of going to individual banks, individuals and businesses will deposit directly with the central bank, which will then direct these deposits to qualifying banks, conditional on these banks satisfying capital structure and other regulatory restrictions. That is, the liquidity warehousing and safekeeping function is transferred to the central bank. In essence, banks will make loans only with "real" (fiat) money borrowed from the central bank, not with bank-created deposits. Other than deposits, banks will raise all their financing—subordinated debt, preferred stock, and equity—as they do in the present system. There is effectively complete deposit insurance, because the central bank is the counterparty for all depositors and hence guarantees the promised repayment to depositors regardless of the size of the deposit.[7] Because there are no bank runs, contagion becomes moot. The deposit interest rate for any given maturity can be set by the central bank or determined via an auction in which banks bid for deposits. Banks would continue to function on the asset side of their balance sheets pretty much the way they do now, making the loans and investing in the securities permissible in the current system.

This is the boldest and most important part of the new architecture. There are other details, to be sure. These are related to questions about whether and how banks can fail, how they should be regulated, the role of market discipline, capital flows, the impact on the payment system, the relationship to shadow banking, and so on. Many of these issues can be dealt with as discussed in the previous chapters, but I will also discuss some of these issues here. Moreover, I will also discuss the potential objections to the proposed design, and I will end with my views on whether we should indeed adopt such a system.

One attractive feature of the new design is a lower likelihood of fire sales and a substantial reduction in the contingent liability of taxpayers in providing a public safety net for banks. Despite its putative benefits in limiting the contagion inherent in bank failures, it is now becoming clear that deposit insurance—as presently designed and implemented—is very costly. And it also induces numerous inefficiencies that in the end make financial crises more precipitous and protracted.[8] There are economic reasons why the overall contingent liability of the central bank under the proposed scheme might be lower than the contingent liability of the government under the existing deposit insurance scheme.

I will explain this in greater detail later, but I want to note at this point that the core assumption that drives the economic motivation for the new proposal is that liquidity risk is pivotal in generating banking crises. This is basically the risk that a bank might suddenly experience a deposit outflow and fail as a result, even though its asset quality (and hence its insolvency risk) had not changed, and that this, in turn, might cause runs on other banks. The proposed design is mainly an attempt to eliminate liquidity risk.

The Proposed New Banking System

Let me begin by revisiting key features of the existing system and then using this as the benchmark to which the new proposed system is compared.

The Existing System

In figure 10.1, I pictorially summarize the existing banking system in the United States and many other developed countries. This figure emphasizes the relatively independent nature of deposit inflows—absent contagion

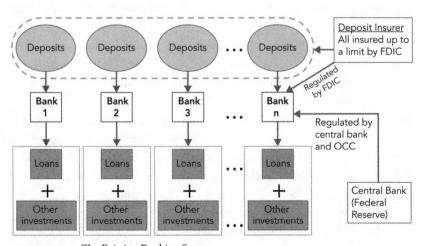

FIGURE 10.1 The Existing Banking System.

during financial crises—to individual banks and the segmented nature of bank regulation.

The figure is self-explanatory. The key points to note are, first, that each bank's deposits are treated as being distinct from any other bank's deposits and insured that way by the FDIC and, second, that each bank's investments in loans and securities, as well as its ability to sustain the size of its balance sheet with those investments, are determined significantly by the size of its own deposit balance at any point in time.

The existing banking system has its roots in the way banks originated centuries ago from warehouses where commodities and precious metals were stored for safekeeping.[9] These traditional banks engaged in relationship lending, in which combining deposit taking and lending, in conjunction with the sale of loan commitments and the provision of cash management and other services, generated economic benefits through synergies.[10] These sorts of benefits are still important for banks, so I will consider them later when I assess the overall merits of the new design.

The existing system reflects the traditional role banks played in serving as the "plumbing" for the payments system. Banks literally provided the physical infrastructure for the financial system. However, this role has been diminishing, as other institutions—including those in shadow banking— have arisen to provide money-like claims that serve as close substitutes for fiat money. As a consequence, banks are now part of a much broader and more fluid financial landscape. Yet they remain the most important players.

If we embrace the view, for now, that liquidity risk—sudden deposit outflows for reasons unrelated to bank solvency risk—is important,[11] then the existing system has a major disadvantage. This disadvantage arises from the fact that the federal deposit insurer provides deposit insurance for *all* (insured) banks, and yet the insurance is provided to the individual depositors of *each* bank. This robs the deposit insurer of a lot of the benefit of pooling and diversification, since the insurer has a liability when a bank suffers a negative deposit supply shock but no offsetting benefit—other than the absence of a liability—when some other bank experiences a positive deposit supply shock. In other words, if people pull their deposits out of a bank in Omaha and put them in a bank in St. Louis, causing the Omaha bank to fail, the FDIC is liable to cover the claims of the failed bank's depositors, but it derives little benefit from the inflow of deposits in the St. Louis bank.

If the government is going to insure all deposits anyway, it seems awfully convoluted to design a system in which all deposits do not flow into the coffers of the deposit insurer for subsequent redistribution.

This drawback can be avoided by centralizing deposits. In figure 10.2, I pictorially summarize the new proposed scheme.

The Basic Design: Under the proposed new system, the central bank is the repository for all deposits in the economy. One can imagine central bank branches all over the country accepting consumer and business deposits, in much the same way that commercial bank branches accept deposits today. Each commercial bank would then have to borrow the deposits it wants from the central bank. In essence, each bank can make loans only with fiat money. The central bank can set the prices and quantities of deposits supplied to different banks, as well as other terms of lending. Prices can be determined via an auction or set by some body akin to the Federal Open Market Committee. One could actually think of this as fed funds loans.

The other terms of lending would include capital requirements. Thus, for example, if there is a 10 percent leverage ratio, then to obtain an additional $9 in deposits from the central bank, the requesting bank would have to show that there is $1 in additional funding being provided by equity, so that the incremental $10 in assets on the balance sheet will be accompanied by an addition of $1 in equity.[12] Risk-based capital requirements can be included along with a leverage ratio, as in the present system.

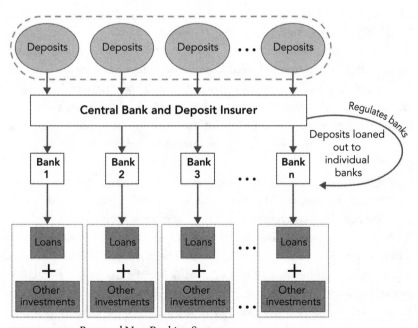

FIGURE 10.2 Proposed New Banking System.

The central bank could also prohibit certain investments by the bank and could employ credit-allocation directives as in the present system.[13] Deposits would be fully insured, and all claims by depositors would be on the central bank. Thus, this scheme effectively combines the Federal Reserve and the FDIC into a single entity. The central bank would supervise banks to ensure that they are managing their risks prudently.

Mutual funds and other institutions could issue money-like claims, but they would not have access to the central bank's "deposit window," meaning they would essentially be issuing uninsured, money-like claims, as in the present system.

Implications for the Payment System: The risk-free nature of deposits would be transparent due to the claims of depositors being on the central bank. All the risk-sharing benefits of (demand) deposits would be maintained without any need to make the bank opaque by having it withhold information about its assets.[14] The payment system would be safeguarded because it would effectively be run by the central bank.

Non-bank payment systems can also be easily accommodated harmoniously. One can imagine players in these alternative payment systems (e.g., PayPal) depositing their aggregate balances with the central bank. This can improve on the present situation in which these alternative payment systems are necessarily linked to banks—for example, at present one needs to have a bank account when using PayPal.

Ability of Banks to Create Deposits through Lending: Although people usually think of deposits creating loans, recent research has highlighted that the causality is often reversed—banks create deposits when they make loans.[15] Under the proposed scheme, the creation of a deposit account in the process of lending will require the bank to purchase fed funds from the central bank. In other words, the depositor of the bank will be the central bank itself. Liquidity creation via fake receipts issued by banks would no longer be possible.

Liquidity and Insolvency Risks for Banks: Access to the "deposit window" at the central bank means that banks no longer have to deal with liquidity risk. The central bank can make use of cross-sectional smoothing of deposit supply shocks in different geographies. Thus, if one region experiences a large deposit outflow, it can be offset by a large deposit inflow in another region. What still remains, of course, is bank-specific insolvency risk. Banks can still fail due to this risk. But since these failures are now primarily due to insolvency problems, the inability of the central bank to distinguish between insolvency and illiquidity in real time in deciding whether to intervene in a bank failure is no longer a challenge.[16] Central bank intervention can therefore be based on a clear identification of insolvency concerns as being the driver of the bank's impending failure.[17] Essentially, this scheme provides banks with "liquidity insurance," as long as there is sufficient capital to ensure solvency, thereby eliminating the need for large unproductive liquidity buffers. An added benefit of this will be that these liquidity buffers will be more productively channeled into lending by banks, increasing credit supply for borrowers.

Non-Deposit Funding for Banks: Banks would no longer have a need for wholesale funding—that is purchased (uninsured) jumbo deposits. They would continue to raise financing from non-depository sources— subordinated debt, preferred stock, and equity—as they do at present.

Money-Market Funds (MMFs) and Quasi-Deposits: Claims similar to deposits, like claims on MMFs, would be uninsured alternatives to (central) bank deposits. However, banks would no longer be dependent on any form of financing from MMFs, so there would be little reason for the central bank to intervene in case insolvency concerns about MMFs induced fund outflows. If banks wished to continue to provide funding to institutions in the shadow banking system through repos, they would be able to do so.

Regulatory Portfolio Restrictions on Banks and Credit-Allocation Directives: I see little reason for any major changes in the asset portfolio restrictions that regulation currently imposes on banks. Moreover, credit- allocation directives like the Community Reinvestment Act may be continued, but the way these regulations are defined will obviously have to be altered, since it will no longer be possible to define geographic areas (metropolitan statistical areas) from which specific banks raise their deposits.

The Advantages of the New System

As you read my discussion of the proposed advantages, keep in mind that a central predicate of this whole discussion is that liquidity risk is the main problem we are trying to solve. The principal advantages of the proposed banking system are:

1. Diminished liquidity risk and lower likelihood of asset fire sales
2. Greater transparency and better market discipline
3. More effective protection of depositors and better risk sharing
4. Enhanced ability of the central bank to deal with "too big to fail" (TBTF)
5. A better protected payments system

6. Reduced volatility of capital flows
7. Elimination of liquidity requirements on banks

I will now discuss each of the above.

   1. Diminished liquidity risk and lower likelihood of fire sales: As I explained earlier, the accumulation of all deposits at the central bank means that bank-specific deposit supply shocks can be diversified to a substantial extent. At present, this diversification is achieved indirectly through the federal funds market in which banks with surplus liquidity lend it to banks with a shortage of liquidity. Not only is the proposed scheme a much more direct way to achieve what the fed funds market achieves, but it also avoids the problem of the fed funds market itself experiencing hiccups that would lead to episodes of insufficient liquidity in the system.[18] The central bank can enable any individual bank to overcome a decline in its short-term funding at any point in time. Even if a large number of banks face correlated declines in their short-term non-deposit funding due to their insolvency risk, the central bank can continue to provide enough deposit funding, as long as these banks are willing to put up the necessary equity. This way, reductions in lending as well as fire sales by these banks can be avoided.

   2. Greater transparency and better market discipline: The proposed banking system also facilitates greater transparency. Because no individual bank faces the risk of a deposit runoff due to the disclosure of adverse information about the bank, the central bank should feel far less constrained in revealing the results of bank examinations and stress tests, no matter how adverse. Similarly, banks themselves are likely to voluntarily disclose more information, because they are assured that this will not adversely affect the availability of deposits.

   Transparency has obvious benefits when it comes to the cost of capital for banks. Opaqueness increases the "lemons premium" in the cost of external financing.[19] Banks often point out that an increase in capital requirements damages banks, because they face a high equity cost of capital.[20] One reason for this high equity cost of capital is, of course, the very high leverage that banks typically operate with. Another reason may be that banks are often viewed as being more opaque to investors than most other firms, and regulators are reluctant to compel them to disclose more because of the fear that greater transparency could lead to deposit runoffs and greater fragility. This fear vanishes under the proposed banking system.

   3. More effective protection of depositors and better risk sharing: A significant benefit of the proposed banking system is that depositors will exhibit *no* concern with the financial health of any bank. Systemic risk may still be an issue, in the sense that if depositors view the entire banking system as having assets with deteriorating values, they might begin to doubt the ability of the central bank to fully repay depositors, and this could precipitate large-scale deposit withdrawals from the central bank. This possibility, which is essentially a form of sovereign risk, undeniably exists for many countries. But it is not a significant concern for the United States.

If depositors are unconcerned about the financial health of any bank and view their claims as being truly riskless, two issues are dealt with effectively. First, the so-called shortage of riskless assets like Treasuries that has been extensively discussed since the financial crisis[21] would all but disappear. This is because a deposit with the central bank is like purchasing a Treasury security that can be redeemed on demand by presenting it to the government. Second, because their claims would be riskless, depositors would be able to make use of perfect risk sharing. Moreover, this would be possible regardless of how transparent the bank is, so we would not need banks to be opaque to preserve depositor risk sharing.

An additional implication of riskless deposits is that depositors would be immune to any individual bank's credit risk.[22]

4. Enhanced ability of the central bank to deal with "too big to fail" (TBTF): TBTF emerged as a major issue during the financial crisis, and reducing/eliminating taxpayer-funded bailouts of TBTF institutions was a goal of the Dodd-Frank Act. A major contention in the TBTF debate is that the TBTF policy encourages large and complex institutions to be excessively leveraged and take excessive risk. But TBTF is not easy to eliminate because of a fundamental time inconsistency problem. Regulators may wish to precommit to not treat any institution as TBTF, but in the face of the prospect of system-wide contagion due to the impending failure of a systemically important institution, bailing out the institution is often viewed as compelling at the time.[23]

Under the proposed new system, problems of TBTF are considerably simplified. The location of deposits with the central bank means that there is much less fear of contagion due to the failure of an individual institution, no matter how large. This means that when an institution is faced with failure, the reason will be insolvency, and the central bank—freed from any confounding of insolvency and illiquidity risks—can choose to help the bank put more equity capital on its balance sheet to reduce insolvency risk or let the bank fail if this equity infusion is not forthcoming.

5. A better protected payment system: The proposal also enhances the safety of the payment system. The reduction of deposit withdrawal risk means that the part of the payment system that is linked to bank deposits will be safer. A simple example is to consider what would have happened in Greece during the tumultuous summer of 2015 if Greek citizens had deposited their euros directly with the ECB rather than with individual Greek banks. There would have been no need for the suspension of convertibility, restrictions on the size of deposit withdrawals, and other disruptions that occurred. The insolvency concerns related to Greek banks could have been dealt with separately from issues related to the bank-dependent payment system in Greece.

6. Reduced volatility of capital flows: A key problem in today's financial system is that capital markets are very fluid and there is high volatility in capital flows. These volatile capital flows sometimes result in runs, like the repo runs we observed in shadow banking during the 2007–2009 financial crisis. Often these capital flows are in response to shifts in market sentiment or irrational changes in beliefs,[24] and are therefore quite destructive.

The pivotal role for the central bank in determining the distribution of bank deposits in this proposal would transparently lead to lower volatility in capital flows.

7. Elimination of Liquidity Requirements on Banks: Subsequent to the 2007–2009 crisis, the Basel III Accord came up with new requirements to reduce the vulnerability of banks to another crisis. One of these is a liquidity requirement that consists of two ratios that banks must maintain to make sure they are sufficiently liquid. Essentially, compliance with these ratios is viewed as ensuring that banks can withstand a drying up of short-term funding for a while. I have argued in detail in a research paper that these liquidity ratios are misguided and are the result of a misreading of the crisis.[25] Moreover, they actually do harm, since they freeze loanable bank funds into immobility, and sometimes a great deal of funds. Consider JP Morgan Chase in 2016. It held $524 billion in "high quality liquid assets"—read "not loans"—on a $1.3 trillion deposit base. What a staggering waste of the bank's lending capacity! Under the proposed scheme, liquidity requirements would be unnecessary, and these funds could be productively invested in the economy.

Connections to Other Proposals

Perhaps the earliest plan similar to this proposal is called the "Chicago plan."[26] While several variations exist, the common element is that the power to create money is separated from the power to distribute it. Commercial banks retain the latter power and continue to provide a range of asset-side services, but deposit accounts rest with the central bank. A recent report commissioned by the prime minister of Iceland proposes investigating the merits of a "sovereign" money system in which commercial banks would not be allowed to create money.[27] This power would be exclusively with the central bank. The proposal shares many features with the Swiss referendum and the proposal discussed here.

Another proposal that is worth comparing this proposal to is "narrow banking."[28] With narrow banking, the bank is provided access to insured deposits but is restricted to investing in very safe securities—like US Treasury bonds—on the asset side. That is, the word "narrow" refers to what the bank can do on the asset side of its balance sheet—no lending. In terms of the three economic functions of banks that I first alluded to in chapter 1, banks would *not* serve the functions of creating funding liquidity and protecting the confidentiality of their borrowers' information. They could still provide warehousing and safeguarding of cash and securities and help to reduce verification costs in contracting. Narrow banking thus addresses the insolvency problem that causes banks to fail.

By contrast, the proposal here addresses the illiquidity problem that many still believe was a big factor in the 2007–2009 crisis. Indeed, by removing the illiquidity problem from the picture, this proposal allows the central bank to focus squarely on just the insolvency problem without denying banks the ability to provide the economic services of screening and monitoring borrowers and reducing informational frictions.

Possible Objections to the Proposed Scheme

The proposed scheme is not without its drawbacks. I discuss them next, keeping the most important objection for last.

1. Greater power in the hands of a public authority, and the specter of politics
2. Privacy concerns
3. Possible misallocation of deposits by the central bank
4. Banks losing deposit-related rents
5. Potential loss of synergies between the asset and liability sides of the bank's balance sheet and deposit-related services provided by banks, including money creation
6. Addressing the "wrong" problem

I now discuss each of these in turn.

1. Greater power in the hands of a public authority and the specter of politics: It is not only libertarians who may object to this proposal on the grounds that it puts more power in the hands of the central bank, a public authority. It seems to smack of greater de facto control of the financial system by a quasi-government agency.[29] Some shudder at the idea of the government knowing every deposit and every withdrawal an individual makes. What if one wants to write a check to donate to a political party opposed to the one in power?

Of course, politics intrudes into banking even today. To see this, consider the point made by Ed Kane[30] and even more forcefully by Charles Calomiris and Stephen Haber in their book[31] that a nation's banking system is essentially the outcome of political forces. Kane hypothesizes that political reasons lead most countries (including the United States) to establish a regulatory culture that involves politically directed subsidies to some groups of borrowers. Moreover, this is accompanied by a politically motivated design of bank regulation that undermines the quality of bank supervision and eventually leads to financial crises. In their book, Calomiris and Haber point out that not only is politics an integral part of banking in all countries, but it also determines whether societies suffer repeated banking crises (like Argentina and the United States) or never suffer banking crises (like Canada).

As I discussed in the earlier chapters, not only did the intrusion of politics into banking play a role in the last crisis, but it also tends to skew the allocation of bank credit on the basis of the political ideology and preferences of the party in power even during normal, non-crisis times. Concerns that politics may influence the way the central bank allocates deposits to banks in different regions cannot be taken lightly. The system would need a huge amount of central bank transparency and mechanical rules of deposit disbursement that leave the central bank with little discretion. But this is not without cost either. Tying the hands of the central bank deprives it of policy flexibility to deal with unanticipated events.

2. Privacy concerns: Centralizing deposits with a quasi-government agency raises obvious privacy concerns. Of course, tax authorities like the IRS already know a lot about us. But centralizing all bank deposits at the central bank takes this loss of privacy to a different level—it has the feel of giving the government a mechanism to peek into one's bedroom.

3. The central bank misallocating deposits: An obvious question that arises with my proposal is: how will the central bank determine how to allocate deposits across banks? One way for the Federal Reserve to do this would be to create an auction in which deposits are priced and allocated to banks based on supply and demand, with pre-specified eligibility requirements, akin to those for discount window borrowing, as well as capital requirements. Even if the deposit interest rate is set by the Federal Reserve through some process, say, one that is similar to that used by the Federal Open Market Committee (FOMC), the system could work. Of course, determining quantity allocations in the absence of an auction may be challenging. Could politics influence this allocation as well?

4. Banks losing deposit-related rents: It is widely believed that banks earn rents because they have access to deposits, especially core deposits. Some of these rents arise because banks are able to obtain these deposits relatively cheaply due to deposit insurance, among other things. From a social welfare standpoint, it is not clear that these rents should go entirely to banks, but research has found that the availability of deposit-related rents can induce banks to make more prudent asset choices and be more trustworthy lenders than non-banks,[32] a point I will return to in the final chapter. In any case, this is an issue related to how a given surplus should be divided between banks and the safety net provider. The setting of the deposit interest rate by the central bank can achieve any desired division. The bigger issue is whether the central bank can provide depositors all of the services they consume as effectively as profit-maximizing banks, competing for deposits, are currently doing. There is good reason to question this in light of the performance of the public sector relative to the private sector in other industries.

5. Potential loss of synergies between the depository and lending activities of the bank: It has been pointed out that the reason why depository institutions dominate the loan commitment market is that keeping on-balance-sheet liquidity is costly for an institution, and both deposit taking and selling loan commitments require the institution to keep such liquidity.[33] Thus, there are economies of scope in using this liquidity to meet deposit withdrawals as well as loan commitment takedowns. This is a specific example of the more general point that there are synergies for banks between deposit taking and lending. That is, loan commitments aside, if a bank's borrowers are also its depositors, there are two benefits. One is that the borrower's depository history provides valuable information to the bank that is considering a relationship loan to that borrower.[34] A second benefit is that when a borrower with a deposit account at the bank defaults on a loan, the bank can claim the deposits as repayment using the concept of "banker's offset." This strengthens the borrower's repayment incentive.[35] It is an important economic benefit of having banks create money through the deposit taking and lending process.

The proposed system would take away this economic benefit and the resulting advantage banks have over non-depository lenders in the credit market.

6. Addressing the "wrong" problem: As I mentioned earlier, the wisdom of this proposal stems from its ability to eliminate bank-specific liquidity risk, which is related to the likelihood that so many depositors at a given bank have an urgent need for liquidity that the bank is unable to meet their withdrawal demands and a bank with healthy assets fails. This bank run could cause panic runs on other banks, causing a crisis. The reason this proposal has gained some traction in countries like Iceland and Switzerland is the belief that the 2007–2009 crisis was a liquidity risk crisis. So more modest proposals like Basel III seek to address the problem through liquidity requirements, and more dramatic proposals like the one here propose to take away from banks their ability to create money. Both initiatives are based on a misreading of the 2007–2009 crisis that it was a liquidity risk crisis. I have presented compelling evidence in previous chapters that the Great Recession was caused by an insolvency risk crisis. The new proposal does not address insolvency risk directly.

So Should We Go for the Proposed System?

If liquidity crises in banking are a big concern, as so many people believe, then the research that has focused on this problem would suggest that something similar to what has been proposed would get rid of the problem. So there is much to like about this proposal if you are a proponent of the liquidity risk view of financial crises.

Nonetheless, I do not endorse this proposal as the new banking system we should adopt. I have four main reasons that are related to the drawbacks discussed above.

Reason no. 1: The first is politics, combined with the inherent inefficiency of public sector institutions compared to private sector institutions. Even with an independent central bank, there may be valid reasons to worry about a quasi-government agency having such control over every bank's deposit supply and the political temptations that may arise.

While there is quite a bit of research on the political economy of banking, most of it is empirical. That is, researchers have analyzed data on how politics affects the allocation of credit by both state-owned and private banks, especially during elections and when there is a change in government.[36] But our foundational theories of the economic functions that banks serve assign no role to politics or the importance of privacy for depositors who may be averse to giving the government really granular, real-time access to all of their financials. The government is viewed merely as a benevolent provider of safety-net guarantees to improve outcomes, and banks are viewed as institutions that protect the confidentiality of information about their borrowers.[37] As we saw earlier, trust is a very important aspect of the relationship customers have with their banks, and many do not trust politically influenced governments as much as they trust their banks.

Add to this the situation that bank branches that gather deposits would be central bank branches rather than branches of profit-maximizing banks. Would the government-run branches provide depositors service of the same quality that banks do today? There are at least two reasons why we might think not. One is that there would not be the kind of competition between the branches of the central bank that we have between the branches of different banks now. The other is that it is not easy for government agencies to replicate private-sector high-powered incentives for individuals to exhibit high performance, given the constraints of civil service wage schemes.

Reason no. 2: The second reason is the loss of synergies from having borrowers being depositors of the same bank. These can be quite substantial.

Reason no. 3: Third, there is the issue of privacy for depositors. I suspect that many would recoil at the idea of a quasi-government institution being able to look, in real time, at every deposit and withdrawal of every individual who uses the banking system. Because the Federal Reserve plays a key role in the payment system even today, it has access to more information about individuals and businesses than most people realize. But at the very least, the optics of the proposed system seem to take it to another level.

How much do people care about privacy? The research on this has found that:[38]

- People say they care about privacy but are willing to relinquish private information when incentivized to do so.
- Small costs (of protecting privacy) can cause consumers' actual choices about privacy to deviate from their stated preferences.
- The introduction of irrelevant but reassuring information about privacy protection makes consumers less likely to avoid surveillance regardless of their stated preferences for privacy. Perhaps this is why private entities like Google, Facebook, and Apple seem to flourish in personal data collection without much objection from those whose data they collect.

It appears, then, that perhaps privacy concerns may not be such a big deal after all, but they still remain a potential cause for reticence to endorse the proposed system.

Reason no. 4: Finally, as I have explained earlier, I do not believe that any of the banking crises we have seen in recent times have been illiquidity crises. If I believed they were, I would be more inclined to endorse the proposed new system. But since the bulk of the empirical evidence points out that what we have experienced were insolvency risk crises, the banking system improvement proposal discussed in the previous chapter may be the way to go. However, for those who still hold on to the view that the 2007–2009 crisis was an illiquidity risk crisis, the proposed new system should be very attractive. I, however, believe it is more important to address insolvency risk, and this can be done through higher capital requirements and strengthening bank culture, while letting banks keep their money-creation function.

Summing Up

In the wake of the 2007–2009 crisis, a radical proposal to transform banking and eliminate bank runs has been put forth. This proposal has been discussed in this chapter.

The proposed new banking system eliminates bank-level deposit gathering and replaces it with all deposits being collected directly by the central bank and then distributed to banks. The non-depository financing of the bank and its lending would remain unchanged. This proposal seeks to eliminate bank-specific liquidity risk. And this it would do very well, while also making the banking system more transparent, providing greater protection for the payment system. But possibly the biggest concerns about it are politics, the potential loss of efficiency in providing depository services by moving away from profit-maximizing banks serving depositors, and the fact that it seems to solve the wrong problem. The proposal is motivated by the view that the 2007–2009 crisis was a liquidity crisis. It was not. It was an insolvency risk crisis. To address insolvency risk, we need much more capital in banking.

Another drawback of the proposed system is that financial system diversity helps create a healthier financial system, and centralization of deposit taking in central banks will lead to less diversity and hence greater risk. For this reason, it is important to continue to have smaller, grass-roots depositories like credit unions and community banks as deposit-gathering intermediaries.

Notes

1. Blackstone 2018.
2. See Bryant 1980, Diamond and Dybvig 1983, and Chari and Jagannathan 1988.
3. See Acharya and Thakor 2016.
4. This means that banks not only invest in risky loans and securities, but they end up with very similar asset portfolios, so if things go badly, they are all financially distressed together. In these circumstances, regulators may wish to bail them all out to avoid a collapse of the whole system. See Merton 1977 for an analysis of how deposit insurance induces banks to be very highly leveraged.
5. See the account of financial crises in Reinhart and Rogoff 2009.
6. See Luttrell, Atkinson, and Rosenblum 2013.
7. This means there would be no contagion-related bank failures through depositors (see Acharya and Thakor 2016).
8. See Demirgüç-Kunt and Detragiache 1999 provide evidence that the recessions following the 2007–2009 crisis were worse and more prolonged in countries with more extensive public safety nets for banks.
9. See Greenbaum, Thakor, and Boot 2015 and Donaldson, Piacentino, and Thakor 2018.
10. Kashyap, Rajan, and Stein 2002 show that banks can take advantage of synergies between selling loan commitments and accepting demand deposits, since both require keeping cash on hand. Song and Thakor 2007 develop a model in which banks that make relationship loans find it optimal to fund them with (core) demand deposits, and banks that make transaction loans find it optimal to fund them with purchased money. How well banks perform their role in providing these services has repercussions for the capital market, as shown by Song and Thakor (2010) who show that banks not only compete with markets, but they also complement them.
11. This is the view in Diamond and Dybvig 1983 and the literature that has developed subsequently using that model.
12. Assuming the capital requirement on the bank was binding prior to the new deposit inflow.
13. For example, the Community Reinvestment Act.
14. As, for example, in Dang, Gorton, Holmström, and Ordoñez 2017.
15. See Donaldson, Piacentino, and Thakor 2018.
16. See Farhi and Tirole 2012, who point out that this confounding of insolvency and illiquidity can lead the central bank to erroneously intervene and provide liquidity to insolvent banks. The view in the literature on central banking, referred to as the "Bagehot rule," is that the central bank, in its role as a lender of last resort, should help a bank out only when the bank is illiquid, not when it is insolvent. See Acharya and Thakor 2016.
17. See Taylor 2009 for a discussion of how the Federal Reserve's initial view that the 2007–2009 crisis was a liquidity crisis caused it to undertake initiatives initially that proved ineffective.

18. Allen and Gale 2000 develop a model in which the fed funds market diversifies away small shocks to bank deposits well but actually makes things worse when a few banks suffer large shocks that are then transmitted through the whole system. Allen and Carletti (2008) discus how mark-to-market accounting exacerbates the propagation of negative shocks across banks.

19. See Myers and Majluf 1984 and Thakor 2015.

20. See, for example, Thakor 2014.

21. See, for example, Krishnamurthy and Vissing Jorgensen 2012.

22. Merton and R. Thakor, forthcoming, argue that the efficient deposit contract from the standpoint of depositors being *customers* of the bank is one that imposes none of the bank's credit risk on the depositors. See also Merton (1993). This is true in the system proposed here.

23. See Acharya and Thakor 2016.

24. See, for example, Shleifer and Vishny 2010 and Gennaioli, Shleifer, and Vishny 2015.

25. See Thakor 2018.

26. See Fisher 1936.

27. See Sigurjonsson 2015.

28. See Pennacchi 2012 and Thakor 2014 for discussions of narrow banking.

29. Goodhart and Jensen 2015 criticize plans like the one I have proposed and refer to them as part of the "currency school." They refer to the existing model as part of the "banking school."

30. See Kane 2015.

31. See Calomiris and Haber 2014.

32. See Merton and R. Thakor 2018.

33. See Kashyap, Rajan, and Stein 2002.

34. Norden and Weber 2010 provide granular empirical evidence on how commercial banks extract information about borrowers from their checking accounts. Ramakrishnan and Thakor (1984) develop a foundational theory of how the ability to improve information processing provides the raison d'etre for banks.

35. See Donaldson, Piacentino, and Thakor 2018 for a theory that has this feature.

36. See, for example, Dinc 2005, Khwaja and Mian 2005, Peek and Rosengren 2005, and Huang and Thakor 2018.

37. See Bhattacharya and Chiesa 1995.

38. See Athey, Catalini, and Tucker 2017. This paper reports the findings of a field experiment with Bitcoin at MIT.

References

Acharya, V., and Anjan Thakor. 2016. "The Dark Side of Liquidity Creation: Leverage Induced Systemic Risk and Implications for the Lender of Last Resort." *Journal of Financial Intermediation* 28:4–21.

Allen, Franklin, and Elena Carletti. 2008. "Mark-to-Market Accounting and Liquidity Pricing." *Journal of Accounting and Economics* 95:358–378.

Allen, Franklin, and Douglas Gale. 2000. "Financial Contagion." *The Journal of Political Economy* 108 (1): 1–33.

Athey, Susan, Christian Catalini, and Catherine Tucker. 2017. "The Digital Privacy Paradox: Small Money, Small Costs, Small Talk." Working Paper, MIT, September 27.

Bhattacharya, Sudipto, and Gabriela Chiesa. 1995. "Proprietary Information, Financial Intermediation, and Research Incentives." *Journal of Financial Intermediation* 4 (4): 328–357.

Blackstone, Brian. 2018. "A Shocking Challenge to the Banking System." *Wall Street Journal*, June 2–3.

Bryant, John. 1980. "A Model of Reserves, Bank Runs and Deposit Insurance." *Journal of Banking and Finance* 4 (4): 335–344.

Calomiris, Charles, and Stephen H. Haber. 2014. *Fragile by Design: The Political Origins of Banking Crises and Scarce Credit*. Princeton, NJ: Princeton University Press.

Chari, V. V., and Ravi Jagannathan. 1988. "Banking Panics, Information and Rational Expectations Equilibrium." *Journal of Finance* 43 (3): 749–761.

Dang, Tri-Vi, Gary Gorton, Bengt Holmström, and Guillermo Ordoñez. 2017. "Banks as Secret Keepers." *American Economic Review* 107 (4): 1005–1029.

Demirgüç-Kunt, Asli, and Enrica Detragiache. 1999. "Does Deposit Insurance Increase Banking System Stability? An Empirical Investigation." World Bank e-Library, November.

Diamond, Douglas W., and Philip H. Dybvig. 1983. "Bank Runs, Deposit Insurance and Liquidity." *Journal of Political Economy* 91 (3): 410–419.

Dinc, I. Serdar. 2005. "Politicians and Banks: Political Influences on Government Owned Banks in Emerging Markets." *Journal of Financial Economics* 77 (2): 453–479.

Donaldson, Jason, Giorgia Piacentino, and Anjan Thakor. 2018. "Warehouse Banking." *Journal of Financial Economics* 129:250–267.

Farhi, Emanuel, and Jean Tirole. 2012. "Collective Moral Hazard, Maturity Mismatch and Systemic Bailouts." *American Economic Review* 102 (1): 60–93.

Fisher, Irvin. 1936. *100% Money*. New York: Adelphi.

Goodhart, Charles A. E., and Meinhard A. Jensen. 2015. A Commentary on Patrizio Laina's "Proposals for Full Reserve Banking." *Economic Thought* 4 (2): 20–31.

Gennaioli, Nicolai, Andrei Shleifer, and Robert Fishny. 2015. "Neglected Risks: The Psychology of Financial Crises." *American Economic Review* 105 (5): 310–314.

Greenbaum, Stuart, Anjan Thakor, and Arnoud Boot. 2015. *Contemporary Financial Intermediation*. 3rd ed. Amsterdam: Elsevier.

Huang, Shen, and Anjan V. Thakor. 2018. "Political Influence on Bank Credit Allocation: Bank Capital Responses, Consumption and Systemic Risk." Working Paper, Washington University in St. Louis, April.

Kane, Edward. 2015 "Regulation and Supervision: An Ethical Perspective." In *The Oxford Handbook on Banking*, 2nd ed., edited by A. Berger, P. Molyneaux, and J Wilson, chapter 21. Oxford: Oxford University Press.

Kashyap, Anil K., Raghuram Rajan, and Jeremy C. Stein. 2002. "Banks as Liquidity Providers: An Explanation for the Co-Existence of Lending and Deposit-Taking." *Journal of Finance* 57 (1): 33–73.

Khwaja, Asim Ijaz, and Atif Mian. 2005. "Do Lenders Favor Politically Connected Firms? Rent Provision in an Emerging Financial Market." *Quarterly Journal of Economics* 120 (4): 1371–1411.

Krishnamurthy, Arvind, and Annette Vissing-Jorgenson. 2012 "The Aggregate Demand for Treasury Debt." *Journal of Political Economy*, 120-2, 233-267.

Luttrell, D., T. Atkinson, and H. Rosenblum. 2013. "Assessing the Costs and Consequences of the 2007–09 Financial Crisis and Its Aftermath." *Federal Reserve Bank of Dallas Economic Letters* 8 (7).

Merton, Robert C. 1977. "An Analytic Derivation of the Cost of Deposit Insurance and Loan Guarantees: An Application of Modern Option Pricing Theory." *Journal of Banking and Finance* 1 (1): 3–11.

Merton, Robert C. 1993. "Operation and Regulation in Financial Intermediation: A Functional Perspective." In *Operation and Regulation of Financial Markets*, edited by P. Englund, 17–67. Stockholm: The Economic Council.

Merton, Robert C., and Richard T. Thakor. Forthcoming. "Customers and Investors: A Framework for Understanding the Evolution of Financial Institutions." NBER WP21258.

Merton, Robert C., and Richard T. Thakor. "Trust in Lending." Working paper, MIT Sloan, August 2018.

Myers, Stewart C., and Nicholas Majluf. 1984. "Corporate Financing and Investment Decisions When Firms Have Information That Investors Do Not Have." *Journal of Financial Economics* 13 (2): 187–221.

Norden, Lars, and Martin Weber. 2010. "Credit Line Usage, Checking Account Activity, and Default Risk of Bank Borrowers." *Review of Financial Studies* 23 (10): 3665–3699.

Peek, Joel, and Eric Rosengren. 2005. "Unnatural Selection: Perverse Incentives and the Misallocation of Credit in Japan." *American Economic Review* 95 (4): 1144–1166.

Pennacchi, George. 2012. "Narrow Banking." *Annual Review of Financial Economics* 4:1–36.

Ramakrishnan, Ram. T. S., and Anjan V. Thakor. 1984. "Information Reliability and a Theory of Financial Intermediation." *Review of Economic Studies* 51 (3): 415–432.

Reinhart, Carmen, and Kenneth Rogoff. 2009. *This Time Is Different: Eight Centuries of Financial Folly*. Princeton, NJ: Princeton University Press.

Shleifer, Andrei, and Robert Vishny. 2010. "Unstable Banking." *Journal of Financial Economics* 97 (3): 306–318.

Sigurjonsson, Frosti. 2015. "Monetary Reform: A Better Monetary System for Iceland." Report Commissioned by the Prime Minister of Iceland, Reykjavik, Iceland.

Song, Fenghua, and Anjan V. Thakor. 2007. "Relationship Banking, Fragility and the Asset-Liability Matching Problem." *Review of Financial Studies* 20 (6): 2129, 2177.

Song, Fenghua, and Anjan Thakor. 2010. "Financial System Architecture and the Co-evolution of Banks and Markets." *Economic Journal* 120 (547): 1021–1055.

Taylor, John B. 2009. "Economic Policy and the Financial Crisis: An Empirical Analysis of What Went Wrong." *Critical Review: A Journal of Politics and Society* 21:341–364.

Thakor, Anjan. 2014. "Bank Capital and Financial Stability: Economic Tradeoff or Faustian Bargain?" *Annual Review of Financial Economics* 6:185–223.

Thakor, Anjan V. 2015. "Strategic Information Disclosure When There Is Fundamental Disagreement." *Journal of Financial Intermediation* 24 (2): 131–153.

Thakor, Anjan. 2018. "Post-Crisis Regulatory Reform in Banking: Focus on Insolvency, Not Illiquidity!" *Journal of Financial Stability* 37, 107–111.

11

Summing Up and Looking Ahead

FINTECH AND BANKING

Introduction

On a recent vacation with some friends, one of my friends mentioned that his daughter had received some Bitcoins as a gift in 2012. The price of a Bitcoin then was between $10 and $15. When we were having the conversation, the price was around $11,500. Clearly, his daughter had made out like the proverbial bandit with that gift! He wondered if I had invested in Bitcoin.

There is obviously a lot of excitement these days not only about Bitcoin, virtual currencies, crypto tokens, and other possible alternatives to traditional fiat currencies, but more broadly about fintech, including P2P lending, and about blockchain technology. But what does it all mean for banking?

Speculation about this abounds. For example, a McKinsey & Company report states:

> Automation is the focus of intense interest in the global banking industry. Many banks are rushing to deploy the latest automation technologies in the hope of delivering the next wave of productivity, cost savings, and improvement in customer experiences. While the results have been mixed thus far, McKinsey expects that early growing pains will ultimately give way to a transformation of banking, with outsized gains for the institutions that master the new capabilities.[1]

Thus, fintech developments are of interest not only because they reflect the evolving impact of technology on financial services but also because they have the potential to transform banking. Thus, in this closing chapter, I will first briefly describe blockchain, Bitcoin, and P2P and then integrate that discussion into thoughts about the future of banking.

The discussion will be a bit speculative, because there is little by way of research on the implications of fintech developments for banking. In closing the book with this chapter, I offer some thoughts on the issues. But in the end, I have more questions than answers.

What Are Blockchain and Bitcoin?

Distributed ledger technology (DLT), of which blockchain is an example, uses cryptographic tools and a distributed consensus process to create a significant innovation in traditional record keeping. That is, Bitcoin is a decentralized and cryptographic ledger of immutable data records that are replicated and distributed to each member/node of a peer-to-peer network.[2] It was invented in 2008 by Satoshi Nakamoto. Bitcoin is also called a cryptocurrency, which means it is a convertible virtual currency.

Any DLT has three features:

- *Veracity:* Multiple copies are made of the entire historical record of ledger entries, and each is verified by consensus.
- *Transparency:* There is a public record of activity that can be seen by all market participants.
- *Disintermediation:* There is a peer-to-peer (P2P) network, so an intermediary (like a bank) is avoided.

Disintermediation is viewed as a major benefit of any DLT, including Bitcoin. The distributed ledger is maintained by its participants, not by a central administrator. Every network participant has an identical copy of the distributed ledger. Based on encrypted technology, changes in the database due to new transactions are grouped together and validated by a network of participants.

The way blockchain works is as follows:

1. *Distributed database:* Each party on a blockchain has access to the entire database and complete history. Each party can verify records of its transaction partners directly.
2. *P2P transmission:* Communication is directly between peers, but each node stores and forwards all information to all other nodes.

3. *Transparency with pseudonymity:* Every transaction is visible to anyone with access to the system. Transactions occur between blockchain addresses.
4. *Irreversibility of records:* Once entered, a record cannot be altered because it is linked to every transaction record that came before.
5. *Computational logic:* Blockchain transactions can be tied to computational logic and programmed, which means transactions can be automatically triggered between nodes.

Blockchain can also raise funds through initial coin offerings (ICOs) at a lower cost than traditional means like initial public offerings (IPOs).

Blockchain can be used for a great many things—cybersecurity, disaster recovery, supply chain, trade finance, title registration, payment processing, loan transactions, document verification, and so on.

What Are the Economic Implications of Blockchain?

Blockchain, like other DLT, affects two key economic costs:[3]

- costs of verification
- costs of networking.

In economic transactions, for an exchange to be executed between market participants, the key attributes of the transaction need to be verified by the parties at various points in time. Blockchain allows participants to perform costless verification, and thus lowers auditing costs.

When DLT is combined with a cryptographic token (like Bitcoin), marketplaces can be "bootstrapped" without involving trusted intermediaries, which means networking or transactions costs can be reduced. Essentially, blockchain is based on trustworthy "pre-trade" transparency. That is, transparency substitutes for the trust that is a central aspect of intermediated transactions.

How will fintech impact banking? Much remains to be learned about this issue, but here I offer some initial thoughts that will hopefully lead to more research.

Use of Digital Currencies Along with Fiat Money: Bitcoin and other cryptocurrencies exist today along with fiat currencies. People use both types of currencies. However, the use of cryptocurrencies is still a small niche practice. What if it grows? Speculations about what will happen if cryptocurrencies grow range from enthusiasm to concern to skepticism. Some think cryptocurrencies will replace fiat currencies. Others worry about potential dangers and are concerned. For example, Randal Quarles, the vice-chairman of the Federal Reserve, warned: "While these digital currencies may not pose major concerns at their current levels of use, more serious financial stability issues may result if they achieve wide-scale usage."

And then there are the skeptics. Carl Icahn, chairman of Icahn Enterprises, said during a CNBC interview in response to a question about Bitcoin: "I just don't get it."

How will fintech impact banking? Much remains to be learned about this issue, but here I offer some initial thoughts on issues like central bank digital currency and P2P versus bank lending that will hopefully inspire future research.

Central Bank Digital Currency: An obvious application of fintech is to the development of a digital currency by the central bank. Rather than viewing things like Bitcoin as a threat, the central bank could simply embrace the technology. This will provide a costless medium of exchange, a stable unit of account, and a secure store of value, and it can be interest bearing.[4] It can eliminate the need for quantitative easing. Moreover, it can facilitate the centralization of deposits at the central bank (recall chapter 10). Bank runs and liquidity crises could become obsolete.[5] However, going down this path is not without possible perils, including cyberattacks.

P2P Lending versus Bank Lending: P2P lending originated as a non-intermediated alternative to bank lending, with savers directly lending to borrowers through a platform as shown in figure 11.1.

The idea with P2P lending is that the layperson would lend directly to another layperson without going through a bank, thereby cutting out an intermediary from the process. The P2P platform is where information about borrowers is stored, so it can be used by savers to make lending decisions.

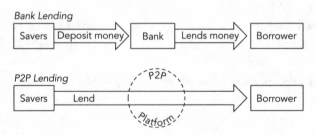

FIGURE 11.1 Bank versus P2P Lending.

Although still very small in volume compared with bank lending, P2P lending platforms have grown in the United States at an average of 84 percent per quarter since 2007.[6] There is also rapid growth in Europe.[7] But it is no longer "peer to peer," because much of the loan financing is now provided by hedge funds and large institutions.[8]

There seems to be a lot of interest in learning more about how P2P lending interacts with bank lending. Although it is a bit early for definitive answers, the evidence thus far indicates that:[9]

- P2P lending grows the most when banks are hit with regulation that increases their cost of lending and when borrowers have the greatest awareness of P2P platforms.
- P2P loans are riskier than bank loans but carry lower risk-adjusted interest rates.

Thus, it appears that P2P platforms are currently "bottom fishing," picking up the relatively risky loans that regulation-constrained banks seem competitively disadvantaged in providing. How this trend evolves in the future will depend on whether P2P lending platforms continue to be trusted by investors.[10]

Metamorphosis of Banking: Recall the three core economic functions of banks that we have seen throughout the book: creating funding liquidity, providing safekeeping services and developing trust, and reducing contracting and verification costs. Blockchain can enable the provision of the last two economic services without requiring trusted intermediaries. The challenge for banks will be to figure out how to embrace this technology—which basically reduces the need for banks—and change the services they provide so they still add significant economic value.

Changes in Contracts at the Intensive Margin: This means that *existing* financial contracts will undergo changes. DLT permits the use of "smart contracts," which are essentially a form of computerized transaction protocol that executes the terms of a contract automatically. That is, smart contracts have terms recorded in a computer language, and execution is done automatically by a computing system, such as a distributed ledger system. Common contractual conditions like payment terms, liens, confidentiality, and enforcement can be satisfied without trusted intermediaries. Enforcement, verification, and compliance costs are reduced. This clearly gives banks the opportunity to significantly lower the costs of their existing contracts in a wide range of activities, including securitization.

Changes in Contracts at the Extensive Margin: This means that fintech will enable the introduction of new financial contracts. Take, for example, the ubiquitous debt contract. Economic theory says that this contract is optimal to use in circumstances in which the financier can observe the borrower's cash flow—from which repayment will be made—only by incurring a verification cost.[11] But if verification costs can be essentially eliminated through blockchain, then why would we use the debt contract? Fintech now offers us a fresh canvas on which to paint all sorts of new contracts. Future research will have to figure out what these contracts might look like, but just imagine a world with no debt contracts, especially in light of our earlier discussions of the harmful effects of excessive consumer and bank leverage.

How Will Banks Compete?

The emergence of blockchain technology and associated developments like Bitcoin and P2P lending are parts of a broader societal trend toward disintermediation. It is a well-established fact that financial intermediation has been an enormously profitable activity for a long time. Not only do financial intermediaries provide valuable economic services, but they are handsomely rewarded for that provision. And those who work in financial services make lots of money. Indeed, many have claimed that the lucrative compensation packages in financial service firms cause too many talented people to choose to work in the financial services industry, at the expense of entrepreneurship, engineering, and so on.[12]

Anytime intermediation is profitable in a value chain, it invites disintermediation. Think of how Michael Dell disrupted the personal computer industry. He observed that while the cost of manufacturing a personal computer had been declining over time, the cost of distribution—getting it from the producer to the end customer—had not. The reason was that the mega retailers—like Circuit City, Best Buy, Walmart, and others—had so much power in the value chain that they could continue to earn profits on distributing personal computers through their stores, and the PC manufacturers had little ability to reduce the profit margins of these retailers. So what was the answer for Dell? Simple. He came up with a business model that bypassed the powerful retail distribution channel. This meant going directly from the PC manufacturer (Dell) to the consumer.

So it is with fintech. Crypto currencies are a way to replace banks as essential intermediaries in the payment system. P2P lending is a way for banks to be supplanted as intermediaries in lending. Eventually, digital currencies that work with mobile phones can provide a centralized alternative to traditional safekeeping of money through banks. Hence, these are developments that portend disintermediation. But if this does occur, what will it mean for economic stability and growth?

To answer this question and see what it means for how banks will compete in the future, let us revisit the four key takeaways from the whole book.

Our first key takeaway is that banks serve three core economic functions: (1) creating funding liquidity and private money by gathering deposits and lending money to borrowers who they screen, monitor, and develop lending relationships with; (2) providing safekeeping services for valuables, maintaining the confidentiality of clients' information, and developing trust; and (3) processing different sorts of information that help reduce contracting costs and the costs of verifying cash flows and asset ownership. Fintech has the potential to serve the third economic function more efficiently than banks, so many contracts that currently involve banks may in the future avoid banks. If banks renew their focus on relationship lending and reacquire public trust, then they are likely to have an advantage in creating funding liquidity and private money through their deposit-gathering and lending functions, as well as in protecting confidentiality of clients' information even in the era of fintech. That is, banks may continue to have an advantage in serving their first two economic functions. In the end, *trust* is likely to be a competitive advantage for (depository) banks over P2P lenders and even shadow banks. Recent research indicates that, due to their deposit-based funding cost advantage, banks are likely to be more trusted than non-bank lenders.[13]

Our second key takeaway is that the core economic functions banks serve help to crystalize the higher purpose of banks and their corporate culture. Articulating and embracing an authentic higher purpose can lead to the development of a culture that generates trust, and this will strengthen one of the last remaining competitive advantages of banks over non-banks.

Our third main takeaway is that due to their various on-balance-sheet and off-balance-sheet activities, banks occupy center stage within the financial system. Thus, to have economic growth with stability, we need to have banks that are not scandal-prone and susceptible to failures that spawn financial crises. Even as fintech grows in importance, this is unlikely to change. There are two reasons for this. One is that there will always be a role for banks as trusted intermediaries between providers and users of capital. Secondly, as fintech evolves, banks will increasingly buy P2P lending platforms and bring them and other types of fintech in-house. This will bring with it changes in organization structure and the types of employees banks hire.

Our final takeaway is that for banks to deliver on their promises of supporting economic growth and also providing financial stability, regulators need to abandon the idea that there is a tradeoff between economic growth and financial stability and that this tradeoff requires them to tolerate undercapitalized banks. We need substantially higher levels of capital in banking, and we need to remove the burden of onerous liquidity requirements that Basel III has imposed on banks. Not only do these liquidity requirements hinder economic growth, but they may not reduce banking risk. If regulators persist in imposing liquidity requirements in their present form, fintech and other non-bank providers of financial services will grow more rapidly, but for the wrong reason.

Summing It Up and Questions

In the 1980s, banks were challenged by the emergence of money market mutual funds that sucked deposits out of the banking system. Even today, banks have to fight hard for deposits with mutual funds. The *Wall Street Journal* reported on April 30, 2018, "Welcome to the new world of Main Street banking, where deposits are heading out the door after years of growth. . . . The higher interest rates now available in money market funds and other investments are luring clients to move their money out of bank accounts that still offer minimal interest rates."[14] Adding to this competition is fintech, which promises to permanently change banking as well as the role of central banks and the conduct of monetary policy. Research is at such an early stage on these issues that it is hard to make conclusive statements, but it appears that for banks to continue to prosper, they will need to articulate an authentic prosocial higher purpose, develop robust corporate cultures, and substantially strengthen their capital positions. It is an exciting time to think about all the possibilities the future holds. When will central bank digital currency become commonplace? Will banks continue to be gatherers of deposits? What new financial contracts will emerge? Stay tuned.

Notes

1. See Berruti, Ross, and Weinberg 2017.
2. See Chartered Accountants 2017 and Blemus 2017.
3. See Catalini and Gans 2016. See also Tapscott and Tapscott (2017).
4. See Bordo and Levin 2017.

5. There is a lot of disagreement on this issue. While former New York Fed president William Dudley said in November 2017 that the Fed had begun thinking about its own digital currency, Governor Quarles said: "I am particularly concerned that a central-bank issued digital currency that's widely held around the globe could be the subject of serious cyberattacks and could be widely used in money laundering and terrorist financing." See Cox 2017.
6. See PricewaterhouseCoopers 2015.
7. See Milne and Parboteeah 2016.
8. See de Roure, Pelizzon, and Thakor 2017.
9. This is based on evidence based on German bank and P2P lending data analyzed in de Roure, Pelizzon, and Thakor 2017.
10. Merton and R. Thakor 2018 develop a theory in which banks are able to weather a loss of trust better than P2P lenders.
11. See Townsend 1979.
12. See, for example, Axelson and Bond 2015.
13. See Merton and R. Thakor 2018.
14. See Rexrode and Ensign 2018.

References

Axelson, Ulf, and Philip Bond. 2015. "Wall Street Occupations." *Journal of Finance* 70 (5): 1949–1996.

Berruti, Frederico, Emily Ross, and Allen Weinberg. 2017. "The Transformative Power of Automation in Banking." *McKinsey & Co.*, November.

Blemus, Stephane. 2017. "Law and Blockchain." Working paper, Université Paris, Sorbonne, December.

Bordo, Michael D., and Andrew T. Levin. 2017. "Central Bank Digital Currency and the Future of Monetary Policy." Hoover Institution Economics Working Paper Series WP17104, August.

Catalini, Christian, and Joshua Gans. 2016. "Some Simple Economics of the Blockchain." MIT Sloan WP5191-16, November 23.

Chartered Accountants. 2017. "The Future of Blockchain: Applications and Implications of Distributed Ledger Technology." *Future Inc.*, January.

Cox, Jeff. 2017. "Fed's Quarles Warns that Digital Currencies like Bitcoin Pose Serious Financial Stability Issues as They Grow." CNBC, November 30.

de Roure, Caleb, Loriana Pelizzon, and Anjan V. Thakor. 2017. "P2P Lenders versus Banks: Cream Skimming or Bottom Fishing?" Working Paper, SAFE-Goethe University and Washington University in St. Louis, December.

Merton, Robert C., and Richard T. Thakor. 2018. "Trust in Lending." MIT Sloan Working Paper, January.

Milne, Alistair, and Paul Parboteeah. 2016. "The Business Models and Economics of Peer-to-Peer Lending." *European Credit Research Institute* 17, May.

PricewaterhouseCoopers. 2015. "Peer Pressure: How Peer-to-Peer Lending Platforms Are Transforming the Consumer Lending Industry." *Technical Report.*

Rexrode, Christina, and Rachel Louise Ensign. 2018. "Regional Banks in Fight for Deposits." *Wall Street Journal*, April 30, B1.

Tapscott, Alex, and Don Tapscott. 2017. "How Blockchain Is Changing Finance." *Harvard Business Review*, March 1.

Townsend, Robert M. 1979. "Optimal Contracts and Competitive Markets with Costly State Verification." *Journal of Economic Theory* 21 (2): 265–293.

Name Index

Subject Index